Longmans' English Classics

EDMUND BURKE'S

SPEECH ON CONCILIATION
WITH AMERICA

EDITED

WITH NOTES AND AN INTRODUCTION

BY

ALBERT S. COOK, Ph.D., L.H.D.

PROFESSOR EMERITUS OF THE ENGLISH LANGUAGE AND LITERATURE
IN YALE UNIVERSITY

LONGMANS, GREEN AND CO.

NEW YORK   CHICAGO   BOSTON   TORONTO

BURKE
ON CONCILIATION
LEC

COPYRIGHT · 1896
BY LONGMANS, GREEN AND CO.

First Edition September 1896
Reprinted January, April and October 1897
May and November 1898, August 1899, June 1900
May 1901, January and November 1902, October 1903
April 1905, October 1906, April 1909, June 1910
September 1911, May 1913, May 1914, February 1916
December 1916, July 1917, May 1919, February 1920
April 1921, December 1921, December 1922, May 1924
May 1925, May 1926, February 1928

To

THE MEMORY OF

CHAUNCEY A. GOODRICH

PROFESSOR IN YALE COLLEGE FROM 1817 TO 1860,

WHO, MORE THAN ANY OTHER AMERICAN,

HAS ILLUSTRATED THE ELO-

QUENCE AND WISDOM

OF BURKE

CONTENTS

PREFACE

ONE of the principal objects aimed at in this edition is to relieve the student from a too exclusive dependence upon Burke for facts and opinions alike, by providing him with historical information and complementary views from other sources. If, as Goldwin Smith asserts (p. xvii), Burke is a rhetorician, and presents only one side of a case, neither the soundness of his judgments nor the quality of his rhetoric can be duly appreciated by him whose knowledge of the relations between England and America is almost wholly derived from Burke's own pages. Payne's otherwise excellent edition seems to me to suffer from the defect just indicated ; yet I cannot refrain from acknowledging my indebtedness to him in several respects, not all of which can be explicitly pointed out. On the other hand, I observe he has frequently laid Goodrich's judicious editing under contribution.

The text is that of Dodsley's second edition (see p. 1), corrected, so far as relates to the preamble of the Chester Act, by collation with the *Statutes of the Realm*. Spelling and punctuation have been freely altered, and in some cases, as in the names of kings, figures have been changed to numeral words, for the sake of self-consistency. Other deviations from my original have been recorded in the Notes. I think I may safely assume that, in all essential respects, no edition of the speech since Dodsley's has had so correct a text as the present, though the differences between this and others would scarcely be discernible save on the closest inspection. The numbering of the paragraphs is an innovation about which tastes will differ; it has convenience of reference in its favour, but on the other hand it may be thought to break the continuity of perusal, and mar the beauty of the page.

The organism of the speech has been displayed somewhat more clearly than hitherto, and in a manner which shows the applicability to the oration of rhetorical principles with which Burke must have been conversant, and which had been observed by one of his great models, Cicero. The mode adopted has been the insertion of subheadings in brackets, wherever an important member of the speech—Exordium, Proof, etc.—begins.

In conclusion, I desire to express, for the publishers and for myself, our sense of the courtesy with which permission has been accorded by various authors and publishers to use extracts from copyright works.

A. S. C.

INTRODUCTION

I. CIRCUMSTANCES LEADING UP TO THE SPEECH ON CONCILIATION WITH AMERICA.

HENRY MORLEY'S HISTORICAL SUMMARY.

Introduction to Morley's Universal Library, No. 38.

THERE had been indirect taxation since the days of our English Commonwealth, when the Navigation Act of 1651 required all colonial exports to England to be shipped only in American or English vessels. After the Restoration, a second Navigation Act, in 1660, ordered that most of the exports from the colonies should be shipped only to England or to an English colony, and in American or English vessels. In 1663 a third Navigation Act required that most of the imports into the colonies should be shipped only from England or an English colony, and in American or English vessels. In 1672 there were added duties upon certain enumerated articles, in passing from one colony to another. This involved the establishment of royal custom-houses and revenue officers in service of the Crown. In Massachusetts these changes were opposed ; the General Court of the colony resolved "that the Acts of Navigation are an invasion of the rights and privileges of the subjects of his Majesty in this colony, they not being represented in the Parliament." In 1680 a notice of the appointment of a collector of the royal customs for New England was torn down at Boston by order of the colonial magistrates. The opposition was not effectual, and the number of revenue officers increased.

In 1696 a Board of Trade was established, consisting of a President and seven members, entitled the Lords Commissioners for Trade and Plantations. Among other duties this body had charge of the execution of the Navigation Acts, and it was to bring the colonies more strictly under royal control. The Board of Trade proposed, therefore, in 1697, the appointment of a captain-general, with absolute power to levy and organize an army without reference to any colonial authority. In 1698 it prohibited the export of colonial woollens even from one colony to another. In 1706 it recommended, but did not obtain, the resumption of charters still held by some of the colonies. In 1714 a Secretary of State was made chief of the Board of Trade. The Duke of Newcastle, who held this office from 1724 to 1748, supposed New England to be an island.

The operations of the Royal African Company, which had been first formed in 1618, reconstituted in 1631, and again in 1663, and which acquired wealth by the trade in slaves, were at the same time promoted. The Treaty of Utrecht, in 1713, contained a contract on the part of Spain that Great Britain alone should supply her colonies with slaves ; and in 1750 Great Britain received, by the treaty of Aix-la-Chapelle, an indemnity of a hundred thousand pounds for giving up this right. When Virginia and South Carolina laid a prohibitory duty on the importation of slaves, their acts were annulled by royal command. In 1750, when the trade in slaves was made independent of this company, the reason given in the British Parliament was that "the slave trade is very advantageous to Great Britain." The colonists of the Southern States of America had therefore endeavored in vain to check the importation of slave labour.

In 1733 the Molasses Act laid duties in the American colonies upon molasses, sugar, and rum imported from any but the British West India Islands. The agent of New York in England protested that this was "divesting the colonists of their rights as the king's natural-born subjects and Englishmen, in levying subsidies upon them against their own consent." In 1732 the American colonists were forbidden to export hats ; in 1750 they were forbidden to erect mills for slitting or rolling iron, or furnaces for making steel.

In 1754 the Mutiny Act, providing for the discipline and quarters of the English army, was extended to the colonies. In 1755 the Earl of Loudoun was sent over as Governor of

Virginia, and commander-in-chief over the thirteen colonies of America. Permanence of the appointment of judges was next struck at; their commissions were issued, which were to run no longer "during good behavior," but "during the king's pleasure." New York in 1761 refused to pay the salary of a chief justice appointed, and he procured for himself from the Board of Trade a grant to be paid from the quitrents of the province. There came claims also in 1761 for writs of assistance authorizing search for goods imported in defiance of the acts of trade.

Thus a long course of unwise policy had raised a spirit of antagonism, and much advance had been made towards the alienation of the American colonies, when there was added for the first time a direct taxation for revenue to the long series of taxations for regulation of trade. At the beginning of the year 1764 the British Parliament voted that it had a right to tax the colonies. George Grenville by the Sugar Act in 1764 laid duties upon sugar and other articles of colonial import. By the Stamp Act in 1765 he imposed in the American colonies a stamp duty, like that in England, upon business documents and newspapers.

This disregard of American feeling not only gave new force to the growing discontent, but provoked the organizing of resistance. Massachusetts proposed a Colonial Congress at New York, which first met on the 7th of October 1765, and twelve days afterwards, on the 19th of October, agreed to a Declaration of Rights.

Just in this critical time the Ministry of Lord Rockingham had newly taken the responsibility of government. Lord Rockingham—himself no speaker; one who had been attacking him was asked, "How could you worry a poor, dumb creature so?"—made Burke his private secretary, brought Burke into the House of Commons, and spoke through the voice of Burke. If Burke did not inspire his American policy, the policy was also Burke's, and Burke was its great interpreter. The Ministry was Whig; but Burke was essentially conservative. He had the practical mind of a statesman; and he strongly dreaded revolutionary change. Inconsiderate zeal to force the colonies into submission to imperial claims, against which opposition was fast rising to revolutionary heat, he met by steady labour in the interests of peace. The Stamp Act was repealed, and Parliament satisfied itself with the assertion of imperial right to tax. Assert by all means, argued Burke, your right to tax the colonies directly for imperial revenue. If you take care never to exercise the right, it will be undisputed. Be taught by the experience that shows the peril of enforcing such a right.

The Rockingham Ministry was followed in July, 1766 by that of the elder Pitt, who took only a small office in his own Ministry, and with it a peerage as Earl of Chatham. The Duke of Grafton took the place at the head of the Treasury vacated by Lord Rockingham, and the Ministry included men who would be foremost in enforcing rights of taxation against the colonists.

American opposition was disarmed by the repeal of the Stamp Act; statues were voted to Pitt and to the king; removal of the active cause of irritation brought back the old spirit of loyalty; while at home the Parliament of 1767 was reversing all the policy of peace. It created a Board of Revenue Commissioners for America; it passed a Tea Act that imposed duties on teas and other imports into the colonies, as means of providing for payment of troops and for the salaries of royal governors and judges; it also declared the New York Assembly incapable of legislation until it had assented to the Quartering Act of 1675. In 1768 the ordering of British troops into Boston, to control the public feeling excited by this policy of coercion, led to the gathering of a convention from all Massachusetts, that urged in vain upon the governor the summoning of the Legislature. In 1769 a new Act of Parliament directed that all cases of treason in the colonies should be tried in the mother country. This drew from Washington the declaration that no man should scruple or hesitate a moment to use arms in defence of freedom. "Yet arms, I would beg leave to add, should be the last resource."

In 1770 the Assembly of Virginia endeavoured to lay restrictions on the slave-trade; but the royal governor was at once directed by the Ministry at home to consent to no laws affecting the interests of the slave-dealers. Attempts of other colonies in the same direction were met in the same way. By 1773 the irritation of the colonists had been urged so far that three ships in the port of Boston bringing cargoes of tea upon which duty was to be raised, were boarded and their tea thrown into the dock.

The Duke of Grafton's Ministry had been succeeded by that of Lord North, who ruled as agent for the king, and during the whole of his disastrous Ministry, from 1770 to 1782, the country suffered from that interference of the king and the king's friends which Burke condemned in 1773 in his *Thoughts on the Cause of the Present Discontents.* . . .

In 1774, at a meeting of the county of Fairfax, with George Washington in the chair, it was resolved "that during our present difficulties and distress no slaves ought to be imported into any of the British colonies on this continent ; and we take this opportunity of declaring our most earnest wishes to see an entire stop forever put to such wicked, cruel, and unnatural trade."

The Government at home met opposition by enactments that virtually deprived Massachusetts of its charter, and placed it under strict British rule. Virginia voted in May, 1774 that an attack upon one colony was an attack upon all British America, and recommended a General Congress, which first met as the Continental Congress at Philadelphia on the 5th of September, 1774. On the 20th of October it signed the agreement that established the American Association. On the day of the separation of this Congress, October 26th, the Congress of Massachusetts organized its militia, and began to prepare for the alternative of forcible resistance. Other colonies followed the example.

In the month of the first meeting of the Continental Congress at Philadelphia there was a general election in England, swayed by strong feeling against the colonists, and a large majority was returned of members pledged to a policy of coercion. Burke entered that Parliament as member for Bristol, then the second town in the kingdom ; and on the 22nd of March, 1775 he laid before the House of Commons thirteen resolutions for reconcilement with America, and made the greatest of all his speeches, that on Conciliation with America.

When Quebec fell the bonfires of loyalty were lighted. England and Chatham were in all colonial hearts. If only that happy moment could have been seized for parting in peace! If, when the British flag was run up on the great stronghold of France, the mother country could have said to the child, "I have done for you all that a parent could do, I have secured to you the dominion of the new world, you have outgrown my protection and control, follow henceforth your own destiny, cultivate your magnificent heritage and be grateful to the arm which helped to win it for you!" Had those unuttered words been spoken, how different might have been the history of our race, perhaps to the end of time!

It is needless and would be painful to recount to Englishmen the annals of a quarrel which fills a too familiar page in English history, and, wretched as it was on both sides, went nearer through its European extension than even the domination of Louis XIV. or the conquests of Napoleon to bringing the head of England low among the nations. Few require to be again told how, when England was burdened by a heavy debt contracted in the war, George Grenville, in an evil hour, bethought him of making the colonies contribute to their own defence, while he enforced at the same time with calamitous industry the fiscal laws and the restrictions on trade ; how to raise revenue for a colonial army he imposed the stamp duty ; how the colonists resisted and Chatham applauded their resistance ; how by Rockingham, with Burke at his side, the stamp duty was repealed, while with the repealing act was unhappily coupled, to save imperial honour, a declaration of the power of Parliament to bind the colonies by its legislation in all cases ; how peace and a measure of good feeling were thereby restored ; how Townshend, usurping command of the government during an eclipse of Chatham, madly reopened the fatal issue by the imposition of a number of import duties ; how Parliament gave a careless assent to Townshend's proposal ; how colonial resistance was renewed ; how, while the

other duties were repealed, pride and obstinacy retained the tea
duty as a proof of power ; how strife again broke out, and ended
only with the destruction of the unity of the British race.
Nor would it be profitable to rehearse arguments which were
mostly in the air, though they had too practical an influence
on the conduct of statesmen and of political assemblies. A
sovereign power there must have been somewhere. Where
could it be but in the Imperial Parliament? Had not the
colonists just acquiesced in an act declaring the power of Parliament to bind them in all cases? Out of the jurisdiction of
Parliament they could not pretend to be, since they had sub-
mitted to laws made by Parliament respecting navigation,
trade, naturalization, and other imperial matters, not to mention the Habeas Corpus Act, or the common law which was
recognized in the colonies, and must have had for its basis the
legislative supremacy of the Parliament of Great Britain.
That there was an essential difference between internal and
external taxation, as Chatham in the interest of peace and
unity contended, few will now maintain. The sovereign power
must include the power of taxation, and taxation is but an exercise of the legislative power in the form of a law enacting
that the impost shall be paid. We rely for our judgment
respecting these questions mainly on Burke. But Burke,
though of all rhetoricians the most philosophic, was still a
rhetorician, and presented only one side of a case. Of this his
essay on the French Revolution is the memorable and disastrous proof. Though he goes deep into everything he seldom
goes to the bottom. You cannot extract from him any definite
theory of the colonial relation, of the authority which an imperial country was entitled really to exercise over colonial dependencies, or of the use of such dependencies if authority
really to be exercised there was none. Was Great Britain
bound to defend the colonies, and were the colonies not bound,
unless they chose, to contribute to the defence? Was each
colonial legislature in the case of a peril calling for common
effort to be at liberty to renounce its share of the burden? It
is said that if England had then done by the American
colonies as she has since done by her other colonies, the result
would have been equally happy. The result is that she bears

the whole burden of imperial defence and all other expenses of the Empire, while the colonies lay protective duties on her goods. Of such an empire neither Burke nor anyone else at that time dreamed. They all, however indistinct their vision might be, had in their mind an empire of real power and solid gain. Would Chatham have thought of allowing the colonies to lay protective duties on British goods, he who talked of forbidding them even to make a nail for a horseshoe? Wisdom spoke, albeit in a crabbed way, by the mouth of Dean Tucker, on whose mind, Tory as he was, the truth had dawned that colonial dependencies were of no real use commercially, inasmuch as you might trade with a colony just as well when it was independent, and of less than no use politically when they were in a chronic state of smothered sedition, and refused to contribute to the defence of the Empire. The Dean advised, if the colonies persisted in their refusal, to bid them begone in peace, an invitation which at that time they would almost certainly have declined. But the voice of wisdom was not recognized even by the philosophic Burke. On the other hand, Burke was surely right in rejecting the plan, countenanced by Adam Smith, of colonial representation in the Imperial Parliament. The difficulty of distance would have been very great, that of the appointment of representatives still greater, especially as the House of Commons was then constituted ; that of a total want of community of interest between states on opposite sides of the Atlantic would have been the greatest of all. The plan of a federal union between the American colonies and Great Britain floated, as some think, before the mind of Chatham. Such a union might have lived with Chatham ; with Chatham it would have died.

At the same time we must recognize the natural sentiment of empire. When Chatham speaks with pride of that "ancient and most noble monarchy" which his genius had raised to the height of glory, and with anguish of its possible dismemberment, his emotion is surely not less generous than any that swelled the bosom of Samuel or John Adams, Patrick Henry, or Thomas Paine. It may even be said that the determination of George III. to hold the colonies at whatever cost of blood and treasure, at whatever risk to his crown, was more compli

mentary to them, if it was less kind, than the proposal of
Dean Tucker at once to show them the door.

JOHN FISKE'S HISTORICAL SUMMARY.

The War of Independence, pp. 58–64, 69–70.

The principle that people must not be taxed except by their
representatives had been to some extent recognized in England
for five hundred years, and it was really the fundamental principle of English liberty, but it was only very imperfectly that
it had been put into practice. In the eighteenth century the
House of Commons was very far from being a body that fairly
represented the people of Great Britain. For a long time
there had been no change in the distribution of seats, and
meanwhile the population had been increasing very differently
in different parts of the kingdom. Thus cities which had
grown up in recent times, such as Sheffield and Manchester, had
no representatives in Parliament, while many little boroughs
with a handful of inhabitants had their representatives.
Some such boroughs had been granted representation by
Henry VIII. in order to create a majority for his measures in
the House of Commons. Others were simply petty towns that
had dwindled away, somewhat as the mountain villages of
New England have dwindled since the introduction of rail-
roads. The famous Old Sarum had members in Parliament
long after it had ceased to have any inhabitants. Seats for
these rotten boroughs, as they were called, were simply bought
and sold. Political life in England was exceedingly corrupt;
some of the best statesmen indulged in wholesale bribery as if it
were the most innocent thing in the world. The country was
really governed by a few great families, some of whose members
sat in the House of Lords and others in the House of Commons.
Their measures were often noble and patriotic in the highest
degree, but when bribery and corruption seemed necessary for
carrying them, such means were employed without scruple.

When George III. came to the throne in 1760, the great
families which had thus governed England for half a century
belonged to the party known as Old Whigs. Under their rule

the power of the crown had been reduced to insignificance, and the modern system of cabinet government by a responsible ministry had begun to grow up. The Tory families during this period had been very unpopular, because of their sympathy with the Stuart pretenders, who had twice attempted to seize the crown and given the country a brief taste of civil war. By 1760 the Tories saw that the cause of the Stuarts was hopeless, and so they were inclined to transfer their affections to the new king. George III. was a young man of narrow intelligence and poor education, but he entertained very strong opinions as to the importance of his kingly office. He meant to make himself a real king, like the king of France or the king of Spain. He was determined to break down the power of the Old Whigs and the system of cabinet government, and, as the Old Whigs had been growing unpopular, it seemed quite possible, with the aid of the Tories, to accomplish this. George was quite decorous in behaviour, and, although subject to fits of insanity which became more troublesome in his later years, he had a fairly good head for business. Industrious as a beaver and obstinate as a mule, he was an adept in political trickery. In the corrupt use of patronage he showed himself able to beat the Old Whigs at their own game, and with the aid of the Tories he might well believe himself capable of reviving for his own benefit the lost power of the crown.

Beside these two parties a third had been for some time growing up, which was in some essential points opposed to both of them. This third party was that of the New Whigs. They wished to reform the representation in Parliament in such wise as to disfranchise the rotten boroughs and give representatives to great towns like Leeds and Manchester. They held that it was contrary to the principles of English liberty that the inhabitants of such great towns should be obliged to pay taxes in pursuance of laws which they had no share in making. The leader of the New Whigs was the greatest Englishman of the eighteenth century, the elder William Pitt, now about to pass into the House of Lords as Earl of Chatham. Their leader next in importance, William Petty, Earl of Shelburne, was in 1765 a young man of eight-and-twenty.

and afterward came to be known as one of the most learned and sagacious statesmen of his time. These men were the forerunners of the great liberal leaders of the nineteenth century, such men as Russell and Cobden and Gladstone. Their first decisive and overwhelming victory was the passage of Lord John Russell's Reform Bill in 1832, but the agitation for reform was begun by William Pitt in 1745, and his famous son came very near winning the victory on that question in 1782.

Now this question of parliamentary reform was intimately related to the question of taxing the American colonies. From some points of view they might be considered one and the same question. At a meeting of Presbyterian ministers in Philadelphia, it was pertinently asked, "Have two men chosen to represent a poor English borough that has sold its votes to the highest bidder any pretence to say that they represent Virginia or Pennsylvania? And have four hundred such fellows a right to take our liberties?" In Parliament, on the other hand, as well as at London dinner tables, and in newspapers and pamphlets, it was repeatedly urged that the Americans need not make so much fuss about being taxed without being represented, for in that respect they were no worse off than the people of Sheffield or Birmingham. To this James Otis replied, "Don't talk to us any more about those towns, for we are tired of such a flimsy argument. If they are not represented, they ought to be ; " and by the New Whigs this retort was greeted with applause.

The opinions and aims of the three different parties were reflected in the long debate over the repeal of the Stamp Act. The Tories wanted to have the act continued and enforced, and such was the wish of the king. Both sections of Whigs were in favour of repeal, but for very different reasons. Pitt and the New Whigs, being advocates of parliamentary reform, came out flatly in support of the principle that there should be no taxation without representation. Edmund Burke and the Old Whigs, being opposed to parliamentary reform and in favour of keeping things just as they were, could not adopt such an argument ; and accordingly they based their condemnation of the Stamp Act upon grounds of pure expediency. They argued that it was not worth while, for the sake of a little

increase of revenue, to irritate three million people and run the
risk of getting drawn into a situation from which there would
be no escape except in either retreating or fighting. There
was much practical wisdom in this Old Whig argument, and
it was the one which prevailed when Parliament repealed the
Stamp Act and expressly stated that it did so only on grounds
of expediency.

There was one person, however, who was far from satisfied
with this result, and that was George III. He was opposed to
parliamentary reform for much the same reason that the Old
Whigs were opposed to it, because he felt that it threatened him
with political ruin. The Old Whigs needed the rotten boroughs
in order to maintain their own control over Parliament and the
country. The king needed them because he felt himself able
to wrest them from the Old Whigs by intrigue and corruption,
and thus hoped to build up his own power. He believed
with good reason, that the suppression of the rotten boroughs
and the granting of fair and equal representation would soon
put a stronger curb upon the crown than ever. Accordingly there were no men whom he dreaded and wished to put
down so much as the New Whigs; and he felt that in the repeal of the Stamp Act, no matter on what ground, they had
come altogether too near winning a victory. He felt that this
outrageous doctrine that people must not be taxed except by
their representatives needed to be sternly rebuked, and thus he
found himself in the right sort of temper for picking a fresh
quarrel with the Americans. . . .

In England the dignified and manly course of the Americans
was generally greeted with applause by Whigs of whatever
sort, except those who had come into the somewhat widening
circle of " the king's friends." The Old Whigs,—Burke, Fox,
Conway, Savile, Lord John Cavendish, and the Duke of Richmond ; and the New Whigs,—Chatham, Shelburne, Camden,
Dunning, Barré, and Beckford ; steadily defended the Americans throughout the whole of the Revolutionary crisis, and
the weight of the best intelligence in the country was certainly
on their side. Could they have acted as a united body, could
Burke and Fox have joined forces in harmony with Chatham
and Shelburne, they might have thwarted the king and pre-

vented the rupture with America. But George III. profited by the hopeless division between these two Whig parties ; and as the quarrel with America grew fiercer, he succeeded in arraying the national pride to some extent upon his side and against the Whigs. This made him feel stronger and stimulated his zeal against the Americans. He felt that if he could first crush Whig principles in America, he could then turn and crush them in England. In this he was correct, except that he miscalculated the strength of the Americans. It was the defeat of his schemes in America that ensured their defeat in England. It is quite wrong and misleading, therefore, to remember the Revolutionary War as a struggle between the British people and the American people. It was a struggle between two hostile principles, each of which was represented in both countries. In winning the good fight, our forefathers won a victory for England as well as for America. What was crushed was George III. and the kind of despotism which he wished to fasten upon America in order that he might fasten it upon England. If the memory of George III. deserves to be execrated, it is especially because he succeeded in giving to his own selfish struggle for power the appearance of a struggle between the people of England and the people of America ; and in so doing, he sowed seeds of enmity and distrust between two glorious nations that, for their own sakes and for the welfare of mankind, ought never for one moment to be allowed to forget their brotherhood.

BUCKLE'S HISTORICAL SUMMARY.

History of Civilization in England, Vol. I., pp. 842–845.

In the reign of George II. a proposal had been made to increase the revenue by taxing the colonies, which, as the Americans were totally unrepresented in Parliament, was simply a proposition to tax an entire people, without even the form of asking their consent. This scheme of public robbery was rejected by that able and moderate man who was then at the head of affairs ; and the suggestion, being generally deemed impracticable, fell to the ground, and seems, indeed, hardly to have

excited attention. But what was deemed by the government
of George II. to be a dangerous stretch of arbitrary power, was
eagerly welcomed by the government of George III. For the
new king, having the most exalted notion of his own authority, and being, from his miserable education, entirely ignorant
of public affairs, thought that to tax the Americans for the
benefit of the English would be a masterpiece of policy. When,
therefore, the old idea was revived, it met with his cordial acquiescence ; and when the Americans showed their intention of
resisting this monstrous injustice, he was only the more confirmed in his opinion that it was necessary to curb their unruly
will. Nor need we be surprised at the rapidity with which
such angry feelings broke out. Indeed, looking, on the one
hand, at the despotic principles which, for the first time since
the Revolution, were now revived at the English court ; and
looking, on the other hand, at the independent spirit of the
colonists,—it was impossible to avoid a struggle between the
two parties ; and the only questions were, as to what form the
contest would take, and towards which side victory was most
likely to incline.

On the part of the English government no time was lost.
Five years after the accession of George III. a bill was brought
into Parliament to tax the Americans; and so complete had
been the change in political affairs that not the least difficulty was found in passing a measure which, in the reign of
George II., no minister had dared to propose. Formerly such
a proposition, if made, would certainly have been rejected :
now the most powerful parties in the state were united in its
favour. The king on every occasion paid a court to the clergy
to which, since the death of Anne, they had been unaccustomed ; he was therefore sure of their support, and they zealously aided him in every attempt to oppress the colonies.
The aristocracy, a few leading Whigs alone excepted, were on
the same side, and looked to the taxation of America as a
means of lessening their own contributions. As to George
III., his feelings on the subject were notorious, and the more
liberal party not having yet recovered from the loss of power
consequent on the death of George II., there was little fear of
difficulties from the cabinet ; it being well known that the

throne was occupied by a prince whose first object was to keep ministers in strict dependence on himself, and who, whenever it was practicable, called into office such weak and flexible men as would yield unhesitating submission to his wishes.

Everything being thus prepared, there followed those events which were to be expected from such a combination. Without stopping to relate details which are known to every reader, it may be briefly mentioned that, in this new state of things, the wise and forbearing policy of the preceding reign was set at naught, and the national councils guided by rash and ignorant men, who soon brought the greatest disasters upon the country, and within a few years actually dismembered the empire. In order to enforce the monstrous claim of taxing a whole people without their consent, there was waged against America a war ill-conducted, unsuccessful, and what is far worse, accompanied by cruelties disgraceful to a civilized nation. To this may be added, that an immense trade was nearly annihilated; every branch of commerce was thrown into confusion; we were disgraced in the eyes of Europe; we incurred an expense of 140,000,000*l.*; and we lost by far the most valuable colonies any nation has ever possessed.

Such were the first fruits of the policy of George III. But the mischief did not stop there. The opinions which it was necessary to advocate in order to justify this barbarous war, recoiled upon ourselves. In order to defend the attempt to destroy the liberties of America, principles were laid down which, if carried into effect, would have subverted the liberties of England. Not only in the court, but in both houses of Parliament, from the episcopal bench, and from the pulpits of the church-party, there were promulgated doctrines of the most dangerous kind—doctrines unsuited to a limited monarchy, and, indeed, incompatible with it. The extent to which this reaction proceeded is known to very few readers, because the evidence of it is chiefly to be found in the parliamentary debates, and in the theological literature, particularly the sermons, of that time, none of which are now much studied. But, not to anticipate matters belonging to another part of this work, it is enough to say that the danger was so imminent

as to make the ablest defenders of popular liberty believe
that everything was at stake; and that if the Americans were
vanquished, the next step would be to attack the liberties of
England, and endeavour to extend to the mother-country the
same arbitrary government which by that time would have
been established in the colonies.

SMYTH'S HISTORICAL SUMMARY.

Lectures on Modern History, Lecture XXXI.

What are the causes that can be mentioned as having produced such unhappy effects on this side of the Atlantic? I
will offer to your consideration such as have occurred to me.
I will mention first those that were natural and not discreditable to us, then those that *were* discreditable.

Of the first kind, then, was a general notion in the English
people that their cause was just. The sovereignty was supposed to be in the parent state ; in the rights of sovereignty
were included the rights of taxation ; England, too, was considered as having protected the Americans from the French in
the war that had been lately concluded. The Americans,
therefore, when they resisted the mother country in her attempts to tax them, were considered on the first account as rebellious, and in the second as ungrateful.

The sentiment, then, of the contest, as far as it was honora-
ble to the inhabitants of this country, originated in the consideration just mentioned. But this sentiment would have
produced no such effect as the American War, had it not
been excited and exasperated by other considerations which I
shall now lay before you, and which were not creditable
to us. . . .

Turning, then, at present, from the causes first mentioned,
an opinion in the people of England that the Americans were
rebellious and ungrateful, and alluding to the causes that were
less honourable in the sentiment, and that were discreditable
to us, and that operated so fatally to the reduction and exas-
peration of the American contest, the first was, I think, a de-
plorable ignorance or inattention to the great leading principles of political economy.

The result of this ignorance or inattention was an indisposition to listen to the arguments of those who laid down from time to time, and explained the proper manner in which colonies might become sources of revenue to the mother country, not by means of taxes and tax-gatherers, but by the interchange of their appropriate products, and by the exertions of the real revenue officers of every country, the merchants, farmers, and manufacturers. This was one of what I consider as the discreditable causes of the war on our part.

Secondly, A very blind, and indeed disgraceful selfishness, in the mere matter of money and payment of taxes ; this was another. It was hence that the country gentlemen of the House of Commons, and the landed interest of England, had actually the egregious folly to support ministers in their scheme of coercing America, from an expectation that their own burdens, their land-tax, for instance, might be made lighter, or at least prevented from becoming heavier.

Thirdly, An overweening national pride, not operating in its more honourable direction to beat off invaders, or repel the approach of insult or injustice, but in making us despise our enemy, vilify the American character, and suppose that nothing could stand opposed to our own good pleasure, or resist the valour of our fleets and armies.

Fourthly, Very high principles of government ; a disposition to push too far the rights of authority ; to insist too sternly on the expediency of control ; to expect the duty of submission to laws without much inquiry into the exact reasonableness of their enactments. These high principles of government operated very fatally, when the question was whether Great Britain could not only claim, but actually exercise, sovereignty over the colonies of America ; whether the people of America could be constitutionally taxed by the Parliament of Great Britain, a parliament in which it could have no representatives.

Fifthly, A certain vulgarity of thinking on political subjects ; narrow, and what will commonly be found popular, notions in national concerns. In these last few words I might perhaps at once comprehend all the causes I have already mentioned. It was thus that men like Mr. Burke, who drew their reasonings from philosophic principles of a general nature, were not comprehended or were disregarded, while the most commonplace declaimer was applauded, and decided the different issues of the dispute.

II. ACCOUNTS AND ESTIMATES OF BURKE.

Buckle, History of Civilization in England, Vol. I., pp. 326–334.

The slightest sketch of the reign of George III. would indeed be miserably imperfect, if it were to omit the name of Edmund Burke. The studies of this extraordinary man not only covered the whole field of political inquiry, but extended to an immense variety of subjects, which, though apparently unconnected with politics, do in reality bear upon them as important adjuncts; since, to a philosophic mind, every branch of knowledge lights up even those that seem most remote from it. The eulogy passed upon him by one who was no mean judge of men might be justified, and more than justified, by passages from his works, as well as by the opinions of the most eminent of his contemporaries. Thus it is that while his insight into the philosophy of jurisprudence has gained the applause of lawyers, his acquaintance with the whole range and theory of the fine arts has won the admiration of artists; a striking combination of two pursuits, often, though erroneously, held to be incompatible with each other. At the same time, and notwithstanding the occupations of political life, we know on good authority that he had paid great attention to the history and filiation of languages; a vast subject, which within the last thirty years has become an important resource for the study of the human mind, but the very idea of which had, in its large sense, only begun to dawn upon a few solitary thinkers. And, what is even more remarkable, when Adam Smith came to London full of those discoveries which have immortalized his name, he found to his amazement that Burke had anticipated conclusions the maturing of which cost Smith himself many years of anxious and unremitting labor.

To these great inquiries, which touch the basis of social

philosophy, Burke added a considerable acquaintance with physical science, and even with the practice and routine of mechanical trades. All this was so digested and worked into his mind, that it was ready on every occasion; not, like the knowledge of ordinary politicians, broken and wasted in fragments, but blended into a complete whole, fused by a genius that gave life even to the dullest pursuits. This, indeed, was the characteristic of Burke, that in his hands nothing was barren. Such was the strength and exuberance of his intellect, that it bore fruit in all directions, and could confer dignity upon the meanest subjects by showing their connexion with general principles, and the part they have to play in the great scheme of human affairs.

But what has always appeared to me still more remarkable in the character of Burke, is the singular sobriety with which he employed his extraordinary acquirements. During the best part of his life, his political principles, so far from being speculative, were altogether practical. This is particularly striking, because he had every temptation to adopt an opposite course. He possessed materials for generalization far more ample than any politician of his time, and he had a mind eminently prone to large views. On many occasions, and indeed whenever an opportunity occurred, he showed his capacity as an original and speculative thinker. But the moment he set foot[1] on political ground, he changed his method. In questions connected with the accumulation and distribution of wealth, he saw that it was possible, by proceeding from a few simple principles, to construct a deductive science available for the commercial and financial interests of the country. Further than this he refused to advance, because he knew that, with this single exception, every department of politics was purely empirical, and was likely long to remain so. Hence it was that he recognized in all its bearings that great doctrine, which even in our own days is too often forgotten, that the aim of the legislator should be, not truth, but expediency. Looking at the actual state of knowledge, he was forced to admit that all political principles have been raised by hasty

1 " Forth," in the editions, is evidently an error.—EDITOR.

induction from limited facts ; and that therefore it is the part of a wise man, when he adds to the facts, to revise the induction, and, instead of sacrificing practice to principles, modify the principles that he may change the practice. Or, to put this in another way, he lays it down that political principles are at best but the product of human reason ; while political practice has to do with human nature and human passions, of which reason forms but a part ; and that, on this account, the proper business of a statesman is to contrive the means by which certain ends may be effected, leaving it to the general voice of the country to determine what those ends shall be, and shaping his own conduct, not according to his own principles, but according to the wishes of the people for whom he legislates, and whom he is bound to obey.

It is these views, and the extraordinary ability with which they were advocated, which make the appearance of Burke a memorable epoch in our political history. We had, no doubt, other statesmen before him who denied the validity of general principles in politics ; but their denial was only the happy guess of ignorance, and they rejected theories which they had never taken the pains to study. Burke rejected them because he knew them. It was his rare merit that, notwithstanding every inducement to rely upon his own generalizations, he resisted the temptation ; that, though rich in all the varieties of political knowledge, he made his opinions subservient to the march of events ; that he recognized as the object of government, not the preservation of particular institutions, nor the propagation of particular tenets, but the happiness of the people at large ; and, above all, that he insisted upon an obedience to the popular wishes which no statesman before him had paid, and which too many statesmen since him have forgotten. Our country, indeed, is still full of those vulgar politicians against whom Burke raised his voice ; feeble and shallow men, who, having spent their little force in resisting the progress of reform, find themselves at length compelled to yield ; and then, so soon as they have exhausted the artifices of their petty schemes, and, by their tardy and ungraceful concessions, have sown the seed of future disaffection, they turn upon the age by which they have been baffled ; they mourn over the degeneracy of mankind ; they lament the decay of public spirit ; and they weep for the fate of a people who have been so regardless of the wisdom of their ancestors as to tamper with a constitution already hoary with the prescription of centuries.

Those who have studied the reign of George III. will easily understand the immense advantage of having a man like Burke to oppose these miserable delusions ; delusions which have been fatal to many countries, and have more than once almost ruined our own. They will also understand that, in the opinion of the king, this great statesman was at best but an eloquent declaimer, to be classed in the same category with Fox and Chatham ; all three ingenious men, but unsafe, unsteady, quite unfit for weighty concerns, and by no means calculated for so exalted an honour as admission into the royal councils. In point of fact, during the thirty years Burke was engaged in public life, he never once held an office in the cabinet ; and the only occasions on which he occupied even a subordinate post were in those very short intervals when the fluctuations of politics compelled the appointment of a liberal ministry.

Indeed, the part taken by Burke in public affairs must have been very galling to a king who thought everything good that was old, and everything right that was established. For, so far was this remarkable man in advance of his contemporaries, that there are few of the great measures of the present generation which he did not anticipate and zealously defend. Not only did he attack the absurd laws against forestalling and regrating, but, by advocating the freedom of trade, he struck at the root of all similar prohibitions. He supported those just claims of the Catholics, which, during his lifetime, were obstinately refused ; but which were conceded, many years after his death, as the only means of preserving the integrity of the empire. He supported the petition of the Dissenters that they might be relieved from the restrictions to which, for the benefit of the Church of England, they were subjected. Into other departments of politics he carried the same spirit. He opposed the cruel laws against insolvents, by which, in the time of George III., our statute book was still defaced; and he vainly attempted to soften the penal code, the increasing severity of which was one of the worst features of that bad reign. He wished to abolish the old plan of enlisting soldiers for life ; a barbarous and impolitic practice, as the English Legislature began to perceive several years later. He attacked the slave-trade ; which, being an ancient usage, the king wished to preserve, as part of the British constitution. He refuted, but, owing to the prejudices of the age, was unable to subvert, the dangerous power exercised by the judges, who, in criminal prosecutions for libel, confined the jury to the mere question of publication; thus taking the real issue into their own hands, and making themselves the arbiters of the fate of those who were so unfortunate as to be placed at their bar. And, what many will think not the least of his merits, he was the first in that long line of financial reformers to whom we are deeply indebted. Notwithstanding the difficulties thrown in his way, he carried through Parliament a series of bills by which several useless places were entirely abolished, and in the single office of paymaster-general effected a saving to the country of 25,000*l*. a year.

These things alone are sufficient to explain the animosity of a prince, whose boast it was that he would bequeath the government to his successor in the same state as that in which he had received it. There was, however, another circumstance by which the royal feelings were still further wounded. The determination of the king to oppress the Americans was so notorious that, when the war actually broke out, it was called "the king's war ; " and those who opposed it were regarded as the personal enemies of their sovereign. In this, however, as in all other questions, the conduct of Burke was governed, not by traditions and principles such as George III. cherished, but by large views of general expediency. Burke, in forming his opinions respecting this disgraceful contest, refused to be guided by arguments respecting the right of either party. He would not enter into any discussion as to whether a mother-country has the right to tax her colonies, or whether the colonies have a right to tax themselves. Such points he left to be mooted by those politicians who, pretending to be guided by principles, are in reality subjugated by prejudice.

For his own part, he was content to compare the cost with the gain. It was enough for Burke, that, considering the power of our American colonies, considering their distance from us, and considering the probability of their being aided by France, it was not advisable to exercise the power ; and it was, therefore, idle to talk of the right. Hence he opposed the taxation of America, not because it was unprecedented, but because it was inexpedient. As a natural consequence, he likewise opposed the Boston Port Bill, and that shameful bill to forbid all intercourse with America, which was not inaptly called the starvation plan ; violent measures, by which the king hoped to curb the colonies, and break the spirit of those noble men whom he hated even more than he feared.

It is certainly no faint characteristic of those times that a man like Burke, who dedicated to politics abilities equal to far nobler things, should, during thirty years, have received from his prince neither favour nor reward. But George III. was a king whose delight it was to raise the humble and exalt the meek. His reign, indeed, was the golden age of successful mediocrity ; an age in which little men were favoured, and great men depressed ; when Addington was cherished as a statesman, and Beattie pensioned as a philosopher ; and when, in all the walks of public life, the first conditions of promotion were, to fawn upon ancient prejudices, and support established abuses.

This neglect of the most eminent of English politicians is highly instructive ; but the circumstances which followed, though extremely painful, have a still deeper interest, and are well worth the attention of those whose habits of mind lead them to study the intellectual peculiarities of great men.

John Morley, Burke, Chap. IV.

The six years during which Burke sat in Parliament for Bristol saw this conflict carried on under the most desperate circumstances. They were the years of the civil war between the English at home and the English in the American colonies. George III. and Lord North have been made scapegoats for sins which were not exclusively their own. They were

only the organs and representatives of all the lurking ignorance and arbitrary humours of the entire community. Burke
discloses in many places, that for once the King and Parliament did not act without the sympathies of the mass. In his
famous speech at Bristol, in 1780, he was rebuking the intol-
erance of those who bitterly taunted him for the support of
the measure for the relaxation of the Penal Code. "It is but
too true," he said in a passage worth remembering, "that the
love, and even the very idea, of genuine liberty is extremely
rare. It is but too true that there are many whose whole
scheme of freedom is made up of pride, perverseness, and inso-
lence. They feel themselves in a state of thraldom, they imagine that their souls are cooped and cabined in, unless they
have some man, or some body of men, dependent on their
mercy. The desire of having some one below them descends
to those who are the very lowest of all ; and a Protestant cob-
bler, debased by his poverty, but exalted by his share of the
ruling church, feels a pride in knowing it is by his generosity
alone that the peer, whose footman's instep he measures, is
able to keep his chaplain from a gaol. This disposition is the
true source of the passion which many men, in very humble
life, have taken to the American war. *Our* subjects in America ; *our* colonies ; *our* dependents. This lust of party power
is the liberty they hunger and thirst for ; and this Siren song
of ambition has charmed ears that we would have thought
were never organized to that sort of music."

This was the mental attitude of a majority of the nation,
and it was fortunate for them and for us that the yeomen and
merchants on the other side of the Atlantic had a more just
and energetic appreciation of the crisis. The insurgents, while
achieving their own freedom, were indirectly engaged in fighting the battle of the people of the mother country as well.
Burke had a vehement correspondent who wrote to him (1777)
that if the utter ruin of this country were to be the consequence of her persisting in the claim to tax America, then he
would be the first to say, *Let her perish !* If England prevails,
said Horace Walpole, English and American liberty is at an
end ; if one fell, the other would fall with it. Burke, seeing
this, " certainly never could and never did wish," as he says

of himself, "the colonists to be subdued by arms. He was fully persuaded that if such should be the event, they must be held in that subdued state by a great body of standing forces, and perhaps of foreign forces. He was strongly of opinion that such armies, first victorious over Englishmen, in a conflict for English constitutional rights and privileges, and afterwards habituated (though in America) to keep an English people in a state of abject subjection, would prove fatal in the end to the liberties of England itself." [1] The way for this remote peril was being sedulously prepared by a widespread deterioration among popular ideas, and a fatal relaxation of the hold which they had previously gained in the public mind. In order to prove that the Americans had no right to their liberties, we were every day endeavouring to subvert the maxims which preserve the whole spirit of our own. To prove that the Americans ought not to be free, we were obliged to depreciate the value of freedom itself. The material strength of the Government, and its moral strength alike, would have been reinforced by the defeat of the colonists, to such an extent as to have seriously delayed or even jeopardized English progress, and therefore that of Europe too. As events actually fell out, the ferocious administration of the law in the last five or six years of the eighteenth century was the retribution for the lethargy or approval with which the mass of the English community had watched the measures of the government against their fellow-Englishmen in America.

It is not necessary here to follow Burke minutely through the successive stages of parliamentary action in the American war. He always defended the settlement of 1766; the Stamp Act was repealed, and the constitutional supremacy and sovereign authority of the mother country was preserved in a Declaratory Act. When the project of taxing the colonies was revived, and relations with them were becoming strained and dangerous, Burke came forward with a plan for leaving the General Assemblies of the colonies to grant supplies and aids, instead of giving and granting supplies in Parliament, to be raised and paid in the colonies. Needless to say that it was rejected, and perhaps it was not feasible. Henceforth

[1] *Appeal from the New to the Old Whigs.*

Burke could only watch in impotence the blunders of government, and the disasters that befell the national arms. But his protests against the war will last as long as our literature.

Of all Burke's writings none are so fit to secure unqualified and unanimous admiration as the three pieces on this momentous struggle: the *Speech on American Taxation* (April 19, 1774); the *Speech on Conciliation with America* (March 22, 1775); and the *Letter to the Sheriffs of Bristol* (1777). Together they hardly exceed the compass of the little volume which the reader now has in his hands. It is no exaggeration to say that they compose the most perfect manual in our literature, or in any literature, for one who approaches the study of public affairs, whether for knowledge or for practice. They are an example without fault of all the qualities which the critic, whether a theorist or an actor, of great political situations, should strive by night and by day to possess. If the subject with which they deal were less near than it is to our interests and affections as free citizens, these three performances would still abound in the lessons of an incomparable political method. If their subject were as remote as the quarrel between the Corinthians and Corcyra, or the war between Rome and the Allies, instead of a conflict to which the world owes the opportunity of the most important of political experiments, we should still have everything to learn from the author's treatment: the vigorous grasp of masses of compressed detail, the wide illumination from great principles of human experience, the strong and masculine feeling for the two great political ends of Justice and Freedom, the large and generous interpretation of expediency, the morality, the vision, the noble temper. If ever, in the fulness of time—and surely the fates of men and literature cannot have it otherwise—Burke becomes one of the half-dozen names of established and universal currency in education and in common books, rising above the waywardness of literary caprice or intellectual fashions, as Shakespeare and Milton and Bacon rise above it, it will be the mastery, the elevation, the wisdom, of these far-shining discourses in which the world will in an especial degree recognize the combination of sovereign gifts with beneficent uses.

The pamphlet on the *Present Discontents* is partially obscured or muffled to the modern reader by the space which is given to the cabal of the day. The *Reflections on the French Revolution* over-abounds in declamation, and—apart from its being passionately on one side, and that perhaps the wrong one—the splendour of the eloquence is out of proportion to the reason and the judgment. In the pieces on the American war, on the contrary, Burke was conscious that he could trust nothing to the sympathy or the prepossessions of his readers, and this put him upon an unwonted persuasiveness. Here it is reason and judgment, not declamation ; lucidity, not passion ; that produces the effects of eloquence. No choler mars the page ; no purple patch distracts our minds from the penetrating force of the argument ; no commonplace is dressed up into a vague sublimity. The cause of freedom is made to wear its own proper robe of equity, self-control, and reasonableness.

Not one, but all those great idols of the political marketplace whose worship and service has cost the race so dear, are discovered and shown to be the foolish uncouth stocks and stones that they are. Fox once urged members of Parliament to peruse the *Speech on Conciliation* again and again, to study it, to imprint it on their minds, to impress it on their hearts. But Fox only referred to the lesson which he thought to be contained in it, that representation is the sovereign remedy for every evil. This is by far the least important of its lessons. It is great in many ways. It is greatest as a remonstrance and an answer against the thriving sophisms of barbarous national pride, the eternal fallacies of war and conquest ; and here it is great, as all the three pieces on the subject are so, because they expose with unanswerable force the deep-lying faults of heart and temper, as well as of understanding, which move nations to haughty and violent courses.

The great argument with those of the war party who pretended to a political defense of their position was the doctrine that the English government was sovereign in the colonies as at home ; and in the notion of sovereignty they found inherent the notion of an indefeasible right to impose and exact taxes. Having satisfied themselves of the existence of this sovereignty, and of the right which they took to be its natural property, they saw no step between the existence of an abstract right and the propriety of enforcing it. We have seen an instance of a similar mode of political thinking in our own lifetime. During the great civil war between the Northern and Southern States of the American Union, people in England convinced themselves—some after careful examination of documents, others by cursory glances at second-hand authorities—that the South had a right to secede. The current of opinion was precisely similar in the struggle to which the United States owed their separate existence. Now the idea of a right as a mysterious and reverend abstraction, to be worshipped in a state of naked divorce from expediency and convenience, was one that Burke's political judgment found preposterous and unendurable. He hated the arbitrary and despotic savour which clung about the English assumptions over the colonies. And his repulsion was heightened when he found that these assumptions were justified, not by some permanent advantage which their victory would procure for the mother country or for the colonies, or which would repay the cost of gaining such a victory ; not by the assertion and demonstration of some positive duty, but by the futile and meaningless doctrine that we had a right to do something or other, if we liked.

The alleged compromise of the national dignity implied in a withdrawal of the just claim of the government, instead of convincing, only exasperated him. "Show the thing you contend for to be reason ; show it to be common-sense ; show it to be the means of attaining some useful end ; and then I am content to allow it what dignity you please." [1] The next year he took up the ground still more firmly, and explained it still more impressively. As for the question of the right of taxation, he exclaimed, "It is less than nothing in my consideration. . . . My consideration is narrow, confined, and wholly limited to the policy of the question. I do not examine whether the giving away a man's money be a power excepted and reserved out of the general trust of government. . . . *The question with me is not whether you have a right*

[1] *Speech on American Taxation.*

to render your people miserable, but whether it is not your in-terest to make them happy. It is not what a lawyer tells me I *may* do, but what humanity, reason, and justice tell me I *ought* to do. . . . I am not determining a point of law ; I am restoring tranquillity, and the general character and situation of a people must determine what sort of government is fitted for them." "I am not here going into the distinctions of rights," he cries, "not attempting to mark their boundaries. I do not enter into these metaphysical distinctions. *I hate the very sound of them.* This is the true touchstone of all theories which regard man and the affairs of man : does it suit his nature in general? does it suit his nature as modified by his habits?" He could not bear to think of having legis-lative or political arrangements shaped or vindicated by a delusive geometrical accuracy of deduction, instead of being entrusted to "the natural operation of things, which, left to themselves, generally fall into their proper order."

Apart from his incessant assertion of the principle that man acts from adequate motives relative to his interests, and not on metaphysical speculations, Burke sows, as he marches along in his stately argument, many a germ of the modern philosophy of civilization. He was told that America was worth fighting for. "Certainly it is," he answered, "if fight-ing a people be the best way of gaining them." Every step that has been taken in the direction of progress, not merely in empire, but in education, in punishment, in the treatment of the insane, has shown the deep wisdom, so unfamiliar in that age of ferocious penalties and brutal methods, of this truth— that "the natural effect of fidelity, clemency, kindness in gov-ernors, is peace, good-will, order, and esteem in the governed." Is there a single instance to the contrary? Then there is that sure key to wise politics : " *Nobody shall persuade me, when a whole people are concerned, that acts of lenity are not means of conciliation.*" And that still more famous sentence, "*I do not know the method of drawing up an indictment against a whole people.*"

Goodrich, Select British Eloquence, pp. 237–240.

The variety and extent of his powers in debate was greater than that of any other orator in ancient or modern times. No one ever poured forth such a flood of thought—so many original combinations of inventive genius ; so much knowledge of man and the working of political systems ; so many just remarks on the relation of government to the manners, the spirit, and even the prejudices of a people ; so many wise maxims as to a change in constitutions and laws ; so many beautiful effusions of lofty and generous sentiment ; such exuberant stores of illustration, ornament, and apt illusion ; all intermingled with the liveliest sallies of wit or the boldest flights of a sublime imagination. In actual debate, as a contemporary informs us, he passed more rapidly from one exercise of his own powers to another, than in his printed productions. During the same evening, sometimes in the space of a few moments, he would be pathetic and humorous, acrimonious and conciliating, now giving vent to his indignant feelings in lofty declamation, and again, almost in the same breath, convulsing his audience by the most laughable exhibitions of ridicule or burlesque. In respect to the versatility of Mr. Burke as an orator, Dr. Parr says, "Who among men of eloquence and learning was ever more profoundly versed in every branch of science ? Who is there that can transfer so happily the results of laborious pursuits to the most familiar and popular topics ? Who is there that possesses so extensive, yet so accurate, an acquaintance with every transaction recent or remote ? Who is there that can deviate from his subject for the purposes of delight with such engaging ease, and insensibly conduct his hearers or readers from the severity of reasoning to the festivity of wit ? Who is there that can melt them, if the occasion requires, with such resistless power to grief or pity ? Who is there that combines the charm of inimitable grace and urbanity with such magnificent and boundless expansion ?"

A prominent feature in the character of Mr. Burke, which prepared him for the wide exercise of his powers, was *intellectual independence*. He leaned on no other man's understanding, however great. In the true sense of the term, he never borrowed an idea or an image. Like food in a healthy system, everything from without was perfectly assimilated ; it entered by a new combination into the very structure of his thoughts, as when the blood, freshly formed, goes out to the extremities under the strong palpitations of the heart. On most subjects, at the present day, this is all we can expect of *originality ;* the thoughts and feelings which a man expresses must be *truly his own.*

In the structure of his mind he had a strong resemblance to Bacon, nor was he greatly his inferior in the leading attributes of his intellect. In imagination he went far beyond him. He united more perfectly than any other man the discordant qualities of the philosopher and the poet, and this union was equally the source of some of his greatest excellencies and faults as an orator.

The first thing that strikes us in a survey of his understanding is its remarkable *comprehensiveness.* He had an amplitude of mind, a power and compass of intellectual vision, beyond that of most men that ever lived. He looked on a subject like a man standing upon an eminence, taking a large and rounded view of it on every side, contemplating each of its parts under a vast variety of relations, and those relations often extremely complex or remote. To this wide grasp of original thought he added every variety of information gathered from abroad. There was no subject on which he had not read, no system relating to the interests of man as a social being which he had not thoroughly explored. All these treasures of acquired knowledge he brought home to amplify and adorn the products of his own genius, as the ancient Romans collected everything that was beautiful in the spoils of conquered nations, to give new splendour to the seat of empire.

To this largeness of view he added a surprising *subtlety of intellect.* So quick and delicate were his perceptions that he saw his way clearly through the most complicated relations, following out the finest thread of thought without once letting go his hold, or becoming lost or perplexed in the intricacies of the subject. This subtlety, however, did not usually take the form of mere logical acuteness in the detection of fallacies. He was not remarkable for his dexterity as a disputant. He loved rather to build up than to pull down; he dwelt not so much on the differences of things as on some hidden agreement between them when apparently most dissimilar. The association of *resemblance* was one of the most active principles of his nature. While it filled his mind with all the imagery of the poet, it gave an impulse and direction to his researches as a philosopher. It led him, as his favorite employment, to trace out analogies, correspondencies, or contrasts (which last, as Brown remarks, are the necessary result of a quick sense of resemblance); thus filling up his original comprehensive mind with a beautiful series of associated thoughts, showing often the identity of things which appeared the most unlike, and binding together in one system what might seem the most unconnected or contradictory phenomena. To this he added another principle of association, still more characteristic of the philosopher, that of *cause and effect.* "Why?" "Whence?" "By what means?" "For what end?" "With what results?" these questions from childhood were continually pressing upon his mind. To answer them in respect *to man* in all his multiplied relations as the creature of society, to trace out the working of political institutions, to establish the principles of wise legislation, to lay open the sources of national security and advancement, was the great object of his life; and he here found the widest scope for that extraordinary subtlety of intellect of which we are now speaking. In the two principles just mentioned, we see the origin of Mr. Burke's inexhaustible richness of invention. We see, also, how it was that in his mode of viewing a subject there was never anything ordinary or commonplace. If the topic was a trite one, the manner of presenting it was peculiarly his own. As in the kaleidoscope the same object takes a thousand new shapes and colours under a change of light, so in his mind the most hackneyed theme was transformed and illuminated by the radiance of his genius, or placed in new relations which gave it all the freshness of original thought.

This amplitude and subtlety of intellect, in connection with his peculiar habits of association, prepared the way for another characteristic of Mr. Burke, his remarkable *power of gener-*

alization. Without this he might have been one of the greatest of poets, but not a philosopher or a scientific statesman. "To generalize," says Sir James Mackintosh, "is to philosophize ; and comprehension of mind, joined to the habit of careful and patient observation, forms the true genius of philosophy." But it was not in his case a mere "habit," it was a kind of instinct of his nature, which led him to gather all the results of his thinking, as by an elective affinity, around their appropriate centres ; and, knowing that truths are valuable just in proportion as they have a wider reach, to rise from particulars to generals, and so to shape his statements as to give them the weight and authority of universal propositions. His philosophy, however, was not that of abstract truth ; it was confined to things in the *concrete*, and chiefly to man, society, and government. He was no metaphysician ; he had, in fact, a dislike, amounting to weakness, of all abstract reasonings in politics, affirming, on one occasion, as to certain statements touching the rights of man, that just "in proportion as they were metaphysically true, they were morally and politically false !" He was, as he himself said, "a philosopher in *action ;* " his generalizations embraced the great facts of human society and political institutions as affected by all the interests and passions, the prejudices and frailties, of a being like man. The impression he made was owing, in a great degree, to the remoteness of the ideas which he brought together, the startling novelty and yet justness of his combinations, the heightening power of contrast, and the striking manner in which he connected truths of imperishable value with the individual case before him. It is here that we find the true character and office of Mr. Burke. He was the *man of principles ;* one of the greatest teachers of "civil prudence" that the world has ever seen. A collection of maxims might be made from his writings infinitely superior to those of Rochefoucauld ; equally true to nature, and adapted, at the same time, not to produce selfishness and distrust, but to call into action all that is generous, and noble, and elevated in the heart of man. His high moral sentiment and strong sense of religion added greatly to the force of these maxims ; and, as a result of these fine generalizations, Mr. Burke has this peculiarity, which distinguishes him from every other writer, that he is almost equally instructive whether he is right or wrong as to the particular point in debate. He may fail to make out his case; opposing considerations may induce us to decide against him; and yet every argument he uses is full of instruction : it contains great truths, which, if they do not turn the scale here, may do it elsewhere; so that he whose mind is filled with the maxims of Burke has within him not only one of the finest incentives of genius, but a fountain of the richest thought, which may flow through a thousand channels in all the efforts of his own intellect, to whatever subject those efforts may be directed.

With these qualities and habits of mind, the oratory of Mr. Burke was of necessity *didactic.* His speeches were *lectures,* and, though often impassioned, enlivened at one time with wit, and rising at another into sublimity or pathos, they usually became wearisome to the House from their minuteness and subtlety; as

> He went on refining,
> And thought of convincing while they thought of dining.

We see, then, in the philosophical habits of his mind (admirable as the results were in most respects), why he spoke so often to empty benches, while Fox, by seizing on the strong points of the case, by throwing away intermediate thoughts, and striking at the heart of the subject, never failed to carry the House with him in breathless attention.

His *method* was admirable, in respect at least to his published speeches. No man ever bestowed more care on the arrangement of his thoughts. The exceptions to this remark are apparent, not real. There is now and then a slight irregularity in his mode of transition, which seems purposely thrown in to avoid an air of sameness; and the subordinate heads sometimes spread out so widely, that their connection with the main topic is not always obvious. But there is reigning throughout the whole a massive unity of design like that of a great cathedral, whatever may be the intricacy of its details.

In his *reasonings* (for he was one of the greatest masters of reason in our language, though some have strangely thought him deficient in this respect) Mr. Burke did not usually adopt the outward forms of logic. He has left us, indeed, some beautiful specimens of dialectical ability, but his arguments, in most instances, consisted of the amplest enumeration and the clearest display of all the facts and principles, the analogies, relations, or tendencies which were applicable to the case, and were adapted to settle it on the immutable basis of the nature and constitution of things. Here again he appeared, of necessity, more as a teacher than a logician, and hence many were led to underrate his argumentative powers. The exuberance of his fancy was likewise prejudicial to him in this respect. Men are apt to doubt the solidity of a structure which is covered all over with flowers. As to this peculiarity of his eloquence, Mr. Fox truly said, "It injures his reputation ; it casts a veil over his wisdom. Reduce his language, withdraw his images, and you will find that he is more wise than eloquent ; you will have your full weight of metal, though you melt down the chasing."

In respect to Mr. Burke's *imagery*, however, it may be proper to remark that a large part of it is not liable to any censure of this kind ; many of his figures are so finely wrought into the texture of his style, that we hardly think of them as figures at all. His great fault in other cases is that of giving them too bold a relief, or dwelling on them too long, so that the primary idea is lost sight of in the image. Sometimes the prurience of his fancy makes him low, and even filthy. He is like a man depicting the scenes of nature, who is not content to give us those features of the landscape that delight the eye, but fills out his canvas with objects which are coarse, disgusting, or noisome. Hence no writer in any language has such extremes of imagery as Mr. Burke, from his picture of the Queen of France, "glittering like the morning star, full of life, and splendour, and joy," or of friendship, as "the soft green of the soul, on which the eye loves to repose," to Lord Chatham's administration "pigging together in the same truckle-bed," and Mr. Dundas with his East India bills, "exposed like the imperial sow of augury, lying in the mud with the prodigies of her fertility about her, as evidences of her delicate amours.''

His *language*, though copious, was not verbose. Every word had its peculiar force and application. His chief fault was that of overloading his sentences with secondary thoughts, which weakened the blow by dividing it. His style is, at times, more careless and inaccurate than might be expected in so great a writer. But his mind was on higher things. His idea of a truly fine sentence, as once stated to a friend, is worthy of being remembered. It consists, said he, in a union of thought, feeling, and imagery—of a striking truth and a corresponding sentiment, rendered doubly striking by the force and beauty of figurative language. There are more sentences of this kind in the pages of Mr. Burke than of any other writer.

In conclusion, we may say, without paradox, since oratory is only one branch of the quality we are now considering, that while Mr. Burke was inferior as an orator to Lord Chatham and Mr. Fox, he has been surpassed by no one in the richness and splendour of his eloquence ; and that he has left us something greater and better than all eloquence in his countless lessons of moral and civil wisdom.   •

Payne, Burke's Select Works, I., **xxxiv.–xxxv., xxxviii., xliv.–xlv.**

He expressed his ideas with all the grandeur in which they were conceived ; but the expression was always natural, and occasionally agreeably relieved by familiarity. It approaches to that manner of ''good conversation'' which he himself attributes, as a high excellence, to Cicero. Burke reprehended any attempt to separate the English which is written from the English which is spoken. Plautus and Terence, and the ''beautiful fragments of Publius Syrus,'' he considered to be models of good speaking and writing. He often casts to the winds all literary formality, and writes just as he may have spoken in public or private, freely and unrestrainedly. In this way Burke gave a lasting stimulus to English prose literature, as Wordsworth soon afterwards gave a stimulus to poetry, by the introduction of a fresher and more natural diction. His writings have ever since been the model of all who wish to say anything forcibly, naturally, freely, and in a comparatively small space. The common-sense politician recognises him as his master, and modern satire is indebted to him for originating the *Saturday Review* style. He fell naturally into that manner which was best adapted to take and to keep hold of the practical English mind, and he brought that manner at once to its perfection. . . .

In his manner of working Burke was unlike Sydney Smith, who composed slowly, and seldom corrected what he wrote. Charles Butler tells us that he never sent a manuscript to the press which he had not so often altered that every page was almost a blot, and never received from the press a first proof which he did not almost equally alter. Often the printers never attempted to correct his proofs, finding it less trouble to take the whole matter to pieces and begin afresh. . . .

He was the only man of his day who had pursued the only and infallible path to becoming a real orator, that of *writing* much, and assiduously cultivating literary excellence. Bolingbroke, by universal consent the greatest orator of his time, had done the same thing : so had Chatham, in his early years, although scarcely anything of his labours saw the light. But most of Burke's contemporaries had attained their proficiency in public speaking by the common and less troublesome plan of trying to do it as often as opportunity offered, and hardening themselves against failure. In this way fluency and self-possession are always to be gained, eloquence never. The former go to make up the practical debater : and a few pointed remarks and striking images will be enough, with a clever man, to conceal want of art in combining his ideas, and incompetency to present them in their most effective form. The oratory of the younger Pitt, which is a good example of the speaking of a business-like, practical statesman, has much of this character. It is marked by a certain mechanical fluency, well adapted for bearing the speaker up while he is meditating what he shall say next, but accompanied by a baneful tautology and confusion of method. It is wanting in organic elasticity.

Wraxall, Historical and Posthumous Memoirs, Vol. XI., pp.
30–31, 35–36.

Nature had bestowed on him a boundless imagination, aided
by a memory of equal strength and tenacity. His fancy was
so vivid that it seemed to light up by its own powers, and to
burn without consuming the aliment on which it fed ;
sometimes bearing him away into ideal scenes created by his
own exuberant mind, but from which he sooner or later returned to the subject of debate, descending from his most
aerial flights by a gentle and imperceptible gradation till he
again touched the ground. Learning waited on him like a
handmaid, presenting to his choice all that antiquity had
culled or invented most elucidatory of the topic under discussion. He always seemed to be oppressed under the load and
variety of his intellectual treasures, of which he frequently
scattered portions with a lavish hand to inattentive, impatient, ignorant, hungry, and sleepy auditors, undeserving of
such presents. Nor did he desist, though warned by the clam-
orous vociferation of the House to restrain or to abbreviate
his speeches. Every power of oratory was wielded by him in
turn, for he could be, during the same evening, often within
the space of a few minutes, pathetic and humorous, acrimonious and conciliating, now giving loose to his indignation or
severity, and then, almost in the same breath, calling to his
assistance wit and ridicule. It would be endless to cite instances of this versatility of disposition, and of the rapidity of
his transitions " from grave to gay, from lively to severe," that
I have myself witnessed. . . .

His enunciation was vehement, rapid, and never checked by
any embarrassment ; for his ideas outran his powers of utterance, and he drew from an exhaustless source. But his Irish
accent, which was as strong as if he had never quitted the
banks of the Shannon, diminished to the ear the enchanting
effect of his eloquence on the mind. . . . In brilliancy of
wit Lord North alone could compete with Burke, for Sheridan
had not then appeared. Burke extracted all his images from
classic authorities ; a fact of which he displayed a beautiful
exemplification when he said of Wilkes, borne along in tri-

umph by the mob, that he resembled Pindar elevated on the wings of poetical inspiration—

—Numerisque fertur
Lege solutis.[1]

a pun of admirable delicacy and the closest application.

His personal qualities of temper and disposition by no means corresponded with his intellectual endowments. Throughout his general manner and deportment in Parliament there was a mixture of petulance, impatience, and at times of intractability, which obscured the lustre of his talents. His features and the undulating motions of his head, while under the influence of anger or passion, were eloquently expressive of this irritability, which on some occasions seemed to approach towards alienation of mind. Even his friends could not always induce him to listen to reason and remonstrance, though they sometimes held him down in his seat by the skirts of his coat in order to prevent the ebullitions of his violence or indignation. Gentle, mild, and amenable to argument in private society, of which he formed the delight and the ornament, he was often intemperate and reprehensibly personal in Parliament. Fox, however irritated, never forgot that he was a chief. Burke, in his most sublime flights, was only a partisan. The countenance of the latter, full of intellect but destitute of softness, which rarely relaxed into a smile, did not invite approach or conciliation. His enmities and prejudices, though they originated in principle as well as in conviction, yet became tinged with the virulent spirit of party, and were eventually in many instances inveterate, unjust, and insurmountable. Infinitely more respectable than Fox, he was nevertheless far less amiable. Exempt from his defects and irregularities, Burke wanted the suavity of Fox's manner, his amenity, and his placability. The one procured admirers, the other possessed friends.

Prior, Life of Burke, pp. 498, 507–509.

Nothing is more peculiar to his impassioned style than this difficulty of imitation. To be convinced that such is the case, let any one take a page or two of our English classics, Ad-

[1] Hor., *Odes*, IV., ii., 11-12.—ED.

dison or Johnson for instance, with the design of hitting off their chief characteristics, and he may probably make the resemblance respectable. Let him attempt the manner of Burke, and he will almost certainly fail; he will either overdo or underdo it. Even Sheridan, with all his genius, who had his eye upon this great model in the early part of his career and in several speeches on the impeachment, soon found out that the endeavour was nearly hopeless, and therefore gave it up. . . .

Lord Erskine said that his defect was *episode*. "A public speaker," said he, "should never be episodical—it is a very great mistake. I hold it to be a rule respecting public speaking which ought never to be violated, that the speaker should not introduce into his oratory insular brilliant passages—they always tend to call off the minds of his hearers, and to make them wander from what ought to be the main business of his speech. If he wishes to introduce brilliant passages, *they should run along the line of his subject matter*, and never quit it. Burke's episodes were highly beautiful—I know nothing *more* beautiful, but they were his defects in speaking." Then he introduced one of his most beautiful episodes, taken from a speech on the American war, and repeated by heart the whole of that part of the speech in which he introduces the quotation "Acta parentum," &c.[1] "All this," said he, "is very beautiful, but it ought to be avoided." . . .

A belief prevailed for a short time in the early part of his career of their being written previous to delivery—an impression arising from admitted superiority over those of his contemporaries; but further observation evinced this was not the case. He meditated deeply, and was sometimes heard to express his thoughts aloud. On new or important questions he committed some of the chief heads of his argument to paper, but for the language in which it was conveyed, the colouring, illustration, and the whole artillery of that forcible diction and figurative boldness in which he has not merely no equal, but no competitor for equality, he trusted to a well-stored mind, a retentive memory, and a readiness which, from constant discipline in the school of debate, never failed him.

[1] Page 15 of this edition.—ED.

Of his published speeches we have the authority of Gibbon, who heard them, as well as of still more intimate friends, for the truth of the fact that they received little embellishment in passing through the press. It is well known indeed that the fragments preserved of several of them were written down *after* and not *before* delivery, assisted by the notes and recollection of different members, his friends, and not unfrequently of the public reporters. Some of his happiest sallies were the inspiration of the moment.

John Morley, Burke, Chap. X.

Though it is not wrong to say of Burke that, as an orator, he was transcendent, yet in that immediate influence upon his hearers which is commonly supposed to be the mark of oratorical success, all the evidence is that Burke generally failed. We have seen how his speech against Hastings affected Miss Burney, and how the speech on the Nabob of Arcot's Debts was judged by Pitt not to be worth answering. Perhaps the greatest that he ever made was that on Conciliation with America; the wisest in its temper, the most closely logical in its reasoning, the amplest in appropriate topics, the most generous and conciliatory in the substance of its appeals. Yet Erskine, who was in the House when this was delivered, said that it drove everybody away, including people who, when they came to read it, read it over and over again, and could hardly think of anything else. As Moore says rather too floridly, but with truth—"In vain did Burke's genius put forth its superb plumage, glittering all over with the hundred eyes of fancy—the gait of the bird was heavy and awkward, and its voice seemed rather to scare than attract." Burke's gestures were clumsy; he had sonorous but harsh tones; he never lost a strong Irish accent; and his utterance was often hurried and eager. Apart from these disadvantages of accident which have been overcome by men infinitely inferior to Burke, it is easy to perceive, from the matter and texture of the speeches that have become English classics, that the very qualities which are excellences in literature were drawbacks to the spoken discourses. A listener in Westminster Hall or the

House of Commons, unlike the reader by his fireside in the
next century, is always thinking of arguments and facts that
bear directly on the special issue before him.   What he wishes
to hear is some particularity of event or inference which wil'
either help him to make up his mind, or will justify him i'
his mind is already made up.   Burke never neglected these
particularities, and he never went so wide as to fall for an instant into vagueness, but he went wide enough into the generalities that lent force and light to his view, to weary men who
cared for nothing, and could not be expected to care for anything, but the business actually in hand and the most expedi-
tious way through it.   The contentiousness is not close enough
and rapid enough to hold the interest of a practical assembly,
which, though it was a hundred times less busy than the
House of Commons to-day, seems to have been eager in the
inverse proportion of what it had to do, to get that little
quickly done.

Then we may doubt whether there is any instance of an orator throwing his spell over a large audience, without frequent
resort to the higher forms of commonplace.   Two of the greatest speeches of Burke's time are supposed to have been Grattan's on Tithes and Fox's on the Westminster Scrutiny, and
these were evidently full of the splendid commonplaces of the
first-rate rhetorician.   Burke's mind was not readily set to
these tunes.   The emotion to which he commonly appealed
was that too rare one, the love of wisdom ; and he combined
his thoughts and knowledge in propositions of wisdom so
weighty and strong, that the minds of ordinary hearers were
not on the instant prepared for them.   .   .   .   He is at heart
thinking more of the subject itself than of those on whom it
was his apparent business to impress a particular view of it.
He surrenders himself wholly to the matter, and follows up,
though with a strong and close tread, all the excursions to
which it may give rise in an elastic intelligence—"motion,"
as De Quincey says, "propagating motion, and life throwing
off life."   But then this exuberant way of thinking, this
willingness to let the subject lead, is less apt in public discourse than it is in literature, and from this comes the literary
quality of Burke's speeches.   .   .   .

Flexibility is not to be found in his manner and composition. That derives its immense power from other sources; from passion, intensity, imagination, size, truth, cogency of logical reason. If any one has imbued himself with that exacting love of delicacy, measure, and taste in expression, which was until our own day a sacred tradition of the French, then he will not like Burke. Those who insist on charm, on winning-ness in style, on subtle harmonies and exquisite suggestion, are disappointed in Burke; they even find him stiff and over-coloured. And there are blemishes of this kind. His banter is nearly always ungainly, his wit blunt, as Johnson said of it, and very often unseasonable. We feel that Johnson must have been right in declaring that though Burke was always in search of pleasantries, he never made a good joke in his life. As is usual with a man who has not true humour, Burke is also without true pathos. The thought of wrong or misery moved him less to pity for the victim than to anger against the cause. Again, there are some gratuitous and unredeemed vulgarities; some images whose barbarity makes us shudder, of creeping ascarides and inexpugnable tape-worms. But it is the mere foppery of literature to suffer ourselves to be long detained by specks like these. . . .

Even in the coolest and dryest of his pieces there is the mark of greatness, of grasp, of comprehension. In all its varieties Burke's style is noble, earnest, deep-flowing, because his sentiment was lofty and fervid, and went with sincerity and ardent disciplined travail of judgment. Fox told Francis Horner that Dryden's prose was Burke's great favourite, and that Burke imitated him more than anyone else. We may well believe that he was attracted by Dryden's ease, his copious-ness, his gaiety, his manliness of style, but there can hardly have been any conscious attempt at imitation. Their topics were too different. Burke had the style of his subjects, the amplitude, the weightiness, the laboriousness, the sense, the high flight, the grandeur, proper to a man dealing with im-perial themes, the freedom of nations, the justice of rulers, the fortunes of great societies, the sacredness of law. Burke will always be read with delight and edification, because in the midst of discussions on the local and the accidental, he

scatters apophthegms that take us into the regions of lasting
wisdom.   In the midst of the torrent of his most strenuous
and passionate deliverances, he suddenly rises aloof from his
immediate subject, and in all tranquillity reminds us of some
permanent relation of things, some enduring truth of human
life or society.

Payne, Burke's Select Works, I., xxxii.-xxxiii., xxxv.-xxxvi.,
xlix.

The literature of England is remarkable for the extent in
which it is pervaded by political ideas.   Poets, divines, drama-
tists, and historians, alike illustrate the leading tendency of
the English mind.   In the two former of these classes Burke
had an especial interest.   Hooker and South, Milton and
Dryden, were often to him a real fount of inspiration.   His
philosophical mind readily discerned any analogy which was
convertible to his own purpose, and this faculty in him was
rarely misused.   Burke knew general English literature well ;
and he turned all his knowledge to such account that next to
facts and reasonings upon facts, it became his chief resource.
Burke moreover, like Cicero, had received the training, not of
a politician, but of a man of letters.   When Cicero first appeared in the character of a statesman, politicians used con-
temptuously to call him "the Greek," and "the Scholar."
Every one of Burke's productions exhibits a mind thoroughly
tinctured with scholarship, in the widest sense of the word,
and perfected in it by continuous practice.   His scholarship is
of the Roman rather than the Greek model.   Cicero, Livy, and
Tacitus were familiarised to him by sympathy with their subject-matter.   He was equally acquainted with the poets, and
was often indebted to them for an illustration.   .   .   .
In the sections of his works in which this grave simplicity is
most prominent, Burke frequently employed the impressive
phrases of the Holy Scriptures, affording a signal illustration
of the truth, that he neglects the most valuable repository of
rhetoric in the English language who has not well studied the
English Bible.   .   .   .
If the aims of writing could be reached by simple reasoning

and description, closely and concisely expressed, much of the poetry and the prose of the last century would be unsurpassable. The more sensitive elements in human nature, however, will not consent to be thus desolated, and the formal writer is thwarted at every step by the recoil of his own mechanism. In the literary art, as in all others, nature must be patiently studied. Burke, who never aimed at merely literary fame, and never once, in his mature years, cherished the thought of living to future ages in his works, was well acquainted with the economics of his art. He devoted himself solely to the immediate object before him, with no sidelong glance at the printing press or the library shelf. He reasoned little, or not at all, when he conceived reason to be out of place, or insufficient for his purpose. He never rejected a phrase or a thought because it did not reach the standard required by literary dignity. With all this, his writing always reaches a high standard of practical excellence, and is always careful and workmanlike. It is, moreover, well attuned to the ear. The cadence of Burke's sentences always reminds us that prose writing is only to be perfected by a thorough study of the poetry of the language. Few prose writers were so well acquainted with the general body of English verse, and few have habitually written so fully, so delicately, and so harmoniously.

Goodrich, Select British Eloquence, pp. 207-208.

A few things have come down to us as to his course of reading. He had mastered most of the great writers of antiquity. Demosthenes was his favourite orator, though he was led in after life, by the bent of his genius, to form himself on the model of Cicero, whom he more resembled in magnificence and copiousness of thought. He delighted in Plutarch. He read most of the great poets of antiquity, and was peculiarly fond of Virgil, Horace, and Lucretius, a large part of whose writings he committed to memory. In English he read the Essays of Lord Bacon again and again with increasing admiration, and pronounced them "the greatest works of that great man." Shakspeare was his daily study. But his highest reverence was reserved for Milton, "whose richness of lan-

guage, boundless learning, and Scriptural grandeur of conception," were the first and last themes of his applause. The
philosophical tendency of his mind began now to display itself with great distinctness, and became, from this period, the
master principle of his genius. "Rerum cognoscere *causas*"
seems ever to have been his delight, and soon became the object of all his studies and reflections. He had an exquisite
sensibility to the beauties of nature, of art, and of elegant
composition, but he could never rest here. "Whence this
enjoyment?" "On what principles does it depend?" "How
might it be carried to a still higher point?"—these are questions which seem almost from boyhood to have occurred in-
stinctively to his mind. His attempts at philosophical criticism commenced in college, and led to his producing one of
the most beautiful works of this kind to be found in any language. In like manner, history to him, even at this early
period, was not a mere chronicle of events, a picture of bat-
tles and sieges, or of life and manners; to make it *history*,
it must bind events together by the causes which produced
them. The science of politics and government was in his
mind the science of man; not a system of arbitrary regulations, or a thing of policy and intrigue, but founded on a
knowledge of those principles, feelings, and even prejudices,
which unite a people together in one community—"ties," as
he beautifully expresses it, "which, though light as air, are
strong as links of iron." Such were the habits of thought
to which his mind was tending even from his college days,
and they made him pre-eminently the great PHILOSOPHICAL
ORATOR of our language.

Being intended by his father for the bar, Mr. Burke was
sent to London at the age of twenty, to pursue his studies at
the Middle Temple. But he was never interested in the law.
He saw enough of it to convince him that it is "one of the
first and noblest of human sciences—a science which does
more to quicken and invigorate the understanding, than all
other kinds of learning put together." Still, it was too dry
and technical for a mind like his; and he felt, that, "except
in persons very happily born, it was not apt to open and liberalize the mind in the same proportion." He therefore soon

gave himself up, with all the warmth of his early attachment, to the pursuits of literature and philosophy. His diligence in study was now carried to its highest point. He devoted every moment to severe labour ; spending his evenings, however, in conversation with the ablest men engaged in the same employments, and thus varying, perhaps increasing, the demand for mental exertion. Few men ever studied to greater effect. He early acquired a power which belongs peculiarly to superior minds—that of *thinking* at all times and in every place, and not merely at stated seasons in the retirement of the closet. His mind seems never to have floated on the current of passing events. He was always *working out trains of thought.* His reading, though wide and multifarious, appears from the first to have been perfectly digested. His views on every ⌄bject were formed into a complete system ; and his habits of daily discussing with others whatever he was revolving in his own mind, not only quickened his powers, but made him guarded in statement, and led him to contemplate every subject under a great variety of aspects. His exuberant fancy, which in most men would have been a fatal impediment to any attempt at speculation, was in him the ready servant of the intellect, supplying boundless stores of thought and illustration for every inquiry. Such were his habits of study from this period, during nearly fifty years, down to the time of his death. Once only, as he stated to a friend, did his mind ever appear to flag. At the age of forty-five, he felt weary of this incessant struggle of thought. He resolved to pause and rest satisfied with the knowledge he had gained. But a week's experience taught him the misery of being idle ; and he resumed his labours with the noble determination of the Greek philosopher, γηράσκειν διδασκύμενος, to grow old in learning. Gifted as he was with pre-eminent genius, it is not surprising that diligence like this, which would have raised even moderate abilities into talents of a high order, should have made him from early life an object of admiration to his friends, and have laid the foundation of that richness and amplitude of thought in which he far surpassed every modern orator.

Goodrich, Select British Eloquence, p. 206.

When eleven years old, he was sent to a school at Ballitore, about twenty miles from Dublin, under the care of a Quaker named Shackleton, who was distinguished, not only for the accuracy of his scholarship, but for his extraordinary power of drawing forth the talents of his pupils, and giving a right direction to their moral principles. Mr. Burke uniformly spoke of his instructor in after life with the warmest affection, and rarely failed, during forty years, whenever he went to Ireland, to pay him a visit. He once alluded to him in the House of Commons, in the following terms : " I was educated," said he, "as a Protestant of the Church of England, by a Dissenter who was an honour to his sect, though that sect has ever been considered as one of the purest. Under his eye, I read the Bible, morning, noon, and night ; and have ever since been a happier and better man for such reading." Under these influences, the development of his intellect and of his better feelings was steady and rapid. He formed those habits of industry and perseverance, which were the most striking traits in his character, and which led him to say in after life, " *Nitor in adversum* is the motto for a man like me." He learned that simplicity and frankness, that bold assertion of moral principle, that reverence for the Word of God, and the habit of going freely to its pages for imagery and illustration, by which he was equally distinguished as a man and an orator. At this period, too, he began to exhibit his extraordinary powers of memory. In every task or exercise dependent on this faculty, he easily outstripped all his competitors ; and it is not improbable that he gained, under his early Quaker discipline, those habits of systematic thought, and that admirable arrangement of all his acquired knowledge, which made his memory one vast storehouse of facts, principles, and illustrations, ready for use at a moment's call. At this early period, too, the imaginative cast of his mind was strongly developed. He delighted above all things in works of fancy. The old romances, such as Palmerin of England and Don Belianis of Greece, were his favourite study ; and we can hardly doubt, considering the peculiar susceptibility of his mind,

that such reading had a powerful influence in producing that
gorgeousness of style which characterized so many of his productions in after life.

Goodrich, Select British Eloquence, p. 209.

Every one was struck with the activity of his mind, the
singular extent and variety of his knowledge, his glowing
power of thought, and the force and beauty of his language.
Even Johnson, whose acknowledged supremacy made him in
most cases

> Bear, like the Turk, no brother near the throne,

was soon conciliated or subdued by the conversational powers
of Burke. It was a striking spectacle to see one so proud
and stubborn, who had for years been accustomed to give
forth his *dicta* with the authority of an oracle, submit to contradiction from a youth of twenty-seven. But, though Johnson differed from Burke on politics, and occasionally on other
subjects, he always did him justice. He spoke of him from
the first in terms of the highest respect. "Burke," said he,
"is an extraordinary man. His stream of talk is perpetual;
and he does not talk from any desire of distinction, but
because his mind is full." "He is the *only* man," said he,
at a later period, when Burke was at the zenith of his reputation, "whose common conversation corresponds with the
general fame which he has in the world. Take him up where
you please, he is ready to meet you." "No man of sense,"
he said, "could meet Burke by accident under a gateway to
avoid a shower, without being convinced that he was the first
man in England." A striking confirmation of this remark
occurred some years after, when Mr. Burke was passing
through Litchfield, the birthplace of Johnson. Wishing to
see the Cathedral during the change of horses, he stepped into
the building, and was met by one of the clergy of the place,
who kindly offered to point out the principal objects of
curiosity. "A conversation ensued; but, in a few moments,
the clergyman's pride of local information was completely
subdued by the copious and minute knowledge displayed by

the stranger. Whatever topic the objects before them suggested, whether the theme was architecture or antiquities, some obscure passage in ecclesiastical history, or some question respecting the life of a saint, he touched it as with a sunbeam. His information appeared universal; his mind, clear intellect, without one particle of ignorance. A few minutes after their separation, the clergyman was met hurrying through the street. ' I have had,' said he, ' quite an adventure. I have been conversing for this half hour past with a man of the most extraordinary powers of mind and extent of information which it has ever been my fortune to meet with ; and I am now going to the inn, to ascertain, if possible, who this stranger is.' "

Goldsmith, Retaliation.

Here lies our good Edmund, whose genius was such,
We scarcely can praise it or blame it too much ;
Who, born for the universe, narrowed his mind,
And to party gave up what was meant for mankind ;
Though fraught with all learning, yet straining his throat
To persuade Tommy Townshend to lend him a vote ;
Who, too deep for his hearers, still went on refining,
And thought of convincing, while they thought of dining ;
Though equal to all things, for all things unfit :
Too nice for a statesman, too proud for a wit,
For a patriot too cold, for a drudge disobedient,
And too fond of the right to pursue the expedient.
In short, 'twas his fate, unemployed, or in place, sir,
To eat mutton cold, and cut blocks with a razor.

SUGGESTIONS FOR TEACHERS AND STUDENTS

THE study of a piece of literature, as distinguished from cursory reading of it, may be directed to either one of two principal ends—interpretation, or criticism. The object of interpretation is the understanding of the work,—as a whole, in its organism, and in its details. The object of criticism is the judgment of the work, with reference both to its merits and defects. The object of both interpretation and criticism is intelligent admiration—admiration of that, and that alone, which is truly and eternally admirable.

Whatever study concerns itself with either of these two ends, interpretation or criticism, is literary study. That which is directed to other ends, or to no particular ends, may be useful in its way, and with reference to its own purposes, but has no right to be considered literary study.

The problem of literary teaching consists in the apportionment and adjustment to one another of the various forms of interpretation and criticism. For its solution no precise rules can be given; yet one statement can be made with confidence— that the ambitious, but untrained and inexperienced, teacher is likely to fall into one of two cardinal and opposite errors : either he will aim at an analysis too particularistic, and lose sight of the whole in a consideration of details or constituent parts ; or he will indulge in a synthesis too large, too vague, possibly too sentimental, and in any case not sufficiently built up and elaborated by and with his pupils.

To return to the two main divisions of interpretation and criticism. Interpretation is basic, and in its nature precedes criticism. Criticism is supplementary, but indispensable to any literary culture which aspires to thoroughness. Interpretation involves the making clear to oneself of the meaning and function of the various constituent elements of a given piece of literature, and of the piece of literature as a whole. These constituent elements are such as words, sentences, and paragraphs ; the organic divisions of a work of literary art, such as the Exordium, Statement of Facts, Proof, etc., of an oration ; quotations or allusions ; and figures of speech. On each of these attention should be bestowed ; and to each regard has been paid in the Notes to this book. What has been done in the Notes, however, has been mainly suggestive, and the pupil should be required—and encouraged—to do much more for himself, the results of his inquiries being tested in the class-room.

Criticism, from its very nature, implies comparison—comparison with principles assumed or deduced ; comparison with other productions of the same class ; or, with respect to the opinions enounced by the author, comparison with the statements or opinions of other persons worthy of credence or respect. Thus the structure of Burke's speech might be studied with reference to its conformity or non-conformity to principles deduced from the practice of the ancients, or the speech might be systematically compared with other eminent examples of its class, ancient or modern, and its superiority or inferiority demonstrated. The style might be examined with respect to various qualities, and its specific merits determined. All information directly tending to confirm or disprove the statements, assumptions, or conclusions propounded by Burke would also be valuable in its bearing upon criticism, since it would increase the ability of the student to determine the trustworthiness of Burke as a guide. Finally, the estimates thus formed by the student might be carefully compared with those expressed by critics of established reputation, both among Burke's contemporaries and those of subsequent date.

The student, and at all events the teacher, is strongly advised to go through the Introduction and Notes, classifying the matter according as it bears upon interpretation or criticism, and, under each of these two heads, according to the particular subdivision which is illustrated. If the teacher has once done this with care, he will scarcely need specific suggestions as to how the book should be used.

Both interpretation and criticism, at least in the case of a masterwork like Burke's *Speech on Conciliation*, demand strenuous exercise of the intellectual faculties, as well as continual appeals to the moral nature. The combination of these two kinds of study ought to strengthen the reasoning powers, develop the imagination, cultivate the nobler sensibilities, and fortify the character.

As to the most helpful books, the Introduction and Notes, considered in conjunction with the Index, will afford many useful hints. It may be added, however, that the teacher who desires to be thoroughly equipped for dealing with Burke's American speeches will do well to have at hand the *Annual Register*, the *Parliamentary History*, and the *Statutes at Large*. No compilations from these sources, not even the best, can take their place ; for nothing else can convey such a sense of personal familiarity with the actors in this momentous epoch of English history, and of the motives and passions by which they were actuated ; nothing else will insure an acquaintance, no less desirable because it is rare, with the decrees and other public papers in which their political wisdom was formulated. If those volumes are inaccessible, Lecky's *England in the Eighteenth Century* and Bancroft's *History of the United States* will measurably serve as substitutes. From all these I have quoted freely, but a connected view of events and their causes can hardly be obtained through the medium of extracts, however copious.

The specimen examination papers that follow will serve to illustrate the principles here laid down, and may be taken as types of those by which the instructor should test the student's progress, as he slowly and critically masters the substance, the method, and the style of the speech.

SPECIMEN EXAMINATION PAPERS

I

" REFINED policy ever has been the parent of confusion, and ever will be so, as long as the world endures. Plain good intention, which is as easily discovered at the first view as fraud is surely detected at last, is, let me say, of no mean force in the government of mankind. Genuine simplicity of heart is a healing and cementing principle. My plan, therefore, being formed upon the most simple grounds imaginable, may disappoint some people when they hear it. It has nothing to recommend it to the pruriency of curious ears. There is nothing at all new and captivating in it. It has nothing of the splendour of the project which has been lately laid upon your table by the Noble Lord in the Blue Ribbon."

1. What were the admirable traits in the character of this "Noble Lord"? Why does not history hold him in greater honour? Give reasons for your opinion.

2. Describe the "project" referred to. In what did its "splendour" consist? On what grounds did Burke criticize it?

3. Wherein does Burke think his own plan preferable to that of the "Noble Lord"? If he preferred his own, why does he here seek to disparage it?

4. Summarize each of the resolutions comprised in Burke's plan.

5. In what division of the speech does this passage occur? What is the function of this division, according to the ancient rhetoricians, and how far does Burke conform to their views?

6. Give a list of the words in the passage which Burke evidently employs in order to awaken unfavourable ideas in the hearer's mind. State the precise effect of each of these words.

7. What does Burke mean by "refined policy?" What by "confusion?" What "refined policy" had been employed, or was it proposed to employ, in dealing with the Colonies?

8. (*a*) Would it have been better if Burke had used the expression, "immense force," instead of "no mean force"? Give reasons. (*b*) Why not "pruriency of *itching* ears"?

9. Wherein does Burke here seem to be a follower of the Sermon on the Mount? Did he ever advocate hostility to other nations, and, if so, on what grounds?

II

1. In the early part of the speech, what reasons does Burke adduce against the employment of force in dealing with the Colonies? Had he chosen to introduce these reasons elsewhere, what would have been the proper place for them, and why? Why did he prefer to have them where they stand? Do they not constitute an interruption in their present position, and, if so, why should they not be removed?

2. Under what circumstances is it proper to introduce Scriptural allusions in a speech, and what effect do they produce? State as many reasons as you can why an orator should be familiar with the Bible.

3. Give four instances in which Burke's statements are confirmed by history. Give as many as you can where his statements or views are not substantiated by the best authorities.

4. Under what distinct heads, in the Introduction, does Goodrich discuss Burke? Summarize his opinions under each of these heads.

5. Illustrate Burke's use of irony and sarcasm by quoting three passages illustrating these figures, distinguishing between the two. Do irony and sarcasm render a speech more interesting? if so, explain why.

III

1. Quote a fine passage, not less than three hundred words in length, from the speech. Underscore the words which should be emphasized in its delivery.

2. Goodrich says : "So quick and delicate were his perceptions that he saw his way clearly through the most complicated relations, following out the finest thread of thought without once letting go his hold, or becoming lost or perplexed in the intricacies of the subject."

If this is true, why did Burke apparently dislike subtlety both in reasoning and in practice? Did he merely wish to persuade others that he was a man of plain common-sense, while really displaying remarkable acuteness? If not, how do you reconcile the seeming contradiction?

3. What did the Americans object to in the "Act for the impartial administration of justice"? What was the chief provision of the Boston Port Bill?

4. What arguments did Dean Tucker adduce in favour of allowing the Colonies to separate from England? How does Burke dispose of this proposition? If Burke was right, what shall we think of Tucker's plan? If Tucker was right, what shall we think of Burke's arguments?

CHRONOLOGICAL TABLE.

BURKE'S LIFE.	HISTORY.	ENGLISH AND AMERICAN LITERATURE.
1729. Born, January 12 (probably).	1730. Methodism begins. 1732. Georgia colonized.	1729. Pope, Dunciad with Notes Variorum. 1733. Franklin, Poor Richard's Almanac. 1733–4. Pope, Essay on Man. 1735. Pope, Epistle to Arbuthnot. 1736. Butler, Analogy. 1737. Glover, Leonidas. Shenstone, Schoolmistress. 1738. Johnson, London. 1740. Richardson, Pamela.
	1741. War of the Austrian Succession.	1742. Fielding, Joseph Andrews. Young, Night Thoughts.
1743. Enters Trinity College, Dublin.	1743. Battle of Dettingen. 1745. Battle of Fontenoy. 1745–6. Jacobite Rebellion. 1746. Princeton University founded.	1743. Blair, The Grave. Akenside, Pleasures of the Imagination.
1748. Graduated.		1748. Richardson, Clarissa Harlowe. Thomson, Castle of Indolence.
	1749. University of Pennsylvania founded.	1749. Bolingbroke, Idea of a Patriot King. Fielding, Tom Jones. Johnson, Vanity of Human Wishes.
1750. Goes to London.		1751. Gray, Elegy.
	1753. British Museum founded. 1754. Columbia University founded.	1754. Jonathan Edwards, Freedom of the Will.
	1755. French and Indian War. Expulsion of the Acadians.	1755. Johnson, Dictionary.
1756. Vindication of Natural Society; Sublime and Beautiful. 1756–7. Marries Jane Nugent.	1756. Black Hole of Calcutta. Seven Years' War begun.	

CHRONOLOGICAL TABLE.—*Continued.*

BURKE'S LIFE.	HISTORY.	ENGLISH AND AMERICAN LITERATURE.
1757. European Settlements in America; Abridgment of History of England (in part).	1757. Foundation of England's Indian Empire.	
1759. Annual Register begun. Secretary to Hamilton.	1759. Capture of Quebec and Wolfe's Death.	1759. Goldsmith, The Bee. Johnson, Rasselas.
	1760. Accession of George III.	1762. Macpherson, Ossian.
	1763. Peace of Paris.	
	1763–5. Grenville's Administration.	
1764. Member of "The Club."		1764. Walpole, Castle of Otranto.
1765. Secretary to Lord Rockingham. M.P. for W .ndover.	1765. Stamp Act passed. Watt's steam-engine.	1765. Blackstone, Commentaries.
	1765–6. Rockingham's Administration.	
	1766. Stamp Act repealed.	1766. Goldsmith, Vicar of Wakefield.
	1766–7. Chatham's Administration.	
	1767–70. Grafton's Administration.	
1768. Pu chases Beaconsfield, 24 miles from London.		1768. Gray, Poems.
1769. Present State of the Nation.	1769. Napoleon Bonaparte born.	1769–72. "Junius." Letters.
1770. Present Discontents.	1770. Boston Massacre.	1770. Goldsmith, Deserted Village.
	1770–82. North's Administration.	
1771. Agent for New York.	1771. English Debates reported (had been prohibited since 1738).	1771. Smollett, Humphrey Clinker.
		1772. Timothy Dwight, America.
1773. Visit to France.	1773. Tea thrown into Boston Harbour.	
1774. American Taxation. M.P. for Bristol.	1774. Boston Port Bill. First Congress at Philadelphia.	
1775. Conciliation with America.	1775. Revolutionary War begun. Washington Commander-in-Chief.	1775. Sheridan, Rivals.
	1776. Declaration of Independence.	1776. Gibbon, Decline and Fall, Vol. I. Adam Smith, Wealth of Nations. Thomas Paine, Common Sense.
1777. Letter to Sheriffs of Bristol.	1777. Burgoyne surrenders.	1777. Sheridan, School for Scandal.

CHRONOLOGICAL TABLE.—*Continued.*

BURKE'S LIFE.	HISTORY.	ENGLISH AND AMERICAN LITERATURE.
	1778. Death of Chatham.	
	1778. Alliance of France and America.	
1780. Loses his seat for Bristol. Economic Reform.	1780. Lord George Gordon Riots.	
1781. M.P. for Malton.	1781. Cornwallis surrenders.	
1782. Paymaster of the Forces, but soon resigns.	1782. Rockingham's Second Administration. Shelburne's Administration. End of Revolutionary War. Daniel Webster born.	1782. Cowper, Table Talk. Trumbull, Mc Fingal.
1783. Paymaster again.	1783. Coalition Ministry. Pitt's Administration begun. Washington Irving born. Recognition of independence of United States.	1783. Crabbe, The Village.
1784. Lord Rector of Glasgow University.		
1785. On the Nabob of Arcot's Debts.	1785. London "Times" established.	1785. Cowper, The Task.
1787. Impeachment of Warren Hastings.		1786. Burns, Poems, chiefly in the Scottish Dialect.
1788. Speeches in the Hastings Case.	1788-95. Trial of Warren Hastings.	
	1789. Beginning of French Revolution. Washington first President.	1789. Blake, Songs of Innocence.
1790. Reflections on the Revolution in France.		
1791. Appeal from the New to the Old Whigs. Breaks with Fox.		1791. Boswell, Life of Johnson.
	1793. Reign of Terror in France.	1793. Wordsworth, An Evening Walk. Godwin, Political Justice.
1794. Closing Speeches in the Hastings Case. Death of his Son.		1794. Radcliffe, Mysteries of Udolpho.
1795. Retires to Beaconsfield.		1795. Lewis, The Monk.
1796. Letter to a Noble Lord. Letters on the Regicide Peace, I. and II.	1796. Bonaparte in Italy. Death of Burns. Washington's Farewell Address.	1796. Scott, Translations from Bürger. Coleridge, Poems on Various Subjects.
1797. Death, July 9.	1797. John Adams President.	1797. The Anti-Jacobin.

SPEECH

OF

EDMUND BURKE, ESQ.

ON

MOVING HIS RESOLUTIONS

FOR

CONCILIATION WITH THE COLONIES

MARCH 22, 1775

THE SECOND EDITION

LONDON
PRINTED FOR J. DODSLEY, IN PALL-MALL
MDCCLXXV

SPEECH OF EDMUND BURKE, ESQ.

[*Exordium.*]

1. I HOPE, Sir, that notwithstanding the austerity of
the Chair, your good nature will incline you to some degree of indulgence towards human frailty. You will
not think it unnatural, that those who have an object
depending which strongly engages their hopes and fears, 5
should be somewhat inclined to superstition. As I
came into the House full of anxiety about the event of
my motion, I found, to my infinite surprise, that the
grand penal bill, by which we had passed sentence on
the trade and sustenance of America, is to be returned 10
to us from the other House. I do confess, I could not
help looking on this event as a fortunate omen. I look
upon it as a sort of providential favour, by which we are
put once more in possession of our deliberative capacity,
upon a business so very questionable in its nature, so 15
very uncertain in its issue. By the return of this bill,
which seemed to have taken its flight for ever, we are at
this very instant nearly as free to choose a plan for our
American government as we were on the first day of the
session. If, Sir, we incline to the side of conciliation, 20
we are not at all embarrassed—unless we please to
make ourselves so—by any incongruous mixture of
coercion and restraint. We are therefore called upon,
as it were by a superior warning voice, again to attend
to America; to attend to the whole of it together; and 25

to review the subject with an unusual degree of care
and calmness.

2. Surely it is an awful subject; or there is none so
on this side of the grave. When I first had the honour
5 of a seat in this House, the affairs of that Continent
pressed themselves upon us as the most important and
most delicate object of parliamentary attention. My
little share in this great deliberation oppressed me. I
found myself a partaker in a very high trust; and hav-
10 ing no sort of reason to rely on the strength of my natural abilities for the proper execution of that trust, I
was obliged to take more than common pains to instruct
myself in everything which relates to our Colonies. I
was not less under the necessity of forming some fixed
15 ideas concerning the general policy of the British Empire. Something of this sort seemed to be indispensable, in order, amidst so vast a fluctuation of passions
and opinions, to concentre my thoughts, to ballast
my conduct, to preserve me from being blown about
20 by every wind of fashionable doctrine. I really did
not think it safe or manly to have fresh principles to
seek upon every fresh mail which should arrive from
America.

3. At that period I had the fortune to find myself in
25 perfect concurrence with a large majority in this House.
Bowing under that high authority, and penetrated with
the sharpness and strength of that early impression, I
have continued ever since, without the least deviation,
in my original sentiments. Whether this be owing to
30 an obstinate perseverance in error, or to a religious ad-
herence to what appears to me truth and reason, it is in
your equity to judge.

4. Sir, Parliament, having an enlarged view of objects, made, during this interval, more frequent changes
35 in their sentiments and their conduct than could be

justified in a particular person upon the contracted scale of private information. But though I do not hazard anything approaching to censure on the motives of former Parliaments to all those alterations, one fact is undoubted,—that under them the state of America has 5 been kept in continual agitation. Everything administered as remedy to the public complaint, if it did not produce, was at least followed by, an heightening of the distemper ; until, by a variety of experiments, that important country has been brought into her present sit- 10 uation—a situation which I will not miscall, which I dare not name, which I scarcely know how to comprehend in the terms of any description.

5. In this posture, Sir, things stood at the beginning of the session. About that time, a worthy member of 15 great parliamentary experience, who, in the year 1766, filled the chair of the American Committee with much ability, took me aside, and, lamenting the present aspect of our politics, told me, things were come to such a pass, that our former methods of proceeding in 20 the House would be no longer tolerated. That the public tribunal—never too indulgent to a long and unsuccessful opposition—would now scrutinize our conduct with unusual severity. That the very vicissitudes and shiftings of ministerial measures, instead of con- 25 victing their authors of inconstancy and want of system, would be taken as an occasion of charging us with a predetermined discontent which nothing could satisfy ; whilst we accused every measure of vigour as cruel, and every proposal of lenity as weak and irresolute. The 30 public, he said, would not have patience to see us play the game out with our adversaries : we must produce our hand. It would be expected that those who for many years had been active in such affairs should show that they had formed some clear and decided idea of 35

the principles of Colony government, and were capable
of drawing out something like a platform of the ground
which might be laid for future and permanent tranquillity.

5   6. I felt the truth of what my Honourable Friend represented—but I felt my situation too. His application
might have been made with far greater propriety to
many other gentlemen. No man was indeed ever better
disposed, or worse qualified, for such an undertaking,
10 than myself. Though I gave so far in to his opinion
that I immediately threw my thoughts into a sort of
parliamentary form, I was by no means equally ready
to produce them. It generally argues some degree of
natural impotence of mind, or some want of knowledge
15 of the world, to hazard plans of government except
from a seat of authority. Propositions are made, not
only ineffectually, but somewhat disreputably, when the
minds of men are not properly disposed for their reception ; and, for my part, I am not ambitious of ridicule
20 —not absolutely a candidate for disgrace.

7. Besides, Sir, to speak the plain truth, I have in
general no very exalted opinion of the virtue of paper
government, nor of any politics in which the plan is to
be wholly separated from the execution. But when I
25 saw that anger and violence prevailed every day more
and more, and that things were hastening towards an
incurable alienation of our Colonies, I confess my caution
gave way. I felt this as one of those few moments in
which decorum yields to a higher duty. Public calam-
30 ity is a mighty leveller ; and there are occasions when
any, even the slightest, chance of doing good must be
laid hold on, even by the most inconsiderable person.

8. To restore order and repose to an empire so great
and so distracted as ours, is, merely in the attempt, an
35 undertaking that would ennoble the flights of the high-

est genius, and obtain pardon for the efforts of the
meanest understanding.   Struggling a good while with
these thoughts, by degrees I felt myself more firm.   I
derived, at length, some confidence from what in other
circumstances usually produces timidity.   I grew less 5
anxious, even from the idea of my own insignificance.
For, judging of what you are by what you ought to be,
I persuaded myself that you would not reject a reasonable proposition because it had nothing but its reason
to recommend it.   On the other hand, being totally 10
destitute of all shadow of influence, natural or adventitious, I was very sure that, if my proposition were
futile or dangerous, if it were weakly conceived or im-
properly timed, there was nothing exterior to it, of
power to awe, dazzle, or delude you.   You will see it 15
just as it is, and you will treat it just as it deserves.

[*Status.*]

9. The proposition is peace.   Not peace through the
medium of war; not peace to be hunted through the
labyrinth of intricate and endless negotiations ; not
peace to arise out of universal discord, fomented from 20
principle in all parts of the empire ; not peace to depend
on the juridical determination of perplexing questions,
or the precise marking the shadowy boundaries of a
complex government.   It is simple peace, sought in its
natural course, and in its ordinary haunts ;—it is peace 25
sought in the spirit of peace, and laid in principles
purely pacific.   I propose, by removing the ground of
the difference, and by restoring the *former unsuspecting
confidence of the Colonies in the Mother Country*, to give
permanent satisfaction to your people, and—far from a 30
scheme of ruling by discord—to reconcile them to
each other in the same act, and by the bond of the very

same interest, which reconciles them to British government.

10. My idea is nothing more. Refined policy ever has
been the parent of confusion, and ever will be so, as long
5 as the world endures. Plain good intention, which is as
easily discovered at the first view as fraud is surely detected at last, is, let me say, of no mean force in the government of mankind. Genuine simplicity of heart is a
healing and cementing principle. My plan, therefore,
10 being formed upon the most simple grounds imaginable,
may disappoint some people when they hear it. It has
nothing to recommend it to the pruriency of curious
ears. There is nothing at all new and captivating in it.
It has nothing of the splendour of the project which has
15 been lately laid upon your table by the Noble Lord in
the Blue Ribbon. It does not propose to fill your lobby
with squabbling Colony agents, who will require the in-
terposition of your mace at every instant, to keep the
peace amongst them. It does not institute a magnificent
20 auction of finance, where captivated provinces come to
general ransom by bidding against each other, until you
knock down the hammer, and determine a proportion of
payments beyond all the powers of algebra to equalize
and settle.

25 11. The plan which I shall presume to suggest derives, however, one great advantage from the proposition
and registry of that Noble Lord's project. The idea of
conciliation is admissible. First, the House, in accepting the resolution moved by the Noble Lord, has
30 admitted, notwithstanding the menacing front of our
address, notwithstanding our heavy bill of pains and
penalties, that we do not think ourselves precluded from
all ideas of free grace and bounty.

12. The House has gone farther : it has declared con-
35 ciliation admissible, *previous* to any submission on the

part of America.   It has even shot a good deal beyond
that mark, and has admitted that the complaints of our
former mode of exerting the right of taxation were not
wholly unfounded.   That right thus exerted is allowed
to have had something reprehensible in it, something 5
unwise or something grievous, since, in the midst of
our heat and resentment, we of ourselves have proposed
a capital alteration ; and, in order to get rid of what
seemed so very exceptionable, have instituted a mode
that is altogether new—one that is, indeed, wholly alien 10
from all the ancient methods and forms of Parliament.

13. The *principle* of this proceeding is large enough
for my purpose.   The means proposed by the Noble
Lord for carrying his ideas into execution, I think,
indeed, are very indifferently suited to the end, and this 15
I shall endeavour to show you before I sit down.   But,
for the present, I take my ground on the admitted
principle.   I mean to give peace.   Peace implies reconciliation ; and, where there has been a material dispute,
reconciliation does in a manner always imply concession 20
on the one part or on the other.   In this state of things I
make no difficulty in affirming that the proposal ought to
originate from us.   Great and acknowledged force is not
impaired, either in effect or in opinion, by an unwilling-
ness to exert itself.   The superior power may offer peace 25
with honour and with safety.   Such an offer from such
a power will be attributed to magnanimity.   But the
concessions of the weak are the concessions of fear.
When such a one is disarmed, he is wholly at the mercy
of his superior ; and he loses for ever that time and 30
those chances, which, as they happen to all men, are
the strength and resources of all inferior power.•

14. The capital leading questions on which you must
this day decide are these two : First, whether you ought
to concede ; and, secondly, what your concession ought 35

to be. On the first of these questions we have gained
—as I have just taken the liberty of observing to you—
some ground. But I am sensible that a good deal more
is still to be done. Indeed, Sir, to enable us to deter-
5 mine both on the one and the other of these great
questions with a firm and precise judgment, I think
it may be necessary to consider distinctly the true
nature and the peculiar circumstances of the object
which we have before us. Because, after all our struggle,
10 whether we will or not, we must govern America according to that nature and to those circumstances, and
not according to our own imaginations, not according to
abstract ideas of right; by no means according to mere
general theories of government, the resort to which
15 appears to me, in our present situation, no better than
arrant trifling. I shall therefore endeavour, with your
leave, to lay before you some of the most material of
these circumstances in as full and as clear a manner as I
am able to state them.

[*Statement of Facts.*]

20   15. The first thing that we have to consider with
regard to the nature of the object is the number of
people in the Colonies. I have taken for some years a
good deal of pains on that point. I can by no calculation justify myself in placing the number below two
25 millions of inhabitants of our own European blood and
colour; besides at least 500,000 others, who form no
inconsiderable part of the strength and opulence of the
whole. This, Sir, is, I believe, about the true number.
There is no occasion to exaggerate, where plain truth
30 is of so much weight and importance. But whether I
put the present numbers too high or too low is a matter
of little moment. Such is the strength with which

population shoots in that part of the world, that, state
the numbers as high as we will, whilst the dispute
continues the exaggeration ends. Whilst we are discussing any given magnitude, they are grown to it.
Whilst we spend our time in deliberating on the mode of 5
governing two millions, we shall find we have millions
more to manage. Your children do not grow faster
from infancy to manhood, than they spread from families to communities, and from villages to nations.

16. I put this consideration of the present and the 10
growing numbers in the front of our deliberation;
because, Sir, this consideration will make it evident to a
blunter discernment than yours, that no partial, narrow,
contracted, pinched, occasional system will· be at all
suitable to such an object. It will show you that it 15
is not to be considered as one of those *minima* which are
out of the eye and consideration of the law; not a paltry excrescence of the State; not a mean dependent,
who may be neglected with little damage, and provoked
with little danger. It will prove that some degree of 20
care and caution is required in the handling such an
object; it will show that you ought not, in reason,
to trifle with so large a mass of the interests and feelings
of the human race. You could at no time do so without
guilt; and be assured you will not be able to do it long 25
with impunity.

17. But the population of this country, the great and
growing population, though a very important consideration, will lose much of its weight, if not combined with
other circumstances. The commerce of your Colonies is 30
out of all proportion beyond the numbers of the-people.
This ground of their commerce indeed has been trod
some days ago, and with great ability, by a distinguished
person, at your bar. This gentleman, after thirty-five

years—it is so long since he first appeared at the same
place to plead for the commerce of Great Britain—has
come again before you to plead the same cause, without
any other effect of time than that, to the fire of imagi-
5 nation and extent of erudition, which even then marked
him as one of the first literary characters of his age,
he has added a consummate knowledge in the commercial interest of his country, formed by a long course
of enlightened and discriminating experience.

10   18. Sir, I should be inexcusable in coming after such
a person with any detail, if a great part of the members
who now fill the House had not the misfortune to be
absent when he appeared at your bar.   Besides, Sir, I
propose to take the matter at periods of time somewhat
15 different from his.   There is, if I mistake not, a point
of view, from whence if you will look at this subject, it
is impossible that it should not make an impression
upon you.

    19. I have in my hand two accounts :—one a compara-
20 tive state of the export trade of England to its Colonies, as it stood in the year 1704, and as it stood in the
year 1772 ; the other a state of the export trade of this
country to its Colonies alone, as it stood in 1772, compared with the whole trade of England to all parts of
25 the world—the Colonies included—in the year 1704.
They are from good vouchers : the latter period from
the accounts on your table, the earlier from an original
manuscript of Davenant, who first established the Inspector-General's office, which has been ever since his
30 time so abundant a source of parliamentary information.

    20. The export trade to the Colonies consists of three
great branches :—the African, which, terminating almost
wholly in the Colonies, must be put to the account of
35 their commerce ; the West Indian ; and the North

American.   All these are so interwoven that the attempt
to separate them would tear to pieces the contexture of
the whole ; and, if not entirely destroy, would very
much depreciate the value of all the parts.   I therefore
consider these three denominations to be, what in effect 5
they are, one trade.

21. The trade to the Colonies, taken on the export
side, at the beginning of this century, that is, in the
year 1704, stood thus :—

Exports to North America and the 10	
West Indies	£483,265
To Africa	86,665
	£569,930

22. In the year 1772, which I take as a middle year
between the highest and lowest of those lately laid on 15
your table, the account was as follows :—

To North America and the West	
Indies	£4,791,734
To Africa	866,398
To which if you add the export 20	
trade from Scotland, which	
had in 1704 no existence . .	364,000
	£6,022,132

23. From five hundred and odd thousand, it has
grown to six millions.   It has increased no less than 25
twelvefold.   This is the state of the Colony trade, as
compared with itself at these two periods, within this
century ; and this is matter for meditation.   But this
is not all.   Examine my second account.   See how the
export trade to the Colonies alone in 1772 stood in the 30

other point of view, that is, as compared to the **whole**
trade of England in 1704.

The whole export trade of England,
  including that to the Colonies,
5   in 1704 . . . . £6,509,000
Export to the Colonies alone, in 1772   6,022,000
                                        ——————
                        Difference   £487,000

24. The trade with America alone is now within less
than £500,000 of being equal to what this great commer-
10 cial nation, England, carried on at the beginning of this
century with the whole world ! If I had taken the
largest year of those on your table, it would rather have
exceeded. But, it will be said, is not this American
trade an unnatural protuberance, that has drawn the
15 juices from the rest of the body ? The reverse. It is
the very food that has nourished every other part into
its present magnitude. Our general trade has been
greatly augmented, and augmented more or less in almost every part to which it ever extended — but with
20 this material difference, that of the six millions which
in the beginning of the century constituted the whole
mass of our export commerce, the Colony trade was but
one twelfth part ; it is now (as a part of sixteen millions)
considerably more than a third of the whole. This is
25 the relative proportion of the importance of the Colonies
at these two periods : and all reasoning concerning our
mode of treating them must have this proportion as its
basis, or it is a reasoning weak, rotten, and sophistical.
25. Mr. Speaker, I cannot prevail on myself to hurry
30 over this great consideration. It is good for us to be
here. We stand where we have an immense view of
what is, and what is past. Clouds, indeed, and darkness rest upon the future. Let us, however, before we

descend from this noble eminence, reflect that this growth of our national prosperity has happened within the short period of the life of man. It has happened within sixty-eight years. There are those alive whose memory might touch the two extremities. For instance, 5 my Lord Bathurst might remember all the stages of the progress. He was in 1704 of an age at least to be made to comprehend such things. He was then old enough

—Acta parentum
Jam legere, et quæ sit poterit cognoscere virtus. 10

Suppose, Sir, that the angel of this auspicious youth, foreseeing the many virtues which made him one of the most amiable, as he is one of the most fortunate, men of his age, had opened to him in vision that when, in the fourth generation, the third Prince of 15 the House of Brunswick had sat twelve years on the throne of that nation, which—by the happy issue of moderate and healing counsels—was to be made Great Britain, he should see his son, Lord Chancellor of England, turn back the current of hereditary dignity 20 to its fountain, and raise him to a higher rank of peerage, whilst he enriched the family with a new one—if, amidst these bright and happy scenes of domestic honour and prosperity, that angel should have drawn up the curtain, and unfolded the rising glories of his country, 25 and, whilst he was gazing with admiration on the then commercial grandeur of England, the Genius should point out to him a little speck, scarce visible in the mass of the national interest, a small seminal principle rather than a formed body, and should tell him — 30 "Young man, there is America, which at this day serves for little more than to amuse you with stories of savage men and uncouth manners, yet shall, before you taste of death, show itself equal to the whole of

that commerce which now attracts the envy of the world. Whatever England has been growing to by a progressive increase of improvement, brought in by varieties of people, by succession of civilizing con-
5 quests and civilizing settlements in a series of seventeen hundred years, you shall see as much added to her by America in the course of a single life!" If this state of his country had been foretold to him, would it not require all the sanguine credulity of youth, and all the
10 fervid glow of enthusiasm, to make him believe it? Fortunate man, he has lived to see it! Fortunate indeed, if he lives to see nothing that shall vary the prospect, and cloud the setting of his day!

26. Excuse me, Sir, if, turning from such thoughts,
15 I resume this comparative view once more. You have seen it on a large scale; look at it on a small one. I will point out to your attention a particular instance of it in the single Province of Pennsylvania. In the year 1704, that Province called for £11,459 in value of your
20 commodities, native and foreign. This was the whole. What did it demand in 1772? Why, nearly fifty times as much; for in that year the export to Pennsylvania was £507,909 — nearly equal to the export to all the Colonies together in the first period.

25 27. I choose, Sir, to enter into these minute and particular details, because generalities, which in all other cases are apt to heighten and raise the subject, have here a tendency to sink it. When we speak of the commerce with our Colonies, fiction lags after truth, invention is
30 unfruitful, and imagination cold and barren.

28. So far, Sir, as to the importance of the object, in the view of its commerce, as concerned in the exports from England. If I were to detail the imports, I could show how many enjoyments they procure, which deceive the
35 burthen of life; how many materials which invigorate

the springs of national industry, and extend and animate
every part of our foreign and domestic commerce. This
would be a curious subject indeed—but I must prescribe
bounds to myself in a matter so vast and various.

29. I pass therefore to the Colonies in another point 5
of view—their agriculture. This they have prosecuted
with such a spirit that, besides feeding plentifully their
own growing multitude, their annual export of grain,
comprehending rice, has some years ago exceeded a
million in value. Of their last harvest, I am persuaded 10
they will export much more. At the beginning of the
century some of these Colonies imported corn from the
Mother Country. For some time past, the Old World
has been fed from the New. The scarcity which you
have felt would have been a desolating famine, if this 15
child of your old age, with a true filial piety, with a
Roman charity, had not put the full breast of its youth-
ful exuberance to the mouth of its exhausted parent.

30. As to the wealth which the Colonies have drawn
from the sea by their fisheries, you had all that matter 20
fully opened at your bar. You surely thought these
acquisitions of value, for they seemed even to excite
your envy ; and yet the spirit by which that enterprising
employment has been exercised ought rather, in my
opinion, to have raised your esteem and admiration. 25
And pray, Sir, what in the world is equal to it ? Pass
by the other parts, and look at the manner in which the
people of New England have of late carried on the whale
fisnery. Whilst we follow them among the tumbling
mountains of ice, and behold them penetrating into the 30
deepest frozen recesses of Hudson's Bay and Davis'
Straits, whilst we are looking for them beneath the
Arctic Circle, we hear that they have pierced into the

2

opposite region of polar cold, that they are at the An-
tipodes, and engaged under the frozen Serpent of the
South.   Falkland Island, which seemed too remote and
romantic an object for the grasp of national ambition,
5 is but a stage and resting-place in the progress of their
victorious industry.   Nor is the equinoctial heat more
discouraging to them than the accumulated winter of
both the poles.   We know that whilst some of them
draw the line and strike the harpoon on the coast of
10 Africa, others run the longitude, and pursue their gi-
gantic game along the coast of Brazil.   No sea but what
is vexed by their fisheries ; no climate that is not witness to their toils.   Neither the perseverance of Holland,
nor the activity of France, nor the dextrous and firm
15 sagacity of English enterprise, ever carried this most
perilous mode of hardy industry to the extent to which
it has been pushed by this recent people,—a people who
are still, as it were, but in the gristle, and not yet hard-
ened into the bone of manhood.

20   31. When I contemplate these things ; when I know
that the Colonies in general owe little or nothing to any
care of ours, and that they are not squeezed into this
happy form by the constraints of watchful and suspicious
government, but that, through a wise and salutary neg-
25 lect, a generous nature has been suffered to take her
own way to perfection ; when I reflect upon these effects,
when I see how profitable they have been to us, I feel
all the pride of power sink, and all presumption in the
wisdom of human contrivances melt and die away with-
30 in me.   My rigour relents.   I pardon something to the
spirit of liberty.

[*Digression from Statement.*]

32. I am sensible, Sir, that all which I have asserted in my detail is admitted in the gross ; but that quite a different conclusion is drawn from it. America, gentlemen say, is a noble object. It is an object well worth fighting for. Certainly it is, if fighting a people be the best way of gaining them. Gentlemen in this respect will be led to their choice of means by their complexions and their habits. Those who understand the military art will of course have some predilection for it. Those who wield the thunder of the state may have more confidence in the efficacy of arms. But I confess, possibly for want of this knowledge, my opinion is much more in favour of prudent management than of force ; considering force not as an odious, but a feeble instrument, for preserving a people so numerous, so active, so growing, so spirited as this, in a profitable and subordinate connection with us.

33. First, Sir, permit me to observe that the use of force alone is but *temporary*. It may subdue for a moment, but it does not remove the necessity of subduing again ; and a nation is not governed which is perpetually to be conquered.

34. My next objection is its *uncertainty*. Terror is not always the effect of force ; and an armament is not a victory. If you do not succeed, you are without resource : for, conciliation failing, force remains ; but, force failing, no further hope of reconciliation is left. Power and authority are sometimes bought by kindness, but they can never be begged as alms by an impoverished and defeated violence.

35. A further objection to force is, that you *impair the object* by your very endeavours to preserve it. The thing you fought for is not the thing which you recover,

but depreciated, sunk, wasted, and consumed in the contest.   Nothing less will content me than *whole America.*
I do not choose to consume its strength along with our
own, because in all parts it is the British strength that
5 I consume.   I do not choose to be caught by a foreign
enemy at the end of this exhausting conflict, and still
less in the midst of it.   I may escape, but I can make no
insurance against such an event.   Let me add, that I do
not choose wholly to break the American spirit, because
10 it is the spirit that has made the country.

36. Lastly, we have no sort of *experience* in favour of
force as an instrument in the rule of our Colonies. Their
growth and their utility has been owing to methods
altogether different.   Our ancient indulgence has been
15 said to be pursued to a fault.   It may be so.   But we
know, if feeling is evidence, that our fault was more
tolerable than our attempt to mend it, and our sin far
more salutary than our penitence.

[*Statement of Facts.*]

20   37. These, Sir, are my reasons for not entertaining'
that high opinion of untried force by which many gentlemen, for whose sentiments in other particulars I have
great respect, seem to be so greatly captivated.   But
there is still behind a third consideration concerning this
25 object, which serves to determine my opinion on the sort
of policy which ought to be pursued in the management
of America, even more than its population and its commerce—I mean its *temper and character.*

38. In this character of the Americans, a love of free-
30 dom is the predominating feature which marks and distinguishes the whole ; and as an ardent is always a jealous affection, your Colonies become suspicious, restive,
and untractable, whenever they see the least attempt to
wrest from them by force, or shuffle from them by chi-

cane, what they think the only advantage worth living for. This fierce spirit of liberty is stronger in the English Colonies probably than in any other people of the earth, and this from a great variety of powerful causes; which, to understand the true temper of their minds, 5 and the direction which this spirit takes, it will not be amiss to lay open somewhat more largely.

39. First, the people of the Colonies are descendants of Englishmen. England, Sir, is a nation, which still I hope respects, and formerly adored, her freedom. The 10 Colonists emigrated from you when this part of your character was most predominant, and they took this bias and direction the moment they parted from your hands. They are therefore not only devoted to liberty, but to liberty according to English ideas and on English prin- 1t ciples. Abstract liberty, like other mere abstractions, is not to be found. Liberty inheres in some sensible object; and every nation has formed to itself some favourite point, which, by way of eminence, becomes the criterion of their happiness. It happened, you know, 20 Sir, that the great contests for freedom in this country were from the earliest times chiefly upon the question of taxing. Most of the contests in the ancient commonwealths turned primarily on the right of election of magistrates, or on the balance among the several orders 25 of the State. The question of money was not with them so immediate. But in England it was otherwise. On this point of taxes the ablest pens and most eloquent tongues have been exercised, the greatest spirits have acted and suffered. In order to give the fullest satisfac- 30 tion concerning the importance of this point, it was not only necessary for those who in argument defended the excellence of the English Constitution to insist on this privilege of granting money as a dry point of fact, and to prove that the right had been acknowledged 35

in ancient parchments and blind usages to reside in
a certain body called a House of Commons. They went
much further ; they attempted to prove—and they succeeded — that in theory it ought to be so, from the
5 particular nature of a House of Commons as an immediate representative of the people, whether the old
records had delivered this oracle or not. They took
infinite pains to inculcate, as a fundamental principle,
that in all monarchies the people must in effect them-
10 selves, mediately or immediately, possess the power
of granting their own money, or no shadow of liberty
could subsist. The Colonies draw from you, as with
their life-blood, these ideas and principles. Their love
of liberty, as with you, fixed and attached on this specific
15 point of taxing. Liberty might be safe, or might be
endangered, in twenty other particulars, without their
being much pleased or alarmed. Here they felt its
pulse; and as they found that beat, they thought themselves sick or sound. I do not say whether they were
20 right or wrong in applying your general arguments
to their own case. It is not easy, indeed, to make a
monopoly of theorems and corollaries. The fact is that
they did thus apply those general arguments ; and your
mode of governing them, whether through lenity or
25 indolence, through wisdom or mistake, confirmed them
in the imagination that they, as well as you, had an
interest in these common principles.

40. They were further confirmed in this pleasing error
by the form of their provincial legislative Assemblies.
30 Their governments are popular in a high degree ; some
are merely popular ; in all, the popular representative is
the most weighty ; and this share of the people in their
ordinary government never fails to inspire them with
lofty sentiments, and with a strong aversion from what-
35 ever tends to deprive them of their chief importance.

41. If anything were wanting to this necessary operation of the form of government, religion would have
given it a complete effect.   Religion, always a principle
of energy, in this new people is no way worn out or impaired ; and their mode of professing it is also one main 5
cause of this free spirit.   The people are Protestants,
and of that kind which is the most adverse to all im-
plicit submission of mind and opinion.   This is a persuasion not only favourable to liberty, but built upon it.
I do not think, Sir, that the reason of this averseness in 10
the dissenting churches from all that looks like absolute
government, is so much to be sought in their religious
tenets as in their history.   Every one knows that the
Roman Catholic religion is at least coeval with most of
the governments where it prevails, that it has generally 15
gone hand in hand with them, and received great favour
and every kind of support from authority.   The Church
of England, too, was formed from her cradle under the
nursing care of regular government.   But the dissenting interests have sprung up in direct opposition to all 20
the ordinary powers of the world, and could justify that
opposition only on a strong claim to natural liberty.
Their very existence depended on the powerful and un-
remitted assertion of that claim.   All Protestantism,
even the most cold and passive, is a sort of dissent.   But 25
the religion most prevalent in our Northern Colonies is
a refinement on the principle of resistance ; it is the
dissidence of dissent, and the protestantism of the Protestant religion.   This religion, under a variety of denominations agreeing in nothing but in the communion 30
of the spirit of liberty, is predominant in most of the
Northern Provinces, where the Church of England, notwithstanding its legal rights, is in reality no more than a
sort of private sect, not composing, most probably, the
tenth of the people.   The Colonists left England when 35

this spirit was high, and in the emigrants was the highest of all; and even that stream of foreigners which has been constantly flowing into these Colonies has, for the greatest part, been composed of dissenters from
5 the establishments of their several countries, and have brought with them a temper and character far from alien to that of the people with whom they mixed.

42. Sir, I can perceive by their manner that some gentlemen object to the latitude of this description, be-
10 cause in the Southern Colonies the Church of England forms a large body, and has a regular establishment. It is certainly true. There is, however, a circumstance attending these Colonies, which in my opinion fully counterbalances this difference, and makes the spirit of
15 liberty still more high and haughty than in those to the northward. It is, that in Virginia and the Carolinas they have a vast multitude of slaves. Where this is the case in any part of the world, those who are free are by far the most proud and jealous of their freedom.
20 Freedom is to them not only an enjoyment, but a kind of rank and privilege. Not seeing there that freedom, as in countries where it is a common blessing, and as broad and general as the air, may be united with much abject toil, with great misery, with all the exterior of
25 servitude, liberty looks amongst them like something that is more noble and liberal. I do not mean, Sir, to commend the superior morality of this sentiment, which has at least as much pride as virtue in it; but I cannot alter the nature of man. The fact is so : and these peo-
30 ple of the Southern Colonies are much more strongly, and with a higher and more stubborn spirit, attached to liberty, than those to the northward. Such were all the ancient commonwealths ; such were our Gothic ancestors ; such in our days were the Poles ; and such will be
35 all masters of slaves, who are not slaves themselves. **In**

such a people, the haughtiness of domination combines
with the spirit of freedom, fortifies it, and renders it invincible.

43. Permit me, Sir, to add another circumstance in
our Colonies, which contributes no mean part towards 5
the growth and effect of this untractable spirit. I mean
their education. In no country perhaps in the world
is the law so general a study. The profession itself is
numerous and powerful, and in most provinces it takes
the lead. The greater number of the deputies sent to 10
the Congress were lawyers. But all who read—and most
do read—endeavour to obtain some smattering in that science. I have been told by an eminent bookseller that in
no branch of his business, after tracts of popular devo-
tion, were so many books as those on the law exported to 15
the Plantations. The Colonists have now fallen into the
way of printing them for their own use. I hear that
they have sold nearly as many of Blackstone's Commentaries in America as in England. General Gage marks
out this disposition very particularly in a letter on your 20
table. He states that all the people in his government
are lawyers, or smatterers in law ; and that in Boston
they have been enabled, by successful chicane, wholly to
evade many parts of one of your capital penal constitutions. The smartness of debate will say that this 25
knowledge ought to teach them more clearly the rights
of legislature, their obligations to obedience, and the
penalties of rebellion. All this is mighty well. But
my Honourable and Learned Friend on the floor, who
condescends to mark what I say for animadversion, will 30
disdain that ground. He has heard, as well as I, that
when great honours and great emoluments do not win
over this knowledge to the service of the state, it is a
formidable adversary to government. If the spirit be
not tamed and broken by these happy methods, it is 35

stubborn and litigious. *Abeunt studia in mores.* This
study renders men acute, inquisitive, dextrous, prompt
in attack, ready in defense, full of resources. In other
countries, the people, more simple and of a less mer-
5 curial cast, judge of an ill principle in government only
by an actual grievance ; here they anticipate the evil,
and judge of the pressure of the grievance by the bad·
ness of the principle. They augur misgovernment at a
distance, and snuff the approach of tyranny in every
10 tainted breeze.

    44. The last cause of this disobedient spirit in the
Colonies is hardly less powerful than the rest, as it is not
merely moral, but laid deep in the natural constitution
of things. Three thousand miles of ocean lie between
15 you and them. No contrivance can prevent the effect
of this distance in weakening government. Seas roll,
and months pass, between the order and the execution ;
and the want of a speedy explanation of a single point
is enough to defeat a whole system. You have, indeed,
20 winged ministers of vengeance, who carry your bolts in
their pounces to the remotest verge of the sea. But
there a power steps in, that limits the arrogance of raging
passions and furious elements, and says, "So far shalt
thou go, and no farther." Who are you that should
25 fret and rage, and bite the chains of Nature ? Nothing
worse happens to you than does to all nations who have
extensive empire ; and it happens in all the forms into
which empire can be thrown. In large bodies, the cir·
culation of power must be less vigorous at the extremi-
30 ties. Nature has said it. The Turk cannot govern
Egypt, and Arabia, and Kurdistan, as he governs Thrace ;
nor has he the same dominion in Crimea and Algiers
which he has at Brusa and Smyrna. Despotism itself is
obliged to truck and huckster. The Sultan gets such
35 obedience as he can. He governs with a loose rein, that

ne may govern at all; and the whole of the force and vigour of his authority in his centre is derived from a prudent relaxation in all his borders. Spain, in her provinces, is perhaps not so well obeyed as you are in yours. She complies too; she submits; she watches 5 times. This is the immutable condition, the eternal law, of extensive and detached empire.

45. Then, Sir, from these six capital sources :—of descent; of form of government; of religion in the Northern Provinces; of manners in the Southern; of 10 education; of the remoteness of situation from the first mover of government—from all these causes a fierce spirit of liberty has grown up. It has grown with the growth of the people in your Colonies, and increased with the increase of their wealth; a spirit that, un- 15 happily meeting with an exercise of power in England, which, however lawful, is not reconcilable to any ideas of liberty, much less with theirs, has kindled this flame that is ready to consume us.

[*Proof, or Main Argument.*]

46. I do not mean to commend either the spirit in this 20 excess, or the moral causes which produce it. Perhaps a more smooth and accommodating spirit of freedom in them would be more acceptable to us. Perhaps ideas of liberty might be desired, more reconcilable with an arbitrary and boundless authority. Perhaps we might 25 wish the Colonists to be persuaded that their liberty is more secure when held in trust for them by us, as their guardians during a perpetual minority, than with any part of it in their own hands. But the question is not whether their spirit deserves praise or blame 30 —what, in the name of God, shall we do with it? You have before you the object, such as it is, with all its

glories, with all its imperfections on its head. You see
the magnitude ; the importance ; the temper ; the habits ; the disorders. By all these considerations we are
strongly urged to determine something concerning it.
5 We are called upon to fix some rule and line for our future conduct, which may give a little stability to our politics, and prevent the return of such unhappy delibera-
tions as the present. Every such return will bring the
matter before us in a still more untractable form. For
10 what astonishing and incredible things have we not seen
already ! What monsters have not been generated from
this unnatural contention ! Whilst every principle of
authority and resistance has been pushed, upon both
sides, as far as it would go, there is nothing so solid and
15 certain, either in reasoning or in practice, that has not
been shaken. Until very lately, all authority in America seemed to be nothing but an emanation from yours.
Even the popular part of the Colony Constitution derived all its activity, and its first vital movement, from
20 the pleasure of the Crown. We thought, Sir, that the
utmost which the discontented Colonists could do was
to disturb authority ; we never dreamt they could of
themselves supply it, knowing in general what an operose business it is to establish a government absolutely
25 new. But having, for our purposes in this contention,
resolved that none but an obedient Assembly should sit,
the humours of the people there, finding all passage
through the legal channel stopped, with great violence
broke out another way. Some Provinces have tried their
30 experiment, as we have tried ours ; and theirs has succeeded. They have formed a government sufficient for
its purposes, without the bustle of a revolution, or the
troublesome formality of an election. Evident necessity
and tacit consent have done the business in an instant.
35 So well they have done it, that Lord Dunmore—the ac-

count is among the fragments on your table—tells you
that the new institution is infinitely better obeyed than
the ancient government ever was in its most fortunate
periods.   Obedience is what makes government, and not
the names by which it is called ; not the name of Gov- 5
ernor, as formerly, or Committee, as at present.   This
new government has originated directly from the people, and was not transmitted through any of the ordinary artificial media of a positive constitution.   It was
not a manufacture ready formed, and transmitted to 10
them in that condition from England.   The evil arising from hence is this :—that the Colonists having once
found the possibility of enjoying the advantages of order
in the midst of a struggle for liberty, such struggles
will not henceforward seem so terrible to the settled and 15
sober part of mankind as they had appeared before the
trial.

47. Pursuing the same plan, of punishing by the denial
of the exercise of government, to still greater lengths, we
wholly abrogated the ancient government of Massachu- 20
setts.   We were confident that the first feeling, if not
the very prospect of anarchy, would instantly enforce
a complete submission.   The experiment was tried.   A
new, strange, unexpected face of things appeared.
Anarchy is found tolerable.   A vast province has now 25
subsisted, and subsisted in a considerable degree of
health and vigour, for near a twelvemonth, without governor, without public council, without judges, without
executive magistrates.   How long it will continue in
this state, or what may arise out of this unheard - of 30
situation, how can the wisest of us conjecture ?   Our
late experience has taught us that many of those
fundamental principles, formerly believed infallible,
are either not of the importance they were imagined
to be, or that we have not at all adverted to some 35

other far more important and far more powerful principles, which entirely overrule those we had considered
as omnipotent. I am much against any further experiments which tend to put to the proof any more
5 of these allowed opinions which contribute so much to
the public tranquillity. In effect, we suffer as much
at home by this loosening of all ties, and this concus-
sion of all established opinions, as we do abroad. For,
in order to prove that the Americans have no right
10 to their liberties, we are every day endeavouring to subvert the maxims which preserve the whole spirit of
our own. To prove that the Americans ought not to
be free, we are obliged to depreciate the value of freedom itself ; and we never seem to gain a paltry ad-
15 vantage over them in debate, without attacking some
of those principles, or deriding some of those feelings,
for which our ancestors have shed their blood.

48. But, Sir, in wishing to put an end to pernicious
experiments, I do not mean to preclude the fullest
20 inquiry. Far from it. Far from deciding on a sudden
or partial view, I would patiently go round and round
the subject, and survey it minutely in every possible
aspect. Sir, if I were capable of engaging you to an
equal attention, I would state that, as far as I am capable
25 of discerning, there are but three ways of proceeding
relative to this stubborn spirit, which prevails in your
Colonies, and disturbs your government. These are :—
to change that spirit, as inconvenient, by removing the
causes ; to prosecute it as criminal ; or to comply with
30 it as necessary. I would not be guilty of an imperfect
enumeration ; I can think of but these three. Another
has indeed been started, that of giving up the Colonies ;
but it met so slight a reception that I do not think
myself obliged to dwell a great while upon it. It is
35 nothing but a little sally of anger, like the frowardness

of peevish children, who, when they cannot get all they would have, are resolved to take nothing.

49. The first of these plans, to change the spirit, as inconvenient, by removing the causes, I think is the most like a systematic proceeding. It is radical in its prin- 5 ciple; but it is attended with great difficulties, some of them little short, as I conceive, of impossibilities. This will appear by examining into the plans which have been proposed.

50. As the growing population in the Colonies is evi- 10 dently one cause of their resistance, it was last session mentioned in both Houses, by men of weight, and received not without applause, that, in order to check this evil, it would be proper for the crown to make no further grants of land. But to this scheme there are two objec- 15 tions. The first, that there is already so much unsettled land in private hands as to afford room for an immense future population, although the crown not only withheld its grants, but annihilated its soil. If this be the case, then the only effect of this avarice of desolation, this 20 hoarding of a royal wilderness, would be to raise the value of the possessions in the hands of the great private monopolists, without any adequate check to the growing and alarming mischief of population.

51. But if you stopped your grants, what would be the 25 consequence? The people would occupy without grants. They have already so occupied in many places. You cannot station garrisons in every part of these deserts. If you drive the people from one place, they will carry on their annual tillage, and remove with their flocks and 30 herds to another. Many of the people in the back settlements are already little attached to particular situations. Already they have topped the Appalachian mountains. From thence they behold before them an immense plain, one vast, rich, level meadow; a square of five hundred 35

miles.   Over this they would wander without a possibility of restraint; they would change their manners
with the habits of their life; would soon forget a government by which they were disowned; would become
5 hordes of English Tartars; and, pouring down upon
your unfortified frontiers a fierce and irresistible cavalry,
become masters of your governors and your counsellors,
your collectors and comptrollers, and of all the slaves
that adhered to them.   Such would, and in no long time
10 must be, the effect of attempting to forbid as a crime,
and to suppress as an evil, the command and blessing of
Providence, "Increase and multiply."   Such would be
the happy result of an endeavour to keep as a lair of wild
beasts that earth which God, by an express charter, has
15 given to the children of men.   Far different, and surely
much wiser, has been our policy hitherto.   Hitherto we
have invited our people, by every kind of bounty, to
fixed establishments.   We have invited the husbandman
to look to authority for his title.   We have taught him
20 piously to believe in the mysterious virtue of wax and
parchment.   We have thrown each tract of land, as it
was peopled, into districts, that the ruling power should
never be wholly out of sight.   We have settled all we
could, and we have carefully attended every settlement
25 with government.

52. Adhering, Sir, as I do, to this policy, as well
as for the reasons I have just given, I think this new
project of hedging-in population to be neither prudent
nor practicable.

30   53. To impoverish the Colonies in general, and in particular to arrest the noble course of their marine enter-
prises, would be a more easy task.   I freely confess it.
We have shown a disposition to a system of this kind,—
a disposition even to continue the restraint after the
35 offense; looking on ourselves as rivals to our Colonies,

and persuaded that of course we must gain all that they shall lose. Much mischief we may certainly do. The power inadequate to all other things is often more than sufficient for this. I do not look on the direct and immediate power of the Colonies to resist our violence as 5 very formidable. In this, however, I may be mistaken. But when I consider that we have Colonies for no purpose but to be serviceable to us, it seems to my poor understanding a little preposterous to make them unserviceable, in order to keep them obedient. It is, in 10 truth, nothing more than the old, and, as I thought, exploded problem of tyranny, which proposes to beggar its subjects into submission. But remember, when you have completed your system of impoverishment, that Nature still proceeds in her ordinary course ; that dis- 15 content will increase with misery ; and that there are critical moments in the fortune of all states, when they who are too weak to contribute to your prosperity, may be strong enough to complete your ruin. *Spoliatis arma supersunt.* 20

54. The temper and character which prevail in our Colonies are, I am afraid, unalterable by any human art. We cannot, I fear, falsify the pedigree of this fierce people, and persuade them that they are not sprung from a nation in whose veins the blood of freedom cir- 25 culates. The language in which they would hear you tell them this tale would 'detect the imposition ; your speech would betray you. An Englishman is the unfittest person on earth to argue another Englishman into slavery. 30

55. I think it is nearly as little in our power to change their republican religion as their free descent ; or to substitute the Roman Catholic as a penalty ; or the Church of England as an improvement. The mode of inquisition and dragooning is going out of fashion in the 35

3

Old World, and I should not confide much to their
efficacy in the New. The education of the Americans
is also on the same unalterable bottom with their religion. You cannot persuade them to burn their books
5 of curious science; to banish their lawyers from their
courts of laws; or to quench the lights of their Assemblies, by refusing to choose those persons who are
best read in their privileges. It would be no less impracticable to think of wholly annihilating the popular
10 Assemblies in which these lawyers sit. The army, by
which we must govern in their place, would be far
more chargeable to us, not quite so effectual, and perhaps, in the end, full as difficult to be kept in obedience.

15   56. With regard to the high aristocratic spirit of Virginia and the Southern Colonies, it has been proposed, I
know, to reduce it, by declaring a general enfranchise-
ment of their slaves. This project has had its advocates
and panegyrists; yet I never could argue myself into
20 any opinion of it. Slaves are often much attached to
their masters. A general wild offer of liberty would not
always be accepted. History furnishes few instances of
it. It is sometimes as hard to persuade slaves to be free
as it is to compel freemen to be slaves; and in this
25 auspicious scheme we should have both these pleasing
tasks on our hands at once. But when we talk of en-
franchisement, do we not perceive that the American
master may enfranchise too, and arm servile hands in
defense of freedom?—a measure to which other people
30 have had recourse more than once, and not without
success, in a desperate situation of their affairs.

57. Slaves as these unfortunate black people are, and
dull as all men are from slavery, must they not a little suspect the offer of freedom from that very nation which
35 has sold them to their present masters? from that na-

tion, one of whose causes of quarrel with those masters
is their refusal to deal any more in that inhuman traffic ?
An offer of freedom from England would come rather
oddly, shipped to them in an African vessel, which is
refused an entry into the ports of Virginia or Carolina 5
with a cargo of three hundred Angola negroes. It would
be curious to see the Guinea captain attempting at the
same instant to publish his proclamation of liberty, and
to advertise his sale of slaves.

58. But let us suppose all these moral difficulties got 10
over: The ocean remains. You cannot pump this dry ;
and as long as it continues in its present bed, so long all
the causes which weaken authority by distance will continue. "Ye gods, annihilate but space and time, and
make two lovers happy !"—was a pious and passionate 15
prayer ; but just as reasonable as many of the serious
wishes of very grave and solemn politicians.

59. If then, Sir, it seems almost desperate to think of
any alterative course for changing the moral causes—and
not quite easy to remove the natural — which produce 20
prejudices irreconcilable to the late exercise of our authority ; but that the spirit infallibly will continue, and,
continuing, will produce such effects as now embarrass
us ; the second mode under consideration is, to prosecute
that spirit in its overt acts, as *criminal*. 25

60. At this proposition I must pause a moment. The
thing seems a great deal too big for my ideas of jurisprudence. It should seem, to my way of conceiving
such matters, that there is a very wide difference in
reason and policy between the mode of proceeding on 30
the irregular conduct of scattered individuals, or even of
bands of men, who disturb order within the state, and
the civil dissensions which may, from time to time, on
great questions, agitate the several communities which

compose a great empire. It looks to me to be narrow
and pedantic, to apply the ordinary ideas of criminal
justice to this great public contest. I do not know the
method of drawing up an indictment against a whole
5 people. I cannot insult and ridicule the feelings of
millions of my fellow-creatures, as Sir Edward Coke insulted one excellent individual—Sir Walter Raleigh—at
the bar. I hope I am not ripe to pass sentence on the
gravest public bodies, intrusted with magistracies of
10 great authority and dignity, and charged with the safety
of their fellow-citizens upon the very same title that I
am. I really think that for wise men this is not judicious ; for sober men, not decent ; for minds tinctured
with humanity, not mild and merciful.

15   61. Perhaps, Sir, I am mistaken in my idea of an empire, as distinguished from a single state or kingdom.
But my idea of it is this : that an empire is the aggregate
of many states under one common head, whether this
head be a monarch or a presiding republic. It does, in
20 such constitutions, frequently happen—and nothing but
the dismal, cold, dead uniformity of servitude can prevent its happening—that the subordinate parts have
many local privileges and immunities. Between these
privileges and the supreme common authority the line
25 may be extremely nice.' Of course disputes, often, too,
very bitter disputes, and much ill blood, will arise. But
though every privilege is an exemption—in the case—
from the ordinary exercise of the supreme authority, it
is no denial of it. The claim of a privilege seems rather,
30 *ex vi termini*, to imply a superior power. For to talk
of the privileges of a state or of a person who has no
superior, is hardly any better than speaking nonsense.
Now in such unfortunate quarrels among the compo-
nent parts of a great political union of communities, I
35 can scarcely conceive anything more completely impru-

dent than for the head of the empire to insist that, if
any privilege is pleaded against his will or his acts, [that]
his whole authority is denied; instantly to proclaim rebellion, to beat to arms, and to put the offending provinces
under the ban.   Will not this, Sir, very soon teach the 5
provinces to make no distinctions on their part ?   Will
it not teach them that the government, against which a
claim of liberty is tantamount to high treason, is a government to which submission is equivalent to slavery ?
It may not always be quite convenient to impress depen- 10
dent communities with such an idea.

62. We are indeed, in all disputes with the Colonies,
by the necessity of things, the judge.   It is true, Sir.
But I confess that the character of judge in my own
cause is a thing that frightens me.   Instead of filling 15
me with pride, I am exceedingly humbled by it.   I cannot proceed with a stern, assured, judicial confidence,
until I find myself in something more like a judicial
character.   I must have these hesitations as long as I
am compelled to recollect that, in my little reading upon 20
such contests as these, the sense of mankind has at least
as often decided against the superior as the subordinate
power.   Sir, let me add, too, that the opinion of my
having some abstract right in my favour would not put
me much at my ease in passing sentence, unless I could 25
be sure that there were no rights which, in their exercise
under certain circumstances, were not the most odious of
all wrongs, and the most vexatious of all injustice.   Sir,
these considerations have great weight with me, when I
find things so circumstanced that I see the same party at 30
once a civil litigant against me in a point of right and a
culprit before me ; while I sit as a criminal judge on
acts of his, whose moral quality is to be decided upon
the merits of that very litigation.   Men are every now
and then put, by the complexity of human affairs, into 35

strange situations ; but justice is the same, let the judge
be in what situation he will.

63. There is, Sir, also a circumstance which convinces
me that this mode of criminal proceeding is not—at least
5 in the present stage of our contest—altogether expedient ; which is nothing less than the conduct of those very
persons who have seemed to adopt that mode, by lately
declaring a rebellion in Massachusetts Bay, as they had
formerly addressed to have traitors brought hither, under
10 an act of Henry the Eighth, for trial.   For though rebellion is declared, it is not proceeded against as such,
nor have any steps been taken towards the apprehension
or conviction of any individual offender, either on our
late or our former address ; but modes of public coercion
15 have been adopted, and such as have much more resemblance to a sort of qualified hostility towards an independent power than the punishment of rebellious
subjects.   All this seems rather inconsistent ; but it
shows how difficult it is to apply these juridical ideas to
20 our present case.

64. In this situation, let us seriously and coolly ponder.
What is it we have got by all our menaces, which have
been many and ferocious ?   What advantage have we
derived from the penal laws we have passed, and which,
25 for the time, have been severe and numerous ?   What
advances have we made towards our object, by the sending of a force which, by land and sea, is no contemptible
strength ?   Has the disorder abated ?   Nothing less.
When I see things in this situation, after such confident
30 hopes, bold promises, and active exertions, I cannot, for
my life, avoid a suspicion that the plan itself is not correctly right.

65. If then the removal of the causes of this spirit of
American liberty be, for the greater part, or rather en-

tirely, impracticable ; if the ideas of criminal process be inapplicable, or if applicable, are in the highest degree inexpedient ; what way yet remains ? No way is open but the third and last—to comply with the American spirit as necessary ; or, if you please, to submit to it as 5 a necessary evil.

66. If we adopt this mode, if we mean to conciliate and concede, let us see of what nature the concession ought to be. To ascertain the nature of our concession, we must look at their complaint. The Colonies complain that 10 they have not the characteristic mark and seal of British freedom. They complain that they are taxed in a Parliament in which they are not represented. If you mean to satisfy them at all, you must satisfy them with regard to this complaint. If you mean to please any people, 15 you must give them the boon which they ask,—not what you may think better for them, but of a kind totally different. Such an act may be a wise regulation, but it is no concession ; whereas our present theme is the mode of giving satisfaction.   20

67. Sir, I think you must perceive that I am resolved this day to have nothing at all to do with the question of the right of taxation. Some gentlemen startle—but it is true ; I put it totally out of the question. It is less than nothing in my consideration. I do not indeed wonder, 25 nor will you, Sir, that gentlemen of profound learning are fond of displaying it on this profound subject. But my consideration is narrow, confined, and wholly limited to the policy of the question. I do not examine, whether the giving away a man's money be a power excepted and 30 reserved out of the general trust of government, and how far all mankind, in all forms of polity, are entitled to an exercise of that right by the charter of nature ; or whether, on the contrary, a right of taxation is

necessarily involved in the general principle of legislation, and inseparable from the ordinary supreme power.
These are deep questions, where great names militate
against each other, where reason is perplexed, and an
5 appeal to authorities only thickens the confusion. For
high and reverend authorities lift up their heads on both
sides, and there is no sure footing in the middle. This
point is the great
> Serbonian bog,
> 10   Betwixt Damiata and Mount Casius old,
> Where armies whole have sunk.

I do not intend to be overwhelmed in that bog, though
in such respectable company. The question with me is
—not whether you have a right to render your people
15 miserable, but whether it is not your interest to make
them happy. It is not what a lawyer tells me I *may* do,
but what humanity, reason, and justice tell me I ought
to do. Is a politic act the worse for being a generous
one ? Is no concession proper but that which is made
20 from your want of right to keep what you grant ? Or
does it lessen the grace or dignity of relaxing in the
exercise of an odious claim, because you have your evi-
dence-room full of titles, and your ·magazines stuffed
with arms to enforce them ? What signify all those titles
25 and all those arms ? Of what avail are they, when the
reason of the thing tells me that the assertion of my
title is the loss of my suit, and that I could do nothing
but wound myself by the use of my own weapons ?

68. Such is stedfastly my opinion of the absolute neces-
80 sity of keeping up the concord of this empire by a unity
of spirit, though in a diversity of operations, that if I
were sure the Colonists had at their leaving this country
sealed a regular compact of servitude, that they had
solemnly abjured all the rights of citizens, that they had
85 made a vow to renounce all ideas of liberty for them and

their posterity to all generations; yet I should hold myself obliged to conform to the temper I found universally
prevalent in my own day, and to govern two million of
men, impatient of servitude, on the principles of freedom.   I am not determining a point of law—I am restor- 5
ing tranquillity; and the general character and situation
of a people must determine what sort of government
is fitted for them. That point nothing else can or ought
to determine.

69. My idea, therefore, without considering whether 10
we yield as matter of right, or grant as matter of favour,
is *to admit the people of our Colonies into an interest in
the Constitution ;* and, by recording that admission in
the Journals of Parliament, to give them as strong an
assurance as the nature of the thing will admit, that we 15
mean for ever to adhere to that solemn declaration of
systematic indulgence.

70. Some years ago, the repeal of a revenue act, upon
its understood principle, might have served to show that
we intended an unconditional abatement of the exercise 20
of a taxing power.   Such a measure was then sufficient to
remove all suspicion, and to give perfect content.   But
unfortunate events since that time may make something
further necessary ; and not more necessary for the satisfaction of the Colonies than for the dignity and consist- 25
ency of our own future proceedings.

71. I have taken a very incorrect measure of the disposition of the House, if this proposal in itself would be
received with dislike. I think, Sir, we have few American financiers. But our misfortune is, we are too acute ; 30
we are too exquisite in our conjectures of the future,
for men oppressed with such great and present evils.
The more moderate among the opposers of parliamentary concession freely confess that they hope no good

from taxation ; but they apprehend the Colonists have
further views, and, if this point were conceded, they
would instantly attack the Trade Laws.   These gentlemen are convinced that this was the intention from the
5 beginning, and the quarrel of the Americans with taxation was no more than a cloak and cover to this design.
Such has been the language even of a gentleman of
real moderation, and of a natural temper well adjusted
to fair and equal government.   I am, however, Sir, not
10 a little surprised at this kind of discourse, whenever I
hear it ; and I am the more surprised, on account of the
arguments which I constantly find in company with it,
and which are often urged from the same mouths, and
on the same day.

15   72. For instance, when we allege that it is against
reason to tax a people under so many restraints in trade
as the Americans, the Noble Lord in the Blue Ribbon
shall tell you that the restraints on trade are futile and
useless, of no advantage to us, and of no burthen to those
20 on whom they are imposed ; that the trade to America is
not secured by the Acts of Navigation, but by the natural
and irresistible advantage of a commercial preference.

73. Such is the merit of the Trade Laws in this posture
of the debate.   But when strong internal circumstances
25 are urged against the taxes ; when the scheme is dissected ; when experience and the nature of things are
brought to prove, and do prove, the utter impossibility
of obtaining an effective revenue from the Colonies ;
when these things are pressed, or rather press them-
30 selves, so as to drive the advocates of Colony taxes to
a clear admission of the futility of the scheme,—then,
Sir, the sleeping Trade Laws revive from their trance ;
and this useless taxation is to be kept sacred, not for its
own sake, but as a counter-guard and security of the
35 laws of trade.

74. Then, Sir, you keep up revenue laws which are mischievous, in order to preserve trade laws that are useless. Such is the wisdom of our plan in both its members. They are separately given up as of no value ; and yet one is always to be defended for the sake of the 5 other. But I cannot agree with the Noble Lord, nor with the pamphlet from whence he seems to have bor-rowed these ideas, concerning the inutility of the Trade Laws. For, without idolizing them, I am sure they are still, in many ways, of great use to us ; and in former 10 times they have been of the greatest. They do confine, and they do greatly narrow, the market for the Ameri-cans. But my perfect conviction of this does not help me in the least to discern how the revenue laws form any security whatsoever to the commercial regulations ; 15 or that these commercial regulations are the true ground of the quarrel ; or that the giving way, in any one in-stance of authority, is to lose all that may remain un-conceded.

75. One fact is clear and indisputable. The public 20 and avowed origin of this quarrel was on taxation. This quarrel has indeed brought on new disputes on new questions, but certainly the least bitter, and the fewest of all, on the Trade Laws. To judge which of the two be the real, radical cause of quarrel, we have to see 25 whether the commercial dispute did, in order of time, precede the dispute on taxation. There is not a shadow of evidence for it. Next, to enable us to judge whether at this moment a dislike to the Trade Laws be the real cause of quarrel, it is absolutely necessary to put the 30 taxes out of the question by a repeal. See how the Americans act in this position, and then you will be able to discern correctly what is the true object of the controversy, or whether any controversy at all will re-main. Unless you consent to remove this cause of 35

difference, it is impossible, with decency, to assert **that** the dispute is not upon what it is avowed to be. And **I** would, Sir, recommend to your serious consideration, whether it be prudent to form a rule for punishing peo-
5 ple, not on their own acts, but on your conjectures. Surely it is preposterous at the very best. It is not justifying your anger by their misconduct; but it is converting your ill-will into their delinquency.

76. "But the Colonies will go further."—Alas! alas!
10 when will this speculating against fact and reason end? What will quiet these panic fears which we entertain of the hostile effect of a conciliatory conduct? Is it true that no case can exist in which it is proper for the sov-ereign to accede to the desires of his discontented sub-
15 jects? Is there anything peculiar in this case, to make a rule for itself? Is all authority of course lost, when it is not pushed to the extreme? Is it a certain maxim that, the fewer causes of dissatisfaction are left by gov-ernment, the more the subject will be inclined to resist
20 and rebel?

77. All these objections being in fact no more than suspicions, conjectures, divinations, formed in defiance of fact and experience, they did not, Sir, discourage me from entertaining the idea of a conciliatory concession,
25 founded on the principles which I have just stated.

78. In forming a plan for this purpose, I endeavoured to put myself in that frame of mind which was the most natural and the most reasonable, and which was cer-tainly the most probable means of securing me from all
30 error. I set out with a perfect distrust of my own abilities, a total renunciation of every speculation of my own; and with a profound reverence for the wisdom of our ancestors, who have left us the inheritance of so happy a Constitution, and so flourishing an empire, and,

what is a thousand times more valuable, the treasury of the maxims and principles which formed the one and obtained the other.

79. During the reigns of the kings of Spain of the Austrian family, whenever they were at a loss in the Spanish councils, it was common for their statesmen to say that they ought to consult the genius of Philip the Second. The genius of Philip the Second might mislead them; and the issue of their affairs showed that they had not chosen the most perfect standard. But, Sir, I am sure that I shall not be misled when, in a case of constitutional difficulty, I consult the genius of the English Constitution. Consulting at that oracle—it was with all due humility and piety—I found four capital examples in a similar case before me : those of Ireland, Wales, Chester, and Durham.

80. Ireland, before the English conquest, though never governed by a despotic power, had no Parliament. How far the English Parliament itself was at that time modelled according to the present form, is disputed among antiquarians. But we have all the reason in the world to be assured that a form of Parliament, such as England then enjoyed, she instantly communicated to Ireland; and we are equally sure that almost every successive improvement in constitutional liberty, as fast as it was made here, was transmitted thither. The feudal baronage and the feudal knighthood, the roots of our primitive constitution, were early transplanted into that soil, and grew and flourished there. Magna Charta, if it did not give us originally the House of Commons, gave us at least a House of Commons of weight and consequence. But your ancestors did not churlishly sit down alone to the feast of Magna Charta. Ireland was made immediately a partaker. This benefit of English laws and liberties, I confess, was not at first extended to *all*

Ireland. Mark the consequence. English authority
and English liberties had exactly the same boundaries.
Your standard could never be advanced an inch before
your privileges. Sir John Davies shows, beyond a doubt,
5 that the refusal of a general communication of these
rights was the true cause why Ireland was five hundred
years in subduing ; and after the vain projects of a
military government, attempted in the reign of Queen
Elizabeth, it was soon discovered that nothing could
10 make that country English in civility and allegiance,
but your laws and your forms of legislature. It was not
English arms, but the English Constitution, that conquered Ireland. From that time, Ireland has ever had
a general Parliament, as she had before a partial Par-
15 liament. You changed the people ; you altered the
religion ; but you never touched the form or the vital
substance of free government in that kingdom. You
deposed kings ; you restored them ; you altered the succession to theirs, as well as to your own crown ; but you
20 never altered their constitution ; the principle of which
was respected by usurpation, restored with the restoration of monarchy, and established, I trust for ever, by
the glorious Revolution. This has made Ireland the
great and flourishing kingdom that it is ; and from a
25 disgrace and a burthen intolerable to this nation, has
rendered her a principal part of our strength and ornament. This country cannot be said to have ever for-
mally taxed her. The irregular things done in the confusion of mighty troubles, and on the hinge of great
30 revolutions, even if all were done that is said to have been
done, form no example. If they have any effect in argument, they make an exception to prove the rule. None
of your own liberties could stand a moment, if the casual
deviations from them at such times were suffered to be
35 used as proofs of their nullity. By the lucrative amount

of such casual breaches in the Constitution, judge what
the stated and fixed rule of supply has been in that
kingdom. Your Irish pensioners would starve, if they
had no other fund to live on than taxes granted by English authority. Turn your eyes to those popular grants 5
from whence all your great supplies are come, and learn
to respect that only source of public wealth in the British
Empire.

81. My next example is Wales. This country was said
to be reduced by Henry the Third. It was said more 10
truly to be so by Edward the First. But though then
conquered, it was not looked upon as any part of the
realm of England. Its old constitution, whatever that
might have been, was destroyed ; and no good one was
substituted in its place. The care of that tract was put 15
into the hands of Lords Marchers—a form of government of a very singular kind ; a strange heterogeneous
monster, something between hostility and government ;
perhaps it has a sort of resemblance, according to the
modes of those times, to that of commander-in-chief at 20
present, to whom all civil power is granted as secondary.
The manners of the Welsh nation followed the genius
of the government : the people were ferocious, restive,
savage, and uncultivated ; sometimes composed, never
pacified. Wales, within itself, was in perpetual dis- 25
order ; and it kept the frontier of England in perpetual
alarm. Benefits from it to the state there were none.
Wales was only known to England by incursion and invasion.

82. Sir, during that state of things, Parliament was 30
not idle. They attempted to subdue the fierce spirit of
the Welsh by all sorts of rigorous laws. They prohibited
by statute the sending all sorts of arms into Wales, as
you prohibit by proclamation—with something more of
doubt on the legality—the sending arms to America. 35

They disarmed the Welsh by statute, as you attempted
—but still with more question on the legality—to dis-
arm New England by an instruction. They made an
act to drag offenders from Wales into England for trial,
5 as you have done—but with more hardship—with regard
to America. By another act, where one of the parties
was an Englishman, they ordained that his trial should
be always by English. They made acts to restrain trade,
as you do ; and they prevented the Welsh from the use
10 of fairs and markets, as you do the Americans from
fisheries and foreign ports. In short, when the statute-
book was not quite so much swelled as it is now, you
find no less than fifteen acts of penal regulation on the
subject of Wales.

15   83. Here we rub our hands—"A fine body of precedents for the authority of Parliament and the use of
it ! " I admit it fully ; and pray add likewise to these
precedents, that all the while Wales rid this kingdom
like an incubus ; that it was an unprofitable and op-
20 pressive burthen ; and that an Englishman traveling in
that country could not go six yards from the high road
without being murdered.

84. The march of the human mind is slow. Sir, it
was not until after two hundred years discovered that, by
25 an eternal law, Providence had decreed vexation to violence, and poverty to rapine. Your ancestors did, however, at length open their eyes to the ill husbandry of
injustice. They found that the tyranny of a free people
could of all tyrannies the least be endured, and that
30 laws made against a whole nation were not the most
effectual methods for securing its obedience. Accordingly, in the twenty-seventh year of Henry the Eighth,
the course was entirely altered. With a preamble stat-
ing the entire and perfect rights of the Crown of Eng-
35 land, it gave to the Welsh all the rights and privileges

of English subjects. A political order was established ;
the military power gave way to the civil ; the Marches
were turned into Counties.   But that a nation should
have a right to English liberties, and yet no share at all
in the fundamental security of these liberties—the grant 5
of their own property—seemed a thing so incongruous,
that, eight years after, that is, in the thirty-fifth of that
reign, a complete and not ill-proportioned representation
by counties and boroughs was bestowed upon Wales by
Act of Parliament.   From that moment, as by a charm, 10
the tumults subsided ; obedience was restored ; peace,
order, and civilization followed in the train of liberty.
When the day-star of the English Constitution had
arisen in their hearts, all was harmony within and without—   15

> —Simul alba nautis
>   Stella refulsit,
> Defluit saxis agitatus humor,
> Concidunt venti, fugiuntque nubes,
> Et minax (quod sic voluere) ponto   20
>   Unda recumbit.

85. The very same year the County Palatine of Chester
received the same relief from its oppressions, and the
same remedy to its disorders.   Before this time Chester
was little less distempered than Wales.   The inhabi- 25
tants, without rights themselves, were the fittest to destroy the rights of others ; and from thence Richard the
Second drew the standing army of archers with which
for a time he oppressed England.   The people of Chester applied to Parliament in a petition penned as I shall 30
read to you :—

To the King our Sovereign Lord, in most humble wise
  shewen unto your most excellent Majesty the inhabitants of your Grace's County Palatine of Chester : That
  where the said County Palatine of Chester is and hath 35

been alway hitherto exempt, excluded, and separateò
out and from your high Court of Parliament, to have
any Knights and Burgesses within the said Court; by
reason whereof the said inhabitants have hitherto sus-
5   tained manifold disherisons, losses, and damages, as
well in their lands, goods, and bodies, as in the good,
civil, and politic governance and maintenance of the
common wealth of their said country;—And forasmuch as the said inhabitants have always hitherto
10   been bound by the acts and statutes made and ordained by your said Highness and your most noble
progenitors, by authority of the said Court, as far
forth as other counties, cities, and boroughs have
been, that have had their Knights and Burgesses
15   within your said Court of Parliament, and yet have
had neither Knight ne Burgess there for the said
County Palatine; the said inhabitants, for lack thereof, have been oftentimes touched and grieved with
acts and statutes made within the said Court, as well
20   derogatory unto the most ancient jurisdictions, liberties, and privileges of your said County Palatine, as
prejudicial unto the common wealth, quietness, rest,
and peace of your Grace's most bounden subjects inhabiting within the same.

25   86. What did Parliament with this audacious address?
Reject it as a libel? Treat it as an affront to government? Spurn it as a derogation from the rights of legislature? Did they toss it over the table? Did they
burn it by the hands of the common hangman? They
30   took the petition of grievance, all rugged as it was,
without softening or temperament, unpurged of the
original bitterness and indignation of complaint; they
made it the very preamble to their act of redress, and
consecrated its principle to all ages in the sanctuary of
35   legislation.

87. Here is my third example. It was attended with
the success of the two former. Chester, civilized as well
as Wales, has demonstrated that freedom, and not servi-

tude, is the cure of anarchy ; as religion, and not athe-
ism, is the true remedy for superstition. Sir, this pat-
tern of Chester was followed in the reign of Charles the
Second with regard to the County Palatine of Durham,
which is my fourth example. This county had long 5
lain out of the pale of free legislation. So scrupulously
was the example of Chester followed, that the style of
the preamble is nearly the same with that of the Chester Act; and, without affecting the abstract extent of
the authority of Parliament, it recognises the equity of 10
not suffering any considerable district, in which the
British subjects may act as a body, to be taxed without
their own voice in the grant.

88. Now if the doctrines of policy contained in these
preambles, and the force of these examples in the Acts 15
of Parliament, avail anything, what can be said against
applying them with regard to America ? Are not the
people of America as much Englishmen as the Welsh ?
The preamble of the act of Henry the Eighth says the
Welsh speak a language no way resembling that of his 20
Majesty's English subjects. Are the Americans not as
numerous ? If we may trust the learned and accurate
Judge Barrington's account of North Wales, and take
that as a standard to measure the rest, there is no comparison. The people cannot amount to above 200,000— 25
not a tenth part of the number in the Colonies. Is
America in rebellion ? Wales was hardly ever free from
it. Have you attempted to govern America by penal
statutes ? You made fifteen for Wales. But your legislative authority is perfect with regard to America. Was 30
it less perfect in Wales, Chester, and Durham ? But
America is virtually represented. What ! does the elec-
tric force of virtual representation more easily pass over
the Atlantic than pervade Wales, which lies in your

neighbourhood, or than Chester and Durham, surround-
ed by abundance of representation that is actual and palpable ?   But, Sir, your ancestors thought this sort of
virtual representation, however ample, to be totally in-
5 sufficient for the freedom of the inhabitants of territories
that are so near, and comparatively so inconsiderable.
How then can I think it sufficient for those which are
infinitely greater, and infinitely more remote ?

89. You will now, Sir, perhaps imagine, that I am on
10 the point of proposing to you a scheme for a representation of the Colonies in Parliament.   Perhaps I might be
inclined to entertain some such thought ; but a great
flood stops me in my course. *Opposuit natura.* I cannot remove the eternal barriers of the creation.   The
15 thing, in that mode, I do not know to be possible.   As
I meddle with no theory, I do not absolutely assert the
impracticability of such a representation.   But I do not
see my way to it ; and those who have been more confident have not been more successful.   However, the arm
20 of public benevolence is not shortened ; and there are
often several means to the same end.   What nature has
disjoined in one way, wisdom may unite in another.
When we cannot give the benefit as we would wish, let
us not refuse it altogether.   If we cannot give the prin-
25 cipal, let us find a substitute.   But how ?   Where ?
What substitute ?

90. Fortunately I am not obliged for the ways and
means of this substitute to tax my own unproductive
invention.   I am not even obliged to go to the rich
30 treasury of the fertile framers of imaginary commonwealths : not to the "Republic" of Plato ; not to the
"Utopia" of More ; not to the "Oceana" of Harring-
ton.   It is before me ; it is at my feet,

—And the rude swain
35   Treads daily on it with his clouted shoon.

I only wish you to recognise, for the theory, the ancient constitutional policy of this kingdom with regard to representation, as that policy has been declared in Acts of Parliament ; and, as to the practice, to return to that mode which a uniform experience has marked out to you 5 as best, and in which you walked with security, advantage, and honour, until the year 1763.

91. My resolutions therefore mean to establish the equity and justice of a taxation of America by *grant*, and not by *imposition ;* to mark the *legal competency* of the 10 Colony Assemblies for the support of their government in peace, and for public aids in time of war ; to acknowledge that this legal competency has had *a dutiful and beneficial exercise ;* and that experience has shown the *benefit of their grants,* and the *futility of parliamentary* 15 *taxation as a method of supply.*

92. These solid truths compose six fundamental propositions. There are three more resolutions corollary to these. If you admit the first set, you can hardly reject the others. But if you admit the first, I shall be far 20 from solicitous whether you accept or refuse the last. I think these six massive pillars will be of strength sufficient to support the temple of British concord. I have no more doubt than I entertain of my existence, that, if you admitted these, you would command an imme- 25 diate peace ; and, with but tolerable future management, a lasting obedience in America. I am not arrogant in this confident assurance. The propositions are all mere matters of fact ; and if they are such facts as draw irresistible conclusions even in the stat- 30 ing, this is the power of truth, and not any management of mine.

93. Sir, I shall open the whole plan to you, together with such observations on the motions as may tend to

illustrate them where they may want explanation.   The
first is a resolution—

That the Colonies and Plantations of Great Britain in
North America, consisting of Fourteen separate Governments, and containing Two Millions and upwards
of free inhabitants, have not had the liberty and privilege of electing and sending any Knights and Burgesses, or others, to represent them in the high Court
of Parliament.

10 This is a plain matter of fact, necessary to be laid down,
and—excepting the description—it is laid down in the
language of the Constitution ; it is taken nearly *verba-
tim* from Acts of Parliament.

94. The second is like unto the first :—

15 That the said Colonies and Plantations have been liable
to, and bounden by, several subsidies, payments, rates,
and taxes, given and granted by Parliament, though
the said Colonies and Plantations have not their
Knights and Burgesses in the said high Court of
20 Parliament, of their own election, to represent the
condition of their country; by lack whereof they have
been oftentimes touched and grieved by subsidies
given, granted, and assented to in the said Court, in
a manner prejudicial to the common wealth, quiet-
25 ness, rest, and peace of the subjects inhabiting within
the same.

95. Is this description too hot, or too cold, too strong,
or too weak ?   Does it arrogate too much to the supreme
Legislature ?   Does it lean too much to the claims of the
30 people ?   If it runs into any of these errors, the fault is
not mine.   It is the language of your own ancient Acts
of Parliament :—

Non meus hic sermo, sed quæ præcepit Ofellus.
Rusticus, abnormis sapiens.

It is the genuine produce of the ancient, rustic, manly, home-bred sense of this country. I did not dare to rub off a particle of the venerable rust that rather adorns and preserves, than destroys the metal. It would be a profanation to touch with a tool the stones which construct 5 the sacred altar of peace. I would not violate with modern polish the ingenuous and noble roughness of these truly constitutional materials. Above all things, I was resolved not to be guilty of tampering,—the odious vice of restless and unstable minds. I put my foot in 10 the tracks of our forefathers, where I can neither wander nor stumble. Determining to fix articles of peace, I was resolved not to be wise beyond what was written ; I was resolved to use nothing else than the form of sound words ; to let others abound in their own sense, and 15 carefully to abstain from all expressions of my own. What the Law has said, I say. In all things else I am silent. I have no organ but for her words. This, if it be not ingenious, I am sure is safe.

96. There are indeed words expressive of grievance in 20 this second resolution, which those who are resolved always to be in the right will deny to contain matter of fact, as applied to the present case ; although Parliament thought them true with regard to the counties of Chester and Durham. They will deny that the Americans 25 were ever " touched and grieved " with the taxes. If they consider nothing in taxes but their weight as pecuniary impositions, there might be some pretense for this denial. But men may be sorely touched and deeply grieved in their privileges, as well as in their 30 purses. Men may lose little in property by the act which takes away all their freedom. When a man is robbed of a trifle on the highway, it is not the twopence lost that constitutes the capital outrage. This is not confined to privileges. Even ancient indulgences with- 35

drawn, without offense on the part of those who enjoyed
such favours, operate as grievances.   But were the
Americans then not touched and grieved by the taxes,
in some measure, merely as taxes ?   If so, why were they
5 almost all either wholly repealed or exceedingly reduced ?
Were they not touched and grieved even by the regulating duties of the Sixth of George the Second ?   Else
why were the duties first reduced to one-third in 1764,
and afterwards to a third of that third in the year 1766 ?
10 Were they not touched and grieved by the Stamp Act ?
I shall say they were, until that tax is revived.   Were
they not touched and grieved by the duties of 1767,
which were likewise repealed, and which Lord Hillsborough tells you (for the ministry) were laid contrary
15 to the true principle of commerce ?   Is not the assurance given by that noble person to the Colonies of a
resolution to lay no more taxes on them, an admission
that taxes would touch and grieve them ?   Is not the
resolution of the Noble Lord in the Blue Ribbon, now
20 standing on your Journals, the strongest of all proofs
that parliamentary subsidies really touched and grieved
them ?   Else why all these changes, modifications, re-
peals, assurances, and resolutions ?

97. The next proposition is—

25 That, from the distance of the said Colonies, and from
other circumstances, no method hath hitherto been
devised for procuring a representation in Parliament
for the said Colonies.

This is an assertion of a fact. I go no further on the
30 paper, though, in my private judgment, a useful representation is impossible ; I am sure it is not desired by
them, nor ought it perhaps by us—but I abstain from
opinions.

98. The fourth resolution is—

That each of the said Colonies hath within itself a body,
chosen, in part or in the whole, by the freemen, freeholders, or other free inhabitants thereof, commonly
called the General Assembly, or General Court; with
powers legally to raise, levy, and assess, according to 5
the several usage of such Colonies, duties and taxes
towards defraying all sorts of public services.

99. This competence in the Colony Assemblies is certain. It is proved by the whole tenour of their Acts of
Supply in all the Assemblies, in which the constant style 10
of granting is "an aid to his Majesty;" and acts granting
to the Crown have regularly for near a century passed
the public offices without dispute. Those who have
been pleased paradoxically to deny this right, holding
that none but the British Parliament can grant to the 15
Crown, are wished to look to what is done, not only in
the Colonies, but in Ireland, in one uniform unbroken
tenour every session. Sir, I am surprised that this doctrine should come from some of the law servants of the
Crown. I say that if the Crown could be responsible, 20
his Majesty—but certainly the Ministers, and even these
law officers themselves, through whose hands the acts
pass biennially in Ireland, or annually in the Colonies,
are in an habitual course of committing impeachable
offences. What habitual offenders have been all Presi- 25
dents of the Council, all Secretaries of State, all First
Lords of Trade, all Attorneys and all Solicitors General!
However, they are safe, as no one impeaches them; and
there is no ground of charge against them, except in
their own unfounded theories. 30
100. The fifth resolution is also a resolution of fact :—

That the said General Assemblies, General Courts, or
other bodies legally qualified as aforesaid, have at sundry times freely granted several large subsidies and
public aids for his Majesty's service, according to their 35

abilities, when required thereto by letter from one of
his Majesty's principal Secretaries of State ; and that
their right to grant the same, and their cheerfulness
and sufficiency in the said grants, have been at sundry
5 times acknowledged by Parliament.

To say nothing of their great expenses in the Indian
wars ; and not to take their exertion in foreign ones,
so high as the supplies in the year 1695; not to go back
to their public contributions in the year 1710 ; I shall
10 begin to travel only where the Journals give me light,
resolving to deal in nothing but fact, authenticated by
parliamentary record, and to build myself wholly on that
solid basis.

101. On the 4th of April, 1748, a committee of this
15 House came to the following resolution:—

Resolved, That it is the opinion of this Committee *that
it is just and reasonable* that the several Provinces
and Colonies of Massachusetts Bay, New Hampshire,
Connecticut, and Rhode Island, be reimbursed the
20   expenses they have been at in taking and securing to
the Crown of Great Britain the Island of Cape Breton
and its dependencies.

These expenses were immense for such Colonies.
They were above £200,000 sterling ; money first raised
25 and advanced on their public credit.

102. On the 28th of January, 1756, a message from
the King came to us, to this effect :—

His Majesty, being sensible of the zeal and vigour with
which his faithful subjects of certain Colonies in
30   North America have exerted themselves in defense of
his Majesty's just rights and possessions, recommends
it to this House to take the same into their consideration, and to enable his Majesty to give them such
assistance as may be a *proper reward and encouragement.*

103. On the 3rd of February, 1756, the House came to
a suitable resolution, expressed in words nearly the same
as those of the message, but with the further addition
that the money then voted was an *encouragement* to the
Colonies to exert themselves with vigour. It will not be 5
necessary to go through all the testimonies which your
own records have given to the truth of my resolutions
I will only refer you to the places in the Journals :—

Vol. xxvii.—16th and 19th May, 1757.
Vol. xxviii.—June 1st, 1758 ; April 26th and 30th, 1t
1759 ; March 26th and 31st, and April 28th, 1760 ; Jan.
9th and 20th, 1761.
Vol. xxix.—Jan. 22nd and 26th, 1762 ; March 14th
and 17th, 1763.

104. Sir, here is the repeated acknowledgment of Par- 15
liament that the Colonies not only gave, but gave to
satiety. This nation has formerly acknowledged two
things :—first, that the Colonies had gone beyond their
abilities, Parliament having thought it necessary to re-
imburse them ; secondly, that they had acted legally 20
and laudably in their grants of money, and their maintenance of troops, since the compensation is expressly
given as reward and encouragement. Reward is not
bestowed for acts that are unlawful ; and encouragement
is not held out to things that deserve reprehension. My 25
resolution therefore does nothing more than collect into
one proposition what is scattered through your Journals.
I give you nothing but your own ; and you cannot refuse in the gross what you have so often acknowledged
in detail. The admission of this, which will be so 30
honourable to them and to you, will indeed be mortal to
all the miserable stories by which the passions of the
misguided people have been engaged in an unhappy sys-

tem. The people heard, indeed, from the beginning of
these disputes, one thing continually dinned in their ears,
that reason and justice demanded that the Americans,
who paid no taxes, should be compelled to contribute.
5 How did that fact of their paying nothing stand, when the
taxing system began? When Mr. Grenville began to form
his system of American revenue, he stated in this House
that the Colonies were then in debt two million six
hundred thousand pounds sterling money, and was of
10 opinion they would discharge that debt in four years.
On this state, those untaxed people were actually subject
to the payment of taxes to the amount of six hundred
and fifty thousand a year. In fact, however, Mr. Grenville was mistaken. The funds given for sinking the
15 debt did not prove quite so ample as both the Colonies
and he expected. The calculation was too sanguine ; the
reduction was not completed till some years after, and
at different times in different Colonies. However, the
taxes after the war continued too great to bear any
20 addition with prudence or propriety ; and when the
burthens imposed in consequence of former requisitions
were discharged, our tone became too high to resort
again to requisition. No Colony, since that time, ever
has had any requisition whatsoever made to it.
25   105. We see the sense of the Crown, and the sense of
Parliament, on the productive nature of a *revenue by
grant*. Now search the same Journals for the produce
of the *revenue by imposition.* Where is it ?—let us
know the volume and the page. What is the gross,
30 what is the net produce ? To what service is it applied ?
How have you appropriated its surplus ? What, can
none of the many skilful index-makers that we are now
employing find any trace of it ? Well, let them and
that rest together. But are the Journals, which say
35 nothing of the revenue, as silent on the discontent ?

Oh no! a child may find it. It is the melancholy burthen and blot of every page.

106. I think then I am, from those Journals, justified in the sixth and last resolution, which is—

That it hath been found by experience that the manner 5 of granting the said supplies and aids by the said General Assemblies hath been more agreeable to the said Colonies, and more beneficial and conducive to the public service, than the mode of giving and granting aids in Parliament, to be raised and paid in the 10 said Colonies.

107. This makes the whole of the fundamental part of the plan. The conclusion is irresistible. You cannot say that you were driven by any necessity to an exercise of the utmost rights of legislature. You cannot assert 15 that you took on yourselves the task of imposing Colony taxes from the want of another legal body, that is competent to the purpose of supplying the exigencies of the State without wounding the prejudices of the people. Neither is it true that the body so qualified, and having 20 that competence, had neglected the duty.

108. The question now, on all this accumulated matter, is whether you will choose to abide by a profitable experience, or a mischievous theory ; whether you choose to build on imagination, or fact ; whether you prefer 25 enjoyment, or hope ; satisfaction in your subjects, or discontent ?

109. If these propositions are accepted, everything which has been made to enforce a contrary system must, I take it for granted, fall along with it. On that ground, 30 I have drawn the following resolution, which, when it comes to be moved, will naturally be divided in a proper manner :—

That it may be proper to repeal an act, made in the seventh year of the reign of his present Majesty, inti- 35

tuled, An act for granting certain duties in the British Colonies and Plantations in America ; for allowing
a drawback of the duties of customs upon the exportation from this kingdom of coffee and cocoa-nuts of
5   the produce of the said Colonies or Plantations ; for
discontinuing the drawbacks payable on China earthenware exported to America ; and for more effectually
preventing the clandestine running of goods in the
said Colonies and Plantations.—And that it may be
10   proper to repeal an act, made in the fourteenth year
of the reign of his present Majesty. intituled, An act
to discontinue, in such manner, and for such time, as
are therein mentioned, the landing and discharging,
lading or shipping, of goods, wares, and merchandise,
15   at the town and within the harbour of Boston, in the
Province of Massachusetts Bay, in North America.—
And that it may be proper to repeal an act, made in
the fourteenth year of the reign of his present Majesty,
intituled, An act for the impartial administration o*
20   justice, in the cases of persons questioned for any acts
done by them in the execution of the law, or for the
suppression of riots and tumults, in the Province of
Massachusetts Bay, in New England.—And that it
may be proper to repeal an act, made in the fourteenth
25   year of the reign of his present Majesty, intituled, An
act for the better regulating the government of the
Province of the Massachusetts Bay, in New England.
—And, also, that it may be proper to explain and
amend an act, made in the thirty-fifth year of the
30   reign of King Henry the Eighth, intituled, An act
for the trial of treasons committed out of the King's
Dominions.

110. I wish, Sir, to repeal the Boston Port Bill, because—independently of the dangerous precedent of sus-
35 pending the rights of the subject during the King's
pleasure—it was passed, as I apprehend, with less regularity, and on more partial principles, than it ought.
The corporation of Boston was not heard before it was
condemned.   Other towns, full as guilty as she was, have

not had their ports blocked up. Even the Restraining Bill of the present session does not go to the length of the Boston Port Act. The same ideas of prudence which induced you not to extend equal punishment to equal guilt, even when you were punishing, induced me, who 5 mean not to chastise, but to reconcile, to be satisfied with the punishment already partially inflicted.

111. Ideas of prudence and accommodation to circumstances prevent you from taking away the charters of Connecticut and Rhode Island, as you have taken away 10 that of Massachusetts Colony, though the Crown has far less power in the two former Provinces than it enjoyed in the latter, and though the abuses have been full as great, and as flagrant, in the exempted as in the punished. The same reasons of prudence and accom- 15 modation have weight with me in restoring the charter of Massachusetts Bay. Besides, Sir, the act which changes the charter of Massachusetts is in many particulars so exceptionable that, if I did not wish absolutely to repeal, I would by all means desire to alter it ; as 20 several of its provisions tend to the subversion of all public and private justice. Such, among others, is the power in the governor to change the sheriff at his pleasure, and to make a new returning officer for every special cause. It is shameful to behold such a regulation 25 standing among English laws.

112. The act for bringing persons accused of committing murder under the orders of government to England for trial is but temporary. That act has calculated the probable duration of our quarrel with the Colonies, and 30 is accommodated to that supposed duration. I would hasten the happy moment of reconciliation ; and therefore must, on my principle, get rid of that most justly obnoxious act.

113. The act of Henry the Eighth, for the trial of 35

treasons, I do not mean to take away, but to confine it
to its proper bounds and original intention ; to make
it expressly for trial of treasons—and the greatest treasons may be committed—in places where the jurisdiction
5 of the Crown does not extend.

114. Having guarded the privileges of local legislature, I would next secure to the Colonies a fair and un-
biassed judicature ; for which purpose, Sir, I propose the
following resolution :—

10 That, from the time when the General Assembly or General Court of any Colony or Plantation in North
America shall have appointed, by act of Assembly
duly confirmed, a settled salary to the offices of the
Chief Justice and other Judges of the Superior Court
15 it may be proper that the said Chief Justice and other
Judges of the Superior Courts of such Colony shall
hold his and their office and offices during their good
behaviour ; and shall not be removed therefrom but
when the said removal shall be adjudged by his Maj-
20 esty in Council, upon a hearing on complaint from
the General Assembly, or on a complaint from the
Governor, or Council, or the House of Representatives severally, of the Colony in which the said Chief
Justice and other Judges have exercised the said
25 offices.

115. The next resolution relates to the Courts of
Admiralty. It is this :—

That it may be proper to regulate the Courts of Admiralty, or Vice-Admiralty, authorized by the fifteenth
30 chapter of the Fourth of George the Third, in such
a manner as to make the same more commodious to
those who sue, or are sued, in the said Courts, and to
provide for the more decent maintenance of the Judges
in the same.

35 116. These courts I do not wish to take away ; they
are in themselves proper establishments. This court is

one of the capital securities of the Act of Navigation.
The extent of its jurisdiction, indeed, has been increased;
but this is altogether as proper, and is indeed on many
accounts more eligible, where new powers were wanted,
than a court absolutely new.   But courts incommo- 5
diously situated in effect deny justice ; and a court partaking in the fruits of its own condemnation is a robber.
The Congress complain, and complain justly, of this
grievance.

117. These are the three consequential propositions. 10
I have thought of two or three more, but they come
rather too near detail, and to the province of executive
government, which I wish Parliament always to superin-
tend, never to assume.   If the first six are granted,
congruity will carry the latter three.   If not, the things 15
that remain unrepealed will be, I hope, rather unseemly
encumbrances on the building, than very materially
detrimental to its strength and stability.

[*Refutation of Objections.*]

118. Here, Sir, I should close ; but I plainly perceive
some objections remain, which I ought, if possible, to re- 20
move.   The first will be that, in resorting to the doctrine
of our ancestors, as contained in the preamble to the
Chester Act, I prove too much : that the grievance from
a want of representation, stated in that preamble, goes
to the whole of legislation as well as to taxation ; and 25
that the Colonies, grounding themselves upon that doctrine, will apply it to all parts of legislative authority.

119. To this objection, with all possible deference and
humility, and wishing as little as any man living to
impair the smallest particle of our supreme authority, I 30
answer, that *the words are the words of Parliament, and
not mine;* and that all false and inconclusive inferences

5

drawn from them are not mine, for I heartily disclaim
any such inference. I have chosen the words of an Act
of Parliament, which Mr. Grenville, surely a tolerably
zealous and very judicious advocate for the sovereignty
5 of Parliament, formerly moved to have read at your
table in confirmation of his tenets. It is true that Lord
Chatham considered these preambles as declaring strongly in favour of his opinions. He was a no less powerful
advocate for the privileges of the Americans. Ought
10 I not from hence to presume that these preambles are as
favourable as possible to both, when properly understood ; favourable both to the rights of Parliament, and
to the privilege of the dependencies of this Crown? But,
Sir, the object of grievance in my resolution I have
15 not taken from the Chester, but from the Durham Act,
which confines the hardship of want of representation
to the case of subsidies, and which therefore falls in exactly with the case of the Colonies. But whether the
unrepresented counties were *de jure*, or *de facto*, bound,
20 the preambles do not accurately distinguish, nor indeed
was it necessary ; for whether *de jure* or *de facto*, the
Legislature thought the exercise of the power of taxing
as of right, or as of fact without right, equally a grievance, and equally oppressive.
25   120. I do not know that the Colonies have, in any general way, or in any cool hour, gone much beyond the demand of immunity in relation to taxes. It is not fair
to judge of the temper or dispositions of any man, or any
set of men, when they are composed and at rest, from
30 their conduct or their expressions in a state of disturb-
ance and irritation. It is besides a very great mistake
to imagine that mankind follow up practically any
speculative principle, either of government or of freedom, as far as it will go in argument and logical illation.
35 We Englishmen stop very short of the principles upon

which we support any given part of our Constitution, or
even the whole of it together. I could easily, if I had
not already tired you, give you very striking and convincing instances of it. This is nothing but what is
natural and proper. All government, indeed every 5
human benefit and enjoyment, every virtue, and every
prudent act, is founded on compromise and barter. We
balance inconveniences ; we give and take ; we remit
some rights that we may enjoy others ; and we choose
rather to be happy citizens than subtle disputants. As 10
we must give away some natural liberty to enjoy civil
advantages, so we must sacrifice some civil liberties for
the advantages to be derived from the communion and
fellowship of a great empire. But, in all fair dealings,
the thing bought must bear some proportion to the pur- 15
chase paid. None will barter away the immediate jewel
of his soul. Though a great house is apt to make slaves
haughty, yet it is purchasing a part of the artificial importance of a great empire too dear, to pay for it all
essential rights, and all the intrinsic dignity of human 20
nature. None of us who would not risk his life rather
than fall under a government purely arbitrary. But although there are some amongst us who think our Constitution wants many improvements to make it a complete
system of liberty, perhaps none who are of that opinion 25
would think it right to aim at such improvement by
disturbing his country, and risking everything that is
dear to him. In every arduous enterprise we consider
what we are to lose, as well as what we are to gain ; and
the more and better stake of liberty every people possess, 30
the less they will hazard in a vain attempt to make it
more. These are *the cords of man*. Man acts from
adequate motives relative to his interest, and not on
metaphysical speculations. Aristotle, the great master
of reasoning, cautions us, and with great weight and 35

propriety, against this species of delusive geometrical accuracy in moral arguments, as the most fallacious of all sophistry.

121. The Americans will have no interest contrary to
5 the grandeur and glory of England, when they are not oppressed by the weight of it ; and they will rather be inclined to respect the acts of a superintending Legislature, when they see them the acts of that power which is itself the security, not the rival, of their secondary importance.
10 In this assurance my mind most perfectly acquiesces ; and I confess I feel not the least alarm from the discontents which are to arise from putting people at their ease ; nor do I apprehend the destruction of this Empire from giving, by an act of free grace and indulgence, to two
15 millions of my fellow-citizens some share of those rights upon which I have always been taught to value myself.

122. It is said, indeed, that this power of granting, vested in American Assemblies, would dissolve the unity of the empire ; which was preserved entire, although
20 Wales, and Chester, and Durham were added to it. Truly, Mr. Speaker, I do not know what this unity means, nor has it ever been heard of, that I know, in the constitutional policy of this country. The very idea of subordination of parts excludes this notion of simple and
25 undivided unity. England is the head ; but she is not the head and the members too. Ireland has ever had from the beginning a separate, but not an independent, Legislature ; which, far from distracting, promoted the union of the whole. Everything was sweetly and har-
30 moniously disposed through both islands for the conservation of English dominion, and the communication of English liberties. I do not see that the same principles might not be carried into twenty islands, and with the same good effect. This is my model with regard to
35 America, as far as the internal circumstances of the two

countries are the same. I know no other unity of this
empire than I can draw from its example during these
periods when it seemed to my poor understanding more
united than it is now, or than it is likely to be by the
present methods.   5

123. But since I speak of these methods, I recollect,
Mr. Speaker, almost too late, that I promised, before I
finished, to say something of the proposition of the
Noble Lord on the floor, which has been so lately received, and stands on your Journals. I must be deeply 10
concerned, whenever it is my misfortune to continue a
difference with the majority of this House. But as the
reasons for that difference are my apology for thus
troubling you, suffer me to state them in a very few
words. I shall compress them into as small a body as I 15
possibly can, having already debated that matter at large
when the question was before the committee.

124. First, then, I cannot admit that proposition of a
ransom by auction; because it is a mere project. It is
a thing new; unheard of; supported by no experience; 20
justified by no analogy; without example of our ancestors, or root in the Constitution. It is neither regular
parliamentary taxation, nor colony grant. *Experimentum in corpore vili* is a good rule, which will ever make
me adverse to any trial of experiments on what is cer- 25
tainly the most valuable of all subjects, the peace of this
empire.

125. Secondly, it is an experiment which must be fatal
in the end to our Constitution. For what is it but a
scheme for taxing the Colonies in the antechamber of 30
the Noble Lord and his successors? To settle the quotas and proportions in this House is clearly impossible.
You, Sir, may flatter yourself you shall sit a State auctioneer, with your hammer in your hand, and knock

down to each Colony as it bids.   But to settle—on the
plan laid down by the Noble Lord—the true proportional
payment for four or five and twenty governments, according to the absolute and the relative wealth of each,
5 and according to the British proportion of wealth and
burthen, is a wild and chimerical notion.   This new
taxation must therefore come in by the back-door of the
Constitution.   Each quota must be brought to this
House ready formed ; you can neither add nor alter.
10 You must register it.   You can do nothing further.
For on what grounds can you deliberate either before or
after the proposition ?   You cannot hear the counsel for
all these Provinces, quarrelling each on its own quantity
of payment and its proportion to others.   If you should
15 attempt it, the Committee of Provincial Ways and
Means, or by whatever other name it will delight to be
called, must swallow up all the time of Parliament.

126. Thirdly, it does not give satisfaction to the complaint of the Colonies.   They complain that they are
20 taxed without their consent ; you answer that you will fix
the sum at which they shall be taxed,—that is, you give
them the very grievance for the remedy.   You tell them,
indeed, that you will leave the mode to themselves.   I
really beg pardon—it gives me pain to mention it—but
25 you must be sensible that you will not perform this part
of the compact.   For, suppose the Colonies were to lay
the duties, which furnished their contingent, upon the
importation of your manufactures ; you know you would
never suffer such a tax to be laid.   You know, too, that
30 you would not suffer many other modes of taxation.
So that, when you come to explain yourself, it will be
found that you will neither leave to themselves the quantum nor the mode ; nor indeed anything.   The whole is
delusion from one end to the other.

35   127. Fourthly, this method of ransom by auction, un-

less it be *universally* accepted, will plunge you into great
and inextricable difficulties.   In what year of our Lord
are the proportions of payments to be settled ?   To say
nothing of the impossibility that Colony agents should
have general powers of taxing the Colonies at their dis- 5
cretion, consider, I implore you, that the communication
by special messages, and orders between these agents and
their constituents on each variation of the case, when the
parties come to contend together and to dispute on their
relative proportions, will be a matter of delay, perplex- 10
ity, and confusion that never can have an end.

128. If all the Colonies do not appear at the outcry,
what is the condition of those Assemblies who offer, by
themselves or their agents, to tax themselves up to your
ideas of their proportion ?   The refractory Colonies, who 15
refuse all composition, will remain taxed only to your
old impositions, which, however grievous in principle,
are trifling as to production.   The obedient Colonies in
this scheme are heavily taxed ; the refractory remain
unburthened.   What will you do ?   Will you lay new and 20
heavier taxes by Parliament on the disobedient ?   Pray
consider in what way you can do it.   You are perfectly
convinced that, in the way of taxing, you can do nothing
but at the ports.   Now suppose it is Virginia that refuses
to appear at your auction, while Maryland and North 25
Carolina bid handsomely for their ransom, and are taxed
to your quota—how will you put these Colonies on a par ?
Will you tax the tobacco of Virginia ?   If you do, you
give its death-wound to your English revenue at home,
and to one of the very greatest articles of your own 30
foreign trade.   If you tax the import of that rebellious
Colony, what do you tax but your own manufactures, or
the goods of some other obedient and already well-taxed
Colony ?   Who has said one word on this labyrinth of
detail, which bewilders you more and more as you enter 35

into it ? Who has presented, who can present you, with
a clue to lead you out of it ? I think, Sir, it is impossible
that you should not recollect that the Colony bounds are
so implicated in one another—you know it by your other
5 experiments in the bill for prohibiting the New England
fishery—that you can lay no possible restraints on almost
any of them which may not be presently eluded, if you
do not confound the innocent with the guilty, and burthen those whom, upon every principle, you ought to
10 exonerate.   He must be grossly ignorant of America
who thinks that, without falling into this confusion of
all rules of equity and policy, you can restrain any single
Colony, especially Virginia and Maryland, the central
and' most important of them all.

15   129. Let it also be considered that, either in the present confusion you settle a permanent contingent, which
will and must be trifling, and then you have no effectual
revenue ; or you change the quota at every exigency, and
then on every new repartition you will have a new quarrel.

20   130. Reflect besides, that when you have fixed a quota
for every Colony, you have not provided for prompt and
punctual payment. Suppose one, two, five, ten years'
arrears. You cannot issue a treasury extent against the
failing Colony. You must make new Boston Port Bills,
25 new restraining laws, new acts for dragging men to England for trial.   You must send out new fleets, new
armies.   All is to begin again.   From this day forward
the empire is never to know an hour's tranquillity.   An
intestine fire will be kept alive in the bowels of the Col-
30 onies, which one time or other must consume this whole
empire.   I allow indeed that the empire of Germany
raises her revenue and her troops by quotas and con-
tingents ; but the revenue of the empire, and the army
of the empire, is the worst revenue and the worst army
35 in the world.

131. Instead of a standing revenue, you will therefore have a perpetual quarrel. Indeed the Noble Lord, who proposed this project of a ransom by auction, seemed himself to be of that opinion. His project was rather designed for breaking the union of the Colonies, than 5 for establishing a revenue. He confessed he apprehended that his proposal would not be to *their taste.* I say, this scheme of disunion seems to be at the bottom of the project; for I will not suspect that the Noble Lord meant nothing but merely to delude the nation by 10 an airy phantom which he never intended to realize. But whatever his views may be, as I propose the peace and union of the Colonies as the very foundation of my plan, it cannot accord with one whose foundation is perpetual discord. 15

132. Compare the two. This I offer to give you is plain and simple; the other full of perplexed and intricate mazes. This is mild; that harsh. This is found by experience effectual for its purposes; the other is a new project. This is universal; the other calculated for 20 certain Colonies only. This is immediate in its conciliatory operation; the other remote, contingent, full of hazard. Mine is what becomes the dignity of a ruling people,—gratuitous, unconditional, and not held out as matter of bargain and sale. I have done my duty in 25 proposing it to you. I have indeed tired you by a long discourse; but this is the misfortune of those to whose influence nothing will be conceded, and who must win every inch of their ground by argument. You have heard me with goodness. May you decide with wisdom! 30 For my part, I feel my mind greatly disburthened by what I have done to-day. I have been the less fearful of trying your patience, because on this subject I mean to spare it altogether in future. I have this comfort, that in every stage of the American affairs I have steadily 35

opposed the measures that have produced the confusion, and may bring on the destruction, of this empire. I now go so far as to risk a proposal of my own. If I cannot give peace to my country, I give it to my con-
5 science.

133. "But what," says the financier, "is peace to us without money? Your plan gives us no revenue." No! But it does—for it secures to the subject the power of REFUSAL,—the first of all revenues. Experience is a
10 cheat, and fact a liar, if this power in the subject of proportioning his grant, or of not granting at all, has not been found the richest mine of revenue ever discovered by the skill or by the fortune of man. It does not indeed vote you £152,750 : 11 : 2¾ths, nor any other pal-
15 try limited sum, but it gives the strong box itself, the fund, the bank, from whence only revenues can arise amongst a people sensible of freedom : *Posita luditur arca.* Cannot you, in England; cannot you, at this time of day; cannot you, a House of Commons, trust to the
20 principle which has raised so mighty a revenue, and accumulated a debt of near 140 millions in this country? Is this principle to be true in England, and false everywhere else? Is it not true in Ireland? Has it not hitherto been true in the Colonies? Why should you pre-
25 sume that in any country a body duly constituted for any function will neglect to perform its duty, and abdicate its trust? Such a presumption would go against all governments in all modes. But, in truth, this dread of penury of supply from a free Assembly has no founda-
30 tion in nature. For first observe that, besides the desire which all men have naturally of supporting the honour of their own government, that sense of dignity and that security to property, which ever attends freedom, has a tendency to increase the stock of the free community.
35 Most may be taken where most is accumulated. And

what is the soil or climate where experience has not uniformly proved that the voluntary flow of heaped - up
plenty, bursting from the weight of its own rich luxuri-
ance, has ever run with a more copious stream of revenue
than could be squeezed from the dry husks of oppressed 5
indigence, by the straining of all the politic machinery
in the world ?

134. Next, we know that parties must ever exist in a
free country. We know, too, that the emulations of such
parties, their contradictions, their reciprocal necessities, 10
their hopes, and their fears, must send them all in their
turns to him that holds the balance of the state. The
parties are the gamesters ; but government keeps the
table, and is sure to be the winner in the end. When
this game is played, I really think it is more to be feared 15
that the people will be exhausted than that government
will not be supplied. Whereas, whatever is got by acts
of absolute power ill obeyed, because odious, or by con-
tracts ill kept, because constrained, will be narrow, feeble,
uncertain, and precarious— 20

Ease would retract
Vows made in pain, as violent and void.

135. I, for one, protest against compounding our demands : I declare against compounding, for a poor limited
sum, the immense, ever-growing, eternal debt, which is 25
due to generous government from protected freedom.
And so may I speed in the great object I propose to you,
as I think it would not only be an act of injustice, but
would be the worst economy in the world, to compel the
Colonies to a sum certain, either in the way of ransom, 30
or in the way of compulsory compact.

136. But to clear up my ideas on this subject : a revenue from America transmitted hither—do not delude
yourselves—you never can receive it ; no, not a shilling.

We have experience that from remote countries it is not
to be expected. If, when you attempted to extract revenue from Bengal, you were obliged to return in loan
what you had taken in imposition, what can you expect
5 from North America ? For certainly, if ever there was
a country qualified to produce wealth, it is India ; or an
institution fit for the transmission, it is the East India
Company. America has none of these aptitudes. If
America gives you taxable objects, on which you lay
10 your duties here, and gives you, at the same time, a surplus by a foreign sale of her commodities to pay the
duties on these objects, which you tax at home, she has
performed her part to the British revenue. But with
regard to her own internal establishments, she may—I
15 doubt not she will—contribute in moderation. I say in
moderation ; for she ought not to be permitted to ex-
haust herself. She ought to be reserved to a war ; the
weight of which, with the enemies that we are most
likely to have, must be considerable in her quarter of
20 the globe. There she may serve you, and serve you
essentially.

[*Peroration.*]

137. For that service, for all service, whether of revenue, trade, or empire, my trust is in her interest in the
British Constitution. My hold of the Colonies is in the
25 close affection which grows from common names, from
kindred blood, from similar privileges, and equal protection. These are ties, which, though light as air, are as
strong as links of iron. Let the Colonies always keep
the idea of their civil rights associated with your gov-
30 ernment—they will cling and grapple to you, and no
force under heaven will be of power to tear them from
their allegiance. But let it be once understood that your

government may be one thing, and their privileges another; that these two things may exist without any
mutual relation—the cement is gone, the cohesion is
loosened, and everything hastens to decay and dissolu-
tion.   As long as you have the wisdom to keep the sov- 5
ereign authority of this country as the sanctuary of
liberty, the sacred temple consecrated to. our common
faith, wherever the chosen race and sons of England
worship freedom, they will turn their faces towards you.
The more they multiply, the more friends you will have; 10
the more ardently they love liberty, the more perfect
will be their obedience.   Slavery they can have any
where.   It is a weed that grows in every soil.   They
may have it from Spain, they may have it from Prussia.
But, until you become lost to all feeling of your true 15
interest and your natural dignity, freedom they can have
from none but you.   This is the commodity of price, of
which you have the monopoly.   This is the true Act of
Navigation, which binds to you the commerce of the
Colonies, and through them secures to you the wealth 20
of the world.   Deny them this participation of freedom,
and you break that sole bond, which originally made,
and must still preserve, the unity of the empire.   Do
not entertain so weak an imagination as that your reg-
isters and your bonds, your affidavits and your suffer- 25
ances, your cockets and your clearances, are what form
the great securities of your commerce.   Do not dream
that your letters of office, and your instructions, and
your suspending clauses, are the things that.hold together
the great contexture of the mysterious whole.   These 30
things do not make your government.   Dead instruments, passive tools as they are, it is the spirit of
English communion that gives all their life and efficacy
to them.   It is the spirit of the English Constitution,
which, infused through the mighty mass, pervades, 35

feeds, unites, invigorates, vivifies every part of the empire, even down to the minutest member.

138. Is it not the same virtue which does everything
for us here in England ? Do you imagine then, that it
5 is the Land Tax Act which raises your revenue ? that it
is the annual vote in the Committee of Supply which
gives you your army ? or that it is the Mutiny Bill which
inspires it with bravery and discipline ? No ! surely no !
It is the love of the people ; it is their attachment to
10 their government, from the sense of the deep stake they
have in such a glorious institution, which gives you your
army and your navy, and infuses into both that liberal
obedience, without which your army would be a base
rabble, and your navy nothing but rotten timber.
15   139. All this, I know well enough, will sound wild and
chimerical to the profane herd of those vulgar and mechanical politicians, who have no place among us ; a
sort of people who think that nothing exists but what
is gross and material ; and who therefore, far from being
20 qualified to be directors of the great movement of empire, are not fit to turn a wheel in the machine. But
to men truly initiated and rightly taught, these ruling
and master principles, which, in the opinion of such men
as I have mentioned, have no substantial existence, are
25 in truth everything, and all in all. Magnanimity in
politics is not seldom the truest wisdom ; and a great
empire and little minds go ill together. If we are conscious of our situation, and glow with zeal to fill our
place as becomes our station and ourselves, we ought to
30 auspicate all our public proceedings on America with
the old warning of the Church, *Sursum corda!* We
ought to elevate our minds to the greatness of that trust
to which the order of Providence has called us. By ad-
verting to the dignity of this high calling, our ancestors
35 have turned a savage wilderness into a glorious empire,

and have made the most extensive, and the only honourable conquests, not by destroying, but by promoting, the
wealth, the number, the happiness of the human race.
Let us get an American revenue as we have got an
American empire. English privileges have made it all 5
that it is ; English privileges alone will make it all it
can be.

140. In full confidence of this unalterable truth, I now
—*quod felix faustumque sit!*—lay the first stone of the
Temple of Peace ; and I move you,   10

That the Colonies and Plantations of Great Britain in
    North America, consisting of Fourteen separate gov-
    ernments, and containing Two Millions and upwards
    of free inhabitants, have not had the liberty and priv-
    ilege of electing and sending any Knights and Bur- 15
    gesses, or others, to represent them in the high Court
    of Parliament.

NOTES

BURKE'S RESOLUTIONS.

THE speech was made for the purpose of moving certain resolutions, which therefore, considered politically, form the most important part of the whole. There is, accordingly, the following appendix in Dodsley's edition :—

"As the propositions were opened separately in the body of the speech, the reader perhaps may wish to see the whole of them together, in the form in which they were moved for.

MOVED,

That the Colonies and Plantations of Great Britain in North America, consisting of Fourteen separate Governments, and containing Two Millions and upwards of free inhabitants, have not had the liberty and privilege of electing and sending any Knights and Burgesses, or others, to represent them in the high Court of Parliament.

That the said Colonies and Plantations have been made[1] liable to, and bounden by, several subsidies, payments, rates, and taxes, given and granted by Parliament, though the said Colonies and Plantations have not their Knights and Burgesses in the said high Court of Parliament, of their own election, to represent the condition of their country; *by lack whereof they have been oftentimes touched and grieved by subsidies given, granted, and assented to in the said Court, in a manner prejudicial to the common wealth, quietness, rest, and peace of the subjects inhabiting within the same.*

That, from the distance of the said Colonies, and from other circumstances, no method hath hitherto been devised for procuring a representation in Parliament for the said Colonies.

That each of the said Colonies hath within itself a body, chosen, in part or in the whole, by the freemen, freeholders, or other free inhabitants thereof, commonly called the General Assembly, or General Court; with powers legally to raise, levy, and assess, according to the several usage of such Colonies

---

[1] Otherwise in the speech ; *cf.* 54 15.

duties and taxes towards defraying all sorts of public services.[1]

That the said General Assemblies, General Courts, or other bodies legally qualified as aforesaid, have at sundry times freely granted several large subsidies and public aids for his Majesty's service, according to their abilities, when required thereto by letter from one of his Majesty's principal Secretaries of State ; and that their right to grant the same, and their cheerfulness and sufficiency in the said grants, have been at sundry times acknowledged by Parliament.

That it hath been found by experience, that the manner of granting the said supplies and aids by the said General Assemblies hath been more agreeable to the inhabitants of [2] the said Colonies, and more beneficial and conducive to the public service, than the mode of giving and granting aids and subsidies[3] in Parliament, to be raised and paid in the said Colonies.

That it may be proper to repeal an act, made in the seventh year of the reign of his present Majesty, intituled, An act for granting certain duties in the British Colonies and Plantations in America ; for allowing a drawback of the duties of customs upon the exportation from this kingdom of coffee and cocoa-nuts of the produce of the said Colonies or Plantations ; for discontinuing the drawbacks payable on China earthenware exported to America ; and for more effectually preventing the clandestine running of goods in the said Colonies and Plantations.

That[4] it may be proper to repeal an act, made in the fourteenth year of the reign of his present Majesty, intituled, An act to discontinue, in such manner, and for such time, as are therein mentioned, the landing and discharging, lading or shipping, of goods, wares, and merchandise, at the town and within the harbour of Boston, in the Province of Massachusetts Bay, in North America.

That[4] it may be proper to repeal an act, made in the fourteenth year of the reign of his present Majesty, intituled, An act for the impartial administration of justice, in cases[5] of persons questioned for any acts done by them in the execution of the law, or for the suppression of riots and tumults, in the Province of Massachusetts Bay, in New England.

---

[1] The first four motions and the last had the previous question put on them. The others were negatived.

The words in italics were, by an amendment that was carried, left out of the motion ; which will appear in the Journals, though it is not the practice to insert such amendments in the votes. [*Original Note in Dodsley's Edition.*]

[2] Otherwise in the speech ; *cf.* 61 7.   [3] *Cf.* 61 10.

[4] *Cf.* 62 17.   [5] *Cf.* 62 20.

That it is [1] proper to repeal an act, made in the fourteenth year of the reign of his present Majesty, intituled, An act for the better regulating the government of the Province of the Massachusetts Bay, in New England.

That it is [1] proper to explain and amend an act made in the thirty-fifth year of the reign of King Henry the Eighth intituled, An act for the trial of treasons committed out of the King's Dominions.

That, from the time when the General Assembly or General Court of any Colony or Plantation in North America shall have appointed, by act of Assembly duly confirmed, a settled salary to the offices of the Chief Justice and Judges [2] of the Superior Courts, [2] it may be proper that the said Chief Justice and other Judges of the Superior Courts of such Colony shall hold his and their office and offices during their good behaviour ; and shall not be removed therefrom but when the said removal shall be adjudged by his Majesty in Council, upon a hearing on complaint from the General Assembly, or on a complaint from the Governor, or Council, or the House of Representatives, severally, of the Colony in which the said Chief Justice and other Judges have exercised the said office. [4]

That it may be proper to regulate the Courts of Admiralty, or Vice-Admiralty, authorized by the fifteenth chapter of the Fourth of George the Third, in such a manner as to make the same more commodious to those who sue, or are sued, in the said Courts, *and to provide for the more decent maintenance of the Judges of* [5] *the same.*''

THE RECEPTION OF BURKE'S SPEECH BY THE HOUSE.

(*Annual Register,* [6] xviii. (1775), Fourth Edition, pp. 109-110.)

On this motion, and on the whole matter, the debate was long and animated. It was objected, in general, that these resolutions abandoned the whole object for which we were contending ; that in words, indeed, they did not give up the right of taxing, but they did so in effect. The first resolution, they said, was artfully worded, as containing in appearance nothing but matters of fact ; but, if adopted, con-

---

[1] Otherwise in the speech ; *cf.* 62 23.   [2] *Cf.* 62 28.
[3] *Cf.* 64 14.   [4] *Of.* 64 25.   [5] *Cf.* 64 34.
[6] It should be remembered that the *Annual Register* was instituted, and for many years edited, by Burke, and that this passage may be from his own hand—at any rate had his full approval. A full analysis of the speech immediately precedes our extract.

sequences would follow highly prejudicial to the public good : that the mere truth of a proposition did not of course make it necessary or proper to resolve it. As they had frequently resolved not to admit the unconstitutional claims of the Americans, they could not admit resolutions directly leading to them. They had no assurance that, if they should adopt these propositions, the Americans would make any dutiful returns on their side ; and thus the scheme, pursued through so many difficulties, of compelling that refractory people to contribute their fair proportion to the expenses of the whole empire, would fall to the ground. The House of Lords would not, they said, permit another plan, somewhat of the same kind, so much as to lie on their table ; and the House of Commons had in this session already adopted one which they judged to be conciliatory, upon a ground more consistent with the supremacy of Parliament. It was asserted that the American Assemblies had made provision upon former occasions—but this, they said, was only when pressed by their own immediate danger, and for their own local use. But if the dispositions of the Colonies had been as favourable as they were represented, still it was denied that the American Assemblies ever had a legal power of granting a revenue to the Crown. This they insisted to be a privilege of Parliament only, and a privilege which could not be communicated to any other body whatsoever. In support of this doctrine, they quoted the following clause from that palladium of the English Constitution, and of the rights and liberties of the subject, commonly called the Bill or Declaration of Rights : [1] viz., that "Levying money for, or to the use of the Crown, *by pretence of prerogative*, without grant of Parliament, for a longer time, or in other manner, than the same is or shall be granted, is illegal."

This clause, they insisted, clearly enforced the exclusive right in Parliament of taxing every part of the Empire. And this right, they said, was not only prudent but necessary. The right of taxation must be inherent in the supreme power, and, being the most essential of all others, was the most necessary, not only to be reserved in theory, but exercised in practice, or it would in effect be lost, and all other powers along with it. This principle was carried so far that it was said any minister ought to be impeached who suffered the grant of any sort of revenue from the Colonies to the Crown ; that such a practice in time of war might possibly be tolerated from the necessity of the case, but that a revenue in time of peace could not be granted by any of the Assemblies without subverting the Constitution. In the warmth of prosecuting this idea, it was asserted by more than one gentleman on that side that the

---

[1] Drawn up in 1689, at the accession of William and Mary.

establishment of a Parliament in Ireland did not by any means preclude Great Britain from taxing that kingdom whenever it was thought necessary; that that right had always been maintained, and exercised too, whenever it was judged expedient; and that the British Parliament had no other rule in that exercise than its own discretion; that all inferior Assemblies in this empire were only like the corporate towns in England, which had a power, like them, of making by-laws for their own municipal government, and nothing more.

On the other side it was urged that the clause in the Declaration of Rights, so much relied on, was calculated merely to restrain the prerogative from the raising of any money within the realm without the consent of Parliament; but that it did not at all reach, nor was intended to interfere with, the taxes levied, or grants passed by legal Assemblies out of the kingdom, for the public service. On the contrary, Parliament knew at the time of passing that law that the Irish grants were subsisting, and taxes constantly levied in consequence of them, without their once thinking, either then or at any other time, of censuring the practice, or condemning the mode as unconstitutional. It was also said that different Parliaments, at different periods, had not only recognized the right, but gratefully acknowledged the benefit which the public derived from the taxes levied, and the grants passed, by the American Assemblies. As to the distinctions taken of a time of war and the necessity of the case—they said it was frivolous and wholly groundless. The power of the subject in granting, or of the Crown in receiving, no way differs in time of war from the same power in time of peace; nor is any distinction on such a supposition made in the article of the Bill of Rights. They argued, therefore, that this article of the Bill of Rights is confined to what it was always thought confined, the prerogative in this kingdom, and bound indeed the Crown, but could not, in securing the rights and liberties of the subject in this kingdom, intend to annihilate them everywhere else. That as the Constitution had permitted the Irish Parliament and American Assemblies to make grants to the Crown, and that experience had shown that these grants had produced both satisfaction and revenue, it was absurd to risk all in favour of theories of supremacy, unity, sovereign rights, and other names, which hitherto had led to nothing but confusion and beggary on all sides, and would continue to produce the same miserable effects as long as they were persisted in. That the mover had very wisely avoided these speculative questions, and confined himself to experience; and it would be well if they could persuade themselves to follow that example.

The previous question was moved on the first proposition, and carried by 270 to 78.

THE CONCEPTION OF ORATORY AMONG THE ANCIENTS.

The three main divisions of oratory, according to the an-
sients,[1] who have generally been followed by the moderns,
are the epideictic, the judicial, and the deliberative. The
epideictic, sometimes called the demonstrative or panegyrical,
is concerned with praise or blame. The judicial, otherwise
known as the forensic, has reference to past actions, and is
concerned with the decision of legal points. The deliberative
or political has reference to the future, and is concerned with
the choice of one among several courses of action. Eulogy
falls under the first head, the speeches of lawyers under the
second, and legislative eloquence under the third.

It is evident that Burke's speech belongs to the class of
deliberative oratory, and that its object is not praise or
blame, accusation or defence, but advocacy and dissuasion—
advocacy of one course of action and dissuasion from another.

The ancients recognized five principal divisions of a judicial
or a deliberative speech: (1) the Exordium o Proem, which is
often called the Introduction ; (2) the Statement of Facts ; (3)
the Proof of what we advance ; (4) the Refutation of an opposing view ; and (5) the Peroration.

Unless facts be brought forward, there is no subject-matter
of discourse ; and the proof of our opinion evidently constitutes the most important part of a speech which is intended to
convince others. These two heads correspond to (2) and (3)
above. Then the refutation of our adversary may be as important as the proof of our own contention, if indeed it be not
regarded as a part of it ; and this corresponds to (4). Finally, it
is important to prepare the audience for the favourable reception
of the main part of the speech, and to close with a recapitula-
tion of the arguments employed, or an appeal to the feelings,
or both. These, then, comprise the remaining heads.

In some cases an orator may distinctly state the central
thought or proposition for which he means to contend ; such
central thought or proposition is technically called the Status

[1] Especially Aristotle and Quintilian.

and this may add another to the divisions. Lastly, it may
seem necessary, in certain cases, to abandon the strict order
laid down above, and introduce a Digression, which may either
belong under some other one of the recognized heads, or may
not properly fall under any. In this way it is possible to have
a sevenfold division of a speech, without reckoning subdivi-
sions ; and such, if we classify with ancient rhetoricians, is
the case before us. It will be seen that, for convenience in
studying its structure, Burke's *Speech on Conciliation* has been
divided by the editor into these seven parts.

3 1. Goodrich (*Select British Eloquence*, pp. 215–216) thus
marks the occasion of this speech, and its differences from the
earlier one on American Taxation, which had been delivered on
April 19, 1774 : —

" On the 20th [properly 10th] of February, 1775, Lord North
brought forward an artful scheme, professedly for the purpose of
' conciliating the differences with America,' but really intended
to divide the colonies among themselves, by exempting from
taxation those who, through their General Assemblies, should
' contribute their proportion to the common defense.' Mr.
Burke seized the opportunity thus presented, and endeavoured
to turn the scheme into its true and proper shape—that of
leaving all taxes levied within the colonies to be laid by their
General Assemblies, and thus establishing the great principle
of English liberty, that *taxation and representation are in-
separably conjoined.* This gave rise to his celebrated speech
on Conciliation with America, delivered March 22nd, 1775. It
would seem hardly possible that, in speaking so soon again
on the same subject, he could avoid making his speech, to
some extent, an echo of his former one. But never were two
productions more entirely different. His ' stand-point ' in
the first [that on American Taxation] was *England.* His
topics were the inconsistency and folly of the ministry in
their ' miserable circle of occasional arguments and temporary
expedients ' for raising a revenue in America. His object
was to recall the House to the original principles of the English colonial system—that of regulating the trade of the
colonies, and making it subservient to the interests of the
mother country, while in other respects she left them ' every
characteristic mark of a free people in all their internal concerns.' His ' stand-point ' in the second speech was *America.* His topics were her growing population, agriculture,
commerce, and fisheries ; the causes of her fierce spirit of
liberty ; the impossibility of repressing it by force ; and the

consequent necessity of some concession on the part of England. His object was—waiving all abstract questions about the right of taxation—to show that Parliament ought 'to admit the people of the colonies into an interest in the Constitution' by giving them—like Ireland, Wales, Chester, and Durham—a share in the representation; and to do this by leaving internal taxation to the colonial Assemblies, since no one could think of an actual representation of America in Parliament at the distance of three thousand miles. The two speeches were equally diverse in their spirit. The first was in a strain of incessant attack, full of the keenest sarcasm, and shaped from beginning to end for the purpose of putting down the ministry. The second, like the plan it proposed, was conciliatory; temperate and respectful towards Lord North; designed to inform those who were ignorant of the real strength and feelings of America; instinct with the finest philosophy of man and of social institutions; and intended, if possible, to lead the House, through Lord North's schema, into a final adjustment of the dispute on the true principles of English liberty. It is the most finished of Mr. Burke's speeches; and though it contains no passage of such vividness and force as the description of Hyder Ali in his speech on the Nabob of Arcot's Debts, it will be read probably more than any of his other speeches, for the richness of its style and the lasting character of the instruction it conveys. Twenty years after, Mr. Fox said, in applying its principles to the subject of parliamentary reform, 'Let gentlemen read this speech by day and meditate on it by night; let them peruse it again and again, study it. imprint it on their minds, impress it on their hearts—they will there learn that *representation* is the sovereign remedy for every evil.' Both of Mr. Burke's speeches on America, indeed, are full of material for the orator and statesman. After all that has been written on the origin of our Revolution, there is nowhere else to be found so admirable a summation of the causes which produced it. They both deserve to be studied with the utmost diligence by every American scholar.''

3 2. *Chair.* It may be well to distinguish between the qualities courteously attributed to the Chair in debate, and those possessed by the actual occupant of it on this occasion. The Speaker was Fletcher Norton (1716-1789), who had been in office since January 22, 1770, and was to remain in it until October 31, 1780. On the assembling of this Parliament on November 29, 1774, he had been unanimously re-elected to the position. According to the *Dict. Nat. Biog.,*

"Norton was a shrewd, unprincipled man, of good abilities and offensive manners. His violent temper and lack of discretion unfitted him for the post of Speaker. Though by no means a learned lawyer, he was a bold and able pleader, and was remarkable alike for the clearness of his arguments and the inaccuracy of his statements. According to Lord Mansfield, Norton's 'art was very likely to mislead a judge and jury; and with him I found it more difficult to prevent injustice being done than with any person who ever practised before me.' . . . Junius made a violent attack upon Norton in Letter 39. . . . Churchill satirizes him in *The Duellist* (bk. iii.)." According to a note on the letter of Junius, "He had commenced his political career as a violent Whig, but for some time past . . . had been as warm in the cause of Toryism as the warmest of its oldest supporters." Churchill's character of him, which is no doubt exaggerated, may be inferred from the following extract : —

> He saw poor Freedom breathe her last ;
> He saw her struggle, heard her groan ;
> He saw her helpless and alone,
> Whelmed in that storm which, feared and praised
> By slaves less bold, himself had raised.

The old House of Commons (originally St. Stephen's Chapel), in which the speech was delivered, was destroyed by fire in 1834. It is thus described in Walford's *Old and New London*, vol. ii., pp. 499–500 : —

"The building was of an oblong shape. about ninety feet in length by thirty in width, and had externally at each corner an octagonal tower. It was lighted by five windows on each side, and its walls were supported by substantial buttresses between each window on the outside. It consisted of two storeys, the upper one being used as the House of Commons. . . . The house in itself had nothing very striking to recommend it ; convenience, not ornament, appears to have been the principal object of those who enlarged this ancient chapel and applied it to the use of the Legislature. The galleries, which ran along the sides and west end, were supported by slender iron pillars, crowned with gilt Corinthian capitals, and the walls were wainscoted to the ceiling. The Speaker's chair stood at some distance from the wall ; it was highly ornamented with gilding, and bore the

royal arms above. Before the chair was a table at which sat
the Clerks of the Parliament. In the centre of the room, between the table and the bar, was a capacious area. The seats
for the members occupied each side and both ends of the
room, with the exception of the passages. There were five
rows of seats, rising in gradation above each other, with short
backs, and green morocco cushions."

To complete the picture, one should read the account in
Knight's *London*, vol. ii., pp. 65-66, of the chamber occupied
by the House of Commons : —

"That narrow, dingy room which, to an unaccustomed eye,
looked more like the prison than the palace of the genius of
our English legislation. A strange, underground, cavernous
air it had, indeed, with its one great table occupying half the
penurious floor, and its five tiers of horseshoe benches carried
back to the wainscoted walls—round about so economically
into every angle and coigne of vantage, and the strips of gallery running overhead along each side and at the one end,
and the chandeliers hung, not high near the ceiling, but low
down in mid air, as if there had been some ground-haze, or
other palpable murkiness, floating about and filling the place,
which would have otherwise intercepted the light. The scene,
truly, was apt to awaken the most awkward fancies. A mind
disordered or thrown off its balance by the shock of the sudden, harsh, and complete *bouleversement* of all its previous
impressions of the dignity and splendour of Parliaments might
have been excused, looking down from that end gallery, for
mistaking at the first glance the assembled wisdom, Speaker's
wig and all, for some den of thieves, or a crew of midnight
conspirators. Yet, on better acquaintance, the contracted, un-
adorned, well-packed apartment revealed a character that was
not inappropriate—an earnest, business, workshop character."

Views of the exterior, as it appeared in 1647 and 1830 respectively, may be seen in Walford, iii., 403, 497. A picture
of the interior in 1834—the year of the fire—is in Walford, iii.,
511, and of the interior of the *present* House on p. 510. See
also p. 523.

As to the rank and file of Parliament see *Saturday Review*,
May 30, 1896 (p. 541): —

"In the old days the majority of members of Parliament
were inarticulate. A spectator, casting his eyes along the
serried ranks of fresh-cheeked country gentlemen who sup

ported the Government of the day, exclaimed, 'By Jove! the finest brute votes in Europe !' These gentlemen had either bought their votes or owed them to the nomination of some Lord Lonsdale or Lord Hertford. The Anglo-Indian Nabob who supported Lord North . . . was as capable of taking part in discussion as he was of writing an essay on the currency. He rushed in from Bellamy's, wiping his mouth with his napkin, to vote against anything the party whipper-in ordered. He cried, 'Hear him!' when Charles Fox or Billy Pitt was speaking, and he was only too pleased to be allowed to lie full length along a bench in his boots, sucking oranges or cracking nuts, when Burke was delivering an oration on Conciliation with America. The speaking he left to fellows like Burke, Pitt, Fox, and the lawyers, while he, 'good, easy man,' was quite content if he escaped an election petition.''

3 6. *Superstition.* Anticipating the phrases ''fortunate omen,'' ''providential favour,'' and ''superior warning voice,'' below. Is it to be supposed that Burke was really superstitious ? If not, why did he begin his speech with an apology for this species of human frailty ?

3 8. That which he was about to make.

3 9. *Penal bill.* The introduction of this bill is thus described in the *Parliamentary History*, under Feb. 10, 1775 (xviii., 298–305) :—

''The House having resolved itself into a Committee on the Papers relating to the Disturbances in North America, Lord North moved, 'That leave be given to bring in a Bill to restrain the trade and commerce of the Provinces of Massachusetts Bay and New Hampshire, the Colonies of Connecticut and Rhode Island, and Providence Plantation, in North America, to Great Britain, Ireland, and the British Islands in the West Indies ; and to prohibit such Provinces and Colonies from carrying on any fishery on the Banks of Newfoundland or other places therein to be mentioned, under certain conditions, and for a time to be limited.' He supported his motion by declaring that, as the Americans had refused to trade with this kingdom, it was but just that we should not suffer them to trade with any other nation ; that the restraints of the Act of Navigation were their charter, and that the several relaxations of that law were so many acts of grace and favour ; which, when the Colonies ceased to merit, it was but reasonable the British Legislature should recall. . . . His Lordship added that he was not averse to admitting such alleviations of the Act as would not prove destructive of its great object. First, therefore, he would move it only as temporary, to the end of the year, or to the end of the next session of Parliament. Secondly, he would permit particular persons to be excepted, on certificates from the Governor of their good behaviour, or upon their taking a test of acknowledgment of the rights of Parliament." On this occasion Burke's argument was that "there was a fifth Province for which no provision at all had been made, which was likely to be as great a sufferer as any of the other four, though not in rebellion, or in the neighbourhood of rebellion. . . . This Province was England, which had now several hundreds of thousands of her property in the four Provinces of New England. He then showed that New England was not a staple Colony, and could only pay her debts through the fishery and the trades which depended upon it, and that to stop their fishery would be to beggar the English merchants and manufacturers."

The bill was brought in by a vote of 261 to 85. The debate was resumed on February 24, and again on March 6, when Burke spoke, and the bill was ordered engrossed by a vote of 215 to 61. On March 8 (not May 8, as the *Parl. Hist.*, by a misprint, has it) the bill was read a third time, and Burke again spoke, after which the bill was passed.

3 10. *Returned.* The bill had passed the House of Lords on the previous day, with an amendment added.

3 12. *Fortunate omen.* In this line Burke speaks like a pagan, in the language of Cicero ; in the next like a Christian.

3 19. *First day.* November 29, 1774—nearly four months previous.

3 20. *Conciliation.* Note the first appearance of the word.

4 4. *When I first.* In 1765.

4 7. *Delicate.* Presenting points which require nice and skilful handling. Thus in Burke's *Letter to the Sheriffs of Bristol:* "These *delicate* points ought to be wholly left to the crown."

4 12. *Instruct myself.* Probably there was no one in England so well informed about America as Burke.

4 20. *By every wind.* Alluding to *Eph.* iv. 14.

4 24. *At that period.* In 1766, on the repeal of the **Stamp Act.**

4 25. *Large majority.* 275 to 161.

4 30. *Religious.* Conscientious.

4 33 ff. Irony ; *cf.* **4** 16 ff., **5** 5 ff.

5 7. *Complaint.* Define ; *cf. distemper*, l. 9.

5 11 ff. An example of the figure called by the ancients *dubitatio*, διαπόρησις or ἀπορία, by which an apparent perplexity in characterizing heightens the effect ; *cf.* De Mille's *Elements of Rhetoric*, § 527.

5 14. *Beginning of the session.* November 29, 1774.

5 15. *A worthy member.* Mr. Rose Fuller, member for Rye. He spoke rather frequently in Parliament, and on April 19, 1774, brought in a motion to repeal the American Tea Duty (*Parl. Hist.*, xvii., 1210), and thus gave occasion to Burke's *Speech on American Taxation.*

5 20. *Our former methods.* See if you can gather what these methods had been from an examination of the rest of the paragraph. Who are meant by *our ?*

5 22. *Public tribunal.* What is meant ?

5 24. *That the,* etc. Observe that this is a dependent clause, to which the principal verb must be supplied from a preceding sentence. Is this method of writing to be recommended ?

5 25. *Whilst.* Burke seems to prefer this form to *while.* Find other examples in the speech.

5 33. *Our hand.* What rhetorical figure ?

6 2. *Platform.* Sketch, outline, plan. Thus Bacon, *Of Gardens :* "So I have made a *platform* of a princely garden."

6 10. *Gave . . . in.* Yielded. Dodsley (the edition here followed) has *gave . . . into*, but this can hardly be right.

6 13. *Argues.* Define.

6 15. *Plans of government.* An example of such a plan of government was Locke's Constitution for the Carolinas, on which *cf.* Goldwin Smith, *The United States*, p. 50 : —

" For an ideal constitution the proprietaries of the Carolinas applied to the wisdom of Locke, and the wisdom of Locke gave them a Grand Model which, especially considering that it was intended for the rough population of a new settlement, may be regarded as the most awful of warnings to political castle-builders. It is an ineffable structure of the feudal type, with a hierarchy of hereditary land-owners under the names of Landgraves and Caciques—the latter name being probably intended as a compliment to native sentiment—a division of the land into seignories, and, what seems incredible as a proposal of Locke, a race of hereditary tenants attached like villeins-regardant to the soil. To keep government in the hands of intelligence and property seems to have been the philosopher's aim. This scheme the proprietaries actually tried to put in force. It could produce nothing but disgust, revolt, and confusion. The only thing in it worthy of Locke is complete religious toleration. In the course of the political squabbles which inevitably ensued, South Carolina was severed from North Carolina, and transferred from the proprietaries to a royal governor.''

6 17. *Disreputably.* Discreditably—to those who make them. A rather forced use, evidently due to the parallelism with *ineffectually*.

6 19. *Ambitious of ridicule.* What were the objects of Burke's ambition? Collect evidence on this point.

6 32. *Inconsiderable person. Cf.* Burke's *Present Discontents*, Exordium : '' In cases of tumult and disorder, our law has invested every man, in some sort, with the authority of a magistrate. When the affairs of the nation are distracted, private people are, by the spirit of that law, justified in stepping a little out of their ordinary sphere.'' The whole of the passage is worth comparing.

6 33 ff. Paraphrase this sentence.

7 4. *What in other circumstances.* What does he mean ?

7 11. *Adventitious.* Define.

7 16. Give an outline of the Exordium, or, as it is sometimes called, Proem (*cf.* p. 85), touching all the principal points in their order.

The object of the Exordium, according to Quintilian (Bk. iv., chap. 1), is to secure the good-will and attention of the person or body which is to decide on the merits of the cause, and to render him or them desirous of further information. To this end various considerations must be kept in mind.

Among those relevant to the present speech are the following. The judge—in this case the Commons, as represented by the Speaker—must have reason to consider the orator a good man, not only in the abstract, but with reference to his appearance in the particular cause. The motive which induces him to come forward must be a powerful and worthy one. All suspicion of meanness, or hatred, or ambition, must be far removed from him. The orator must be modest, and must take care not to appear insolent, malignant, overbearing, or reproachful. The judge may be conciliated in any proper way. The matter proposed should seem new and important, and the orator must seem likely to speak concisely and to the point. The style of the Exordium should be simple and inartificial, lest the suspicions of the auditory be aroused. Point out any illustrations of these principles which Burke yields.

Quintilian says that "there is much attraction in an exordium which does not appear to have been composed at home, but to be produced on the spot, and from the suggestion of the subject; it increases the reputation of the speaker for ability, from the facility which he exhibits, and, from wearing the appearance of a plain address, . . . gains him the confidence of his audience; insomuch that though the rest of his speech may be written and carefully studied, the whole of it nevertheless seems almost entirely extemporaneous." Study paragraph 1 of the speech in the light of this doctrine.

Goodrich says (*Select British Eloquence*, p. 266): "There is too much that is fanciful in some parts of this exordium. A man who was wholly absorbed in his subject would not talk thus about himself, or about 'the austerity of the chair,' . . . etc. It was this that made Mr. Hazlitt say, 'Most of his speeches have a sort of parliamentary preamble to them; there is an air of affected modesty and ostentatious trifling in them; he seems fond of coquetting with the House of Commons, and is perpetually calling the Speaker out to dance a minuet with him before he begins.'"

7 17 ff. For the Status in general, see De Mille's *Elements of Rhetoric*, §§ 327, 329. What I have here called the Status may properly be regarded as part of the Exordium, and the principles to be observed in the Exordium should be applied to it also. The *Status*, then, in this speech, is that portion of the Exordium in which the orator *states* precisely what view he proposes to advocate, or what, actions he means to recommend.

7 19. *Labyrinth.* What were the two great labyrinths of antiquity? What description can you give of either?

7 20. *Fomented.* Is Burke here referring to any scheme in particular? Can any part, or the whole of his language, be construed to apply to Lord North's "project" (**8** 14)? If so, then a new rhetorical feature of the Exordium is here exemplified, namely, the belittling of the adversary's position. Here it is indirectly and incidentally done, and is all the more effective on that account.

7 22. *Juridical.* Is there any difference in meaning between this word and "judicial"?

7 23. *Shadowy boundaries.* *Cf.* Pope's *Essay on Man*, ii., 207–208. Where has Burke already employed a figure drawn from the art of painting?

7 25, 26. *Spirit of peace.* *Cf. Lk.* i. 17 ; *Gal.* vi. 1.

7 28. *Unsuspecting confidence*, etc. Burke borrows the expression from the Philadelphia Congress of 1774. *Cf.* his *Letter to the Sheriffs of Bristol:*

"The Congress has used an expression with regard to this pacification which appears to me truly significant. After the repeal of the Stamp Act, 'the colonies fell,' says this Assembly, ' into their ancient state of *unsuspecting confidence in the Mother Country.*' This unsuspecting confidence is the true centre of gravity amongst mankind, about which all the parts are at rest. It is this *unsuspecting confidence* that removes all difficulties, and reconciles all the contradictions which occur in the complexity of all ancient, puzzled, political establishments. Happy are the rulers which have the secret of preserving it!"

8 3 ff. Robert Louis Stevenson (*On Style in Literature : Cont. Rev.*, xlvii., 548–561) thus touches upon a curious peculiarity of literature : "One sound suggests, echoes, demands, and harmonizes with another ; and the art of rightly using these concordances is the final art in literature. It used to be a piece of good advice to all young writers to avoid alliteration; and the advice was sound, in so far as it prevented daubing. None the less for that was it abominable nonsense, and the mere raving of the blindest of the blind who will not see. The beauty of the contents of a phrase, or of a sentence, depends implicitly upon alliteration and upon assonance. The vowel demands to be repeated; the consonant demands to be repeated; and both cry aloud to be perpetually varied. You may follow the adventures of a letter through any passage that has particularly pleased you; find it, perhaps, denied awhile, to tantalize the ear; find it fired again at you in a whole broadside; or find it pass into congenerous sounds, one liquid or labial melting away into another.'' In accordance with this suggestion, follow the adventures of *p* through paragraph 10, and compare this with 6 6–18, and 7 17–27, *e.g.*, "it is *p*eace sought in the spirit of *p*eace, and laid in *p*rinci-*p*les *p*urely *p*acific;'' "*p*ro*p*ortion of *p*ayments beyond all the *p*owers of algebra to equalize and settle.''

6 3–9. Payne says, in a note on the *Present Discontents:* "If he introduces general observations, it is done in such a way as to prepare for the particular points which are to fol-low, and with strict reference to that object. Being the most philosophical, he is naturally the most sententious of ora-tors.''

6 12. *Pruriency.* Referring to 2 *Tim.* iv. 3, where "itch-ing'' means "desirous of hearing something pleasant''; the Lat. has "*prurientes* auribus.''

6 14. *Project.* Not to be confounded with the "penal bill'' mentioned above.

On February 20, 1775, Lord North brought in the follow-ing resolution (*Parl. Hist.*, xviii., 320): "That it is the opinion of this Committee that when the Governor, Coun-cil, and Assembly, or General Court, of any of his Maj-esty's Provinces or Colonies in America, shall propose to make provision, according to the condition, circumstances, and situation of such Province or Colony, for contribut-ing their proportion to the common defence (such propor-tion to be raised under the authority of the General Court, or General Assembly, of such Province or Colony, and dis-posable by Parliament), and shall engage to make provision also for the support of the civil government and the administration of justice in such Province or Colony, it will be proper, if such proposal shall be approved by his Majesty and the two Houses of Parliament, and for so long as such provision shall be made accordingly, to forbear, in respect of such Province or Colony, to levy any duty [*Annual Register*, "duties"], tax, or assessment, or to impose any farther [*Annual Register*, "further"] duty, tax, or assessment, except only such duties as it may be expedient to continue to levy or to impose for the regulation of commerce—the net produce of the duties last mentioned to be carried to the account of such Province or Colony [*Annual Register*, "Province, Colony, or Plantation"] respectively." In commenting upon his resolution, Lord North said (*P. H.*, 322): "It will have been wise, it will have been just, it will have been humane, that we have held out the terms of peace ; if they reject it, their blood must be upon their own hearts. But I have better hopes : there are people, and I hope whole Colonies, that wish for peace ; and by these means I hope they will find their way to it." In the course of an extended debate, Col. Barré said (*P. H.*, 333 and 334): "The Noble Lord's new motion . . . is founded on that wretched, low, shameful, abominable maxim which has predominated in every measure of our late Minister, *divide et impera*. This is to divide the Americans ; this is to break those associations, to dissolve that generous union in which the Americans, as one man, stand in defence of their rights and liberties. . . . The Noble Lord does not expect it will be accepted. It is meant only to propose something specious, which he knows the Americans will refuse, and therefore offers to call down tenfold more vengeance on their devoted heads, rendered thus ten times more odious by refusing such fair, such reasonable, such just, such wise, and such humane offers ; but neither will this snare succeed." Lord North replied (*P. H.*, 334): "Is it foolish, is it mean, when a people heated and misled by evil counsels are running into unlawful combinations, to hold out those terms which will sift the reasonable from the unreasonable? . . . If propositions that the conscientious and the prudent will accept, will at the same time recover them from under the influence and fascination of the wicked, I avow the using that principle which will thus divide the good from the bad, and give support to the friends of peace and good government."

The resolution was reported from the Committee to the House on February 27, debated again, and then agreed to by the House. An admirable summary of the debates is given in the *Annual Register* for 1775, pp. *95-*100 ; the debates themselves in the *Parl. Hist.*, xviii., 819-358. See Lecky's *England*

7

in the Eighteenth Century, iii., 459–461, who says : "The colonists repudiated it as interfering with their absolute right of
disposing as they pleased of their own property, and most later
historians have treated it as wholly delusive. With this view
I am unable to concur. The proposition appears to me to
have been a real and considerable step towards conciliation."

Dodsley quotes the terms of the resolution incorrectly, sub-
stituting "or" for "and" in the phrase of the first sentence,
"and Assembly;" the latter is also the expression in the
Annual Register, p. *95.

According to Lecky, the resolution "was recommended to
the Americans by Lord Dartmouth in language of much force
and of evident sincerity. . . . [Parliament] determines
nothing about the specific sum to be raised. The King trusts
that adequate provision will be made by the colonies, and that
it will be 'proposed in such a way as to increase or diminish according as the public burthens of this kingdom are from time
to time augmented or reduced, in so far as those burthens
consist of taxes and duties which are not a security for the
National Debt. By such a mode of contribution,' he adds,
'the colonies will have full security that they can never be
required to tax themselves without Parliament taxing the
subjects of this kingdom in a far greater proportion.'" "The
conciliatory offer of Lord North was," says Lecky (p. 465)
"emphatically rejected" by the new Continental Congress
which met at Philadelphia on May 10.

8 15. *Noble Lord.* Frederick North (1732–1792), second
Earl of Guilford. He was Prime Minister from 1770–1781. It
is said that during his term of office the national debt was
more than doubled (*Dict. Nat. Biog.*, xli., 161). Portraits of
Lord North may be found in Walford's *Old and New London*, iii., 528, and in Lodge's *Portraits*. He was, of course,
forty-three years of age when Burke's speech was delivered.
His personality, principles, and conduct were so important in
their bearing upon the American Revolution that no apology
will be needed for introducing several characterizations drawn
by competent hands :—

Wraxall, *Hist. and Posth. Memoirs*, ed. Wheatley, i., 361–
364 : "In his person he was of the middle size, heavy, large,

and much inclined to corpulency. There appeared in the cast and formation of his countenance, nay, even in his manner, so strong a resemblance to the royal family of England, that it was difficult not to perceive it. Like them, he had a fair complexion, regular features, light hair, with bushy eyebrows, and grey eyes rather prominent in his head. His face might be indeed esteemed a caricature of the King. . . . His natural affability rendered him, besides, so accessible, and the communicativeness of his temper inclined him so much to conversation, that every member of the House found a facility in becoming known to him. Never, indeed, was a First Minister less intrenched within the forms of his official situation. He seemed, on the contrary, always happy to throw aside his public character and to relapse into an individual. . . . Lord North was powerful, able, and fluent in debate, sometimes repelling the charges made against him with solid argument, but still more frequently eluding or blunting the weapons of his antagonists by the force of wit and humor."

Lecky, *England in the Eighteenth Century*, iii., 137–138 : "The son of the Earl of Guilford, Lord North had entered Parliament in 1754, had accepted a lordship of the Treasury under Pitt in 1759, had been removed from office by Rockingham in 1765, and had again come into office under Pitt as Joint Paymaster of the Forces. He belonged, however, to none of the Whig parties, and he possessed in the highest degree that natural leaning towards authority which was most pleasing to the King. Since the beginning of the reign there had been no arbitrary or unpopular measure which he had not defended. . . . He defended the Stamp Act. He bitterly resisted its repeal. . . . Most of the measures which he advocated in the long course of his ministry were proved by the event to be disastrous and foolish, but he possessed an admirable good sense in the management of details, and he had many of the qualities that lead to eminence both in the closet and in Parliament. His ungainly form, his harsh tones, his slow and laboured utterance, his undisguised indolence, furnished a ready theme for ridicule, but his private character was wholly unblemished. No statesman has ever encountered the storms of political life with a temper which it was more difficult to ruffle, or more impossible to embitter. His almost unfailing tact, his singularly quick and happy wit, and his great knowledge of business, and especially of finance, made him most formidable as a debater, while his sweet and amiable disposition gave him some personal popularity even in the most disastrous moments of his career. Partly through political principle, and partly through weakness of character he continually subordinated his own judgment to that of the King. . . . The growing power of North drew the King more closely to his min-

isters, and he cordially adopted their views on the two great
questions on which English politics were now chiefly concen-
trated.   These questions were the Middlesex election and the
renewed taxation of America. ''

Dict. Nat. Biog., xli., 161, 163 : '' North's government was
what he afterwards called a ' government by departments.'
He himself was rather the agent than the responsible adviser
of the king, who practically directed the policy of the ministry, even on the minutest points.   .   .   .   North was an easy-
going, obstinate man, with a quick wit and a sweet temper.
He was neither a great statesman nor a great orator, though
his tact was unfailing and his powers as a debater were unquestioned. ''

Walpole, *Memoirs of the Reign of George III.*, iv., 78 :
''Two large prominent eyes that rolled about to no purpose
(for he was utterly short-sighted), a wide mouth, thick lips,
and inflated visage, gave him the air of a blind trumpeter. ''

Gibbon dedicated his *Decline and Fall* to Lord North in
these words : '' Were I ambitious of any other patron than the
public, I would inscribe this work to a statesman who, in a
long, a stormy, and at length an unfortunate administration,
had many political opponents, almost without a personal en ·
emy ; who has retained in his fall from power many faithful and
disinterested friends ; and who, under the pressure of severe
infirmity, enjoys the lively vigour of his mind, and the felicity
of his incomparable temper. ''

Wells, *Life and Public Services of Samuel Adams*, i., 226–
227 : '' ' America must fear you before she can love you,' said
Lord North to Alderman Beckford, who recommended a repeal of the late act, and a policy of moderation and kindness.
' Punishment,' he continued, ' will not be extended beyond
the really guilty ; and if rewards shall be found necessary,
rewards shall be given.   But what we do we will do firmly ;
we shall go through our plan, now that we have brought it so
near success.   I am against repealing the last act of Parliament, securing to us a revenue out of America.   I will never
think of repealing it until I see America prostrate at my feet. '
In uttering this threat the Minister defined his policy throughout his premiership.   Courageous, good-humored, and apa-
thetic in temperament, he was devoted to the royal prerogative, and was strict in the performance of his duties.   Opposed
to reforms, and bitterly against concessions to the Americans.
having voted for the Stamp Act and against its repeal, he was
exactly the man to blindly pursue the measures of the head-
strong King, and thus, under Providence, to bring about the
liberty of the Colonies.   It was in November, 1768, that he
was determined to see ' America at his feet.'   In November,
1781, he was fated, as Prime Minister, to hear of the surren-

der of Cornwallis, which virtually ended the war of independence. Then his self-possession deserted him, and he looked back with horror and chagrin upon the measures of his administration, and, reluctantly yielding to a vote of censure from the House of Commons for his American policy before and during the war, the vanquished peer retired from the Cabinet, followed by the execrations of his countrymen.''

Burke, *Letter to a Noble Lord* (1795): ''I do not mean to speak disrespectfully of Lord North. He was a man of admirable parts; of general knowledge; of a versatile understanding; fitted for every sort of business; of infinite wit and pleasantry; of a delightful temper; and with a mind most perfectly disinterested. But it would be only to degrade myself by a weak adulation, and not to honour the memory of a great man, to deny that he wanted something of the vigilance and spirit of command that the time required.''

8 16. *Blue Ribbon.* The broad, dark-blue ribbon worn across the breast, on other occasions than solemn feasts, by Knights of the Garter. The ribbon was designed as a means of suspending the George, or figure of St. George piercing the dragon, which is an emblem of the Order. The Order of the Garter, or of St. George, was instituted by Edward III., probably on January 18, 1344. Lord North was invested a Knight of the Garter on June 18, 1772, "an honour conferred on members of the House of Commons in only three other instances, namely, Sir Robert Walpole, Lord Castlereagh, and Lord Palmerston '' (*Dict. Nat. Biog.*). Of these three, of course Walpole had been North's only predecessor, and the designation may therefore have been employed as a mark of peculiar respect or a means of flattery.

8 18. *Mace.* The symbol of the authority of the House of Commons. See pictures of it in the *Standard Dictionary, s. v.*, and in Walford (iii., 511). For an account of its extraordinary powers see Walford, iii., 513–514.

8 20. *Auction of finance.* Burke is fond of this mode of picturing the idea, and had already employed it at length in the debate on February 20 (*Parl. Hist.*, xviii., 336–337); *cf.* **69** 19, **70** 35.

8 28. *Conciliation.* Observe the progress made since **3** 20.

8 29. *Resolution. Cf.* note on **8** 14.

8 81. *Address.* This address, after protracted debate, had been finally carried on February 7. It is as follows (*Parl. Hist.*, xviii., 297–298) : —

"Most Gracious Sovereign :

"We, your Majesty's most dutiful and loyal subjects, the Lords Spiritual and Temporal, and Commons, in Parliament assembled, return your Majesty our most humble thanks for having been graciously pleased to communicate to us the several papers relating to the present state of the British Colonies in America, which, by your Majesty's command, have been laid before us. We have taken them into our most serious consideration ; and we find that a part of your Majesty's subjects in the Province of the Massachusetts Bay have proceeded so far to resist the authority of the supreme Legislature that a rebellion at this time actually exists within the said Province : and we see with the utmost concern that they have been countenanced and encouraged by unlawful combinations and engagements entered into by your Majesty's subjects in several of the other Colonies, to the injury and oppression of many of their innocent fellow-subjects resident within the kingdom of Great Britain and the rest of your Majesty's dominions. This conduct on their part appears to us the more inexcusable, when we consider with how much temper your Majesty and the two Houses of Parliament have acted in support of the laws and Constitution of Great Britain. We can never so far desert the trust reposed in us as to relinquish any part of the sovereign authority over all your Majesty's dominions which by law is vested in your Majesty and the two Houses of Parliament ; and the conduct of many persons in several of the Colonies during the late disturbances is alone sufficient to convince us how necessary this power is for the protection of the lives and fortunes of all your Majesty's subjects. We ever have been, and always shall be, ready to pay attention and regard to any real grievances of any of your Majesty's subjects, which shall, in a dutiful and constitutional manner, be laid before us ; and whenever any of the Colonies shall make a proper application to us, we shall be ready to afford them every just and reasonable indulgence. At the same time we consider it as our indispensable duty humbly to beseech your Majesty that you will take the most effectual measures to enforce due obedience to the laws and authority of the supreme Legislature ; and we beg leave in the most solemn manner to assure your Majesty that it is our fixed resolution, at the hazard of our lives and properties, to stand by your Majesty against all rebellious attempts in the maintenance of the just rights of your Majesty and the two Houses of Parliament."

See the *Annual Register,* pp. 63-77, for an account of the debates on the Address.

8 32. *Heavy bill.* The "penal bill" of **3** 9. Not *bills,* as some editions have.

9 8. *Capital alteration.* See Lord North's resolution in note on **8** 13.

9 10. *Alien from.* Burke elsewhere uses *alien to.* The former, which is the earlier use in English, seems to be derived from the Lat. *alienus ab ;* the latter from the construction of *alienus* with the dative. See *New Eng. Dict., s. v.*

9 15. *Indifferently.* Poorly.

9 16. *Endeavour to show. Cf.* **69** 6 ff.

9 25. *Peace with honour.* Possibly adapted from Cicero's *cum dignitate otium* ("*id quod est præstantissimum maximeque optabile omnibus sanis et bonis et beatis, cum dignitate otium,*" *Pro Sestio,* 45, 98). Syle remarks : "This phrase has become famous in recent years, from its employment by Disraeli in the speech with which he celebrated his triumphant return from the Congress of Berlin (1878). 'I bring you peace,' said he to the mob of Jingoes who howled under the windows of the Foreign Office ; 'I bring you Peace ; and Peace with Honour.'"

9 30. *That time and those chances. Cf. Jul. Cæs.,* iv., 3, 216–219.

9 34. *Whether you ought. Cf.* **39** 3 ff.

9 35. *What your concession ought to be. Cf.* **39** 7 ff., **53** 8 ff., pp. 80–82.

10 7. *True nature and the peculiar circumstances.* Transition to next main division of the speech, the Statement of Facts.

10 20. On the Statement of Facts in general, see Quintilian, Bk. iv., chap. 2.

10 24. *Two millions.* Bancroft computes the population in 1770 as 1,850,000 whites, and in 1780 at 2,383,000 ; the mean between the two will bear out Burke's statement. Lecky says (iii., 290): "Their number probably slightly exceeded two millions at the time of the Declaration of Independence.'

10 26. *Five hundred thousand others.* Meaning blacks, of whom Bancroft computes 462,000 in 1770, and 562,000 in 1780.

11 1. *Shoots.* Note this poetic word.

11 7 ff. Goodrich says: "This is in Burke's best style. The comparison beautifully illustrates the idea, and justifies his assertion that while ' the dispute continues the exaggeration ends.' "

11 11. *Front.* Beginning. A poetic use ; so Shakespeare has "Summer's front," "April's front."

11 14. *Occasional.* Devised to suit a special *occasion ;* the reverse of *comprehensive.* Why so many adjectives here ?

11 16. *Minima.* Referring to the law maxim, *De minimis non curat lex.*

11 21. *Care and caution.* Dr. Johnson draws an opposite conclusion from such facts as Burke has been adducing, in his famous *Taxation no Tyranny :*—

"But while we are melting in silent sorrow, and in the transports of delicious pity dropping both the sword and balance from our hands, another friend of the Americans thinks it better to awaken another passion, and tries to alarm our interest, or excite our veneration, by accounts of their greatness and their opulence, of the fertility of their land, and the splendour of their towns. We then begin to consider the question with more evenness of mind ; are ready to conclude that those restrictions are not very oppressive which have been found consistent with this speedy growth of prosperity ; and begin to think it reasonable that they, who thus flourish under the protection of our government, should contribute something toward its expense.

"But we are soon told that the Americans, however wealthy, cannot be taxed ; that they are the descendants of men who left all for liberty, and that they have constantly preserved the principles and stubbornness of their progenitors ; that they are too obstinate for persuasion, and too powerful for constraint ; that they will laugh at argument, and defeat violence ; that the continent of North America contains three millions, not of men merely, but of Whigs—of Whigs fierce for liberty, and disdainful of dominion ; that they multiply with the fecundity of their own rattlesnakes, so that every quarter of a century doubles their numbers.

"Men accustomed to think themselves masters do not love to be threatened. This talk is, I hope, commonly thrown away.

or raises passions different from those which it was intended to excite. Instead of terrifying the English hearer to tame acquiescence, it disposes him to hasten the experiment of bending obstinacy before it is become yet more obdurate, and convinces him that it is necessary to attack a nation thus prolific while we may yet hope to prevail. When he is told through what extent of territory we must travel to subdue them, he recollects how far, a few years ago, we travelled in their defence. When it is urged that they will shoot up like the hydra, he naturally considers how the hydra was destroyed.''

11 33. *A distinguished person.* Richard Glover (1712–1785), best known as a poet. Specimens of his *Leonidas* (1737, 1770) and *Athenaid* (pub. 1787), and the whole of his ballad, *Admiral Hosier's Ghost,* may be read in Chambers' *Cyclopædia of English Literature.* The following line from *Leonidas* will be recognized by some readers :—

A reverential murmur breathes applause.

11 34. *At your bar.* Within which none were allowed but officers and members of the House. Mr. Glover had, on March 16, addressed the House in behalf of a petition presented on February 2 by the West India Planters, ''praying the House to take into their most serious consideration that great political system of the Colonies heretofore so very beneficial to the Mother Country and her dependencies, and adopt such measures as to them shall seem meet to prevent the evils with which the petitioners are threatened, and to preserve the intercourse between the West India islands and the Northern Colonies '' (*Parl. Hist.*, xviii., 221)—they having been threatened with loss of trade by a non-importation agreement entered into by Congress on Sept. 5, 1774. For this speech he received a piece of plate worth 300*l.* from the West India merchants (*Dict. Nat. Biog.*).

Thirty-five years. Here Burke seems to have been in error. On January 20, 1742, the Lord Mayor of London presented a petition signed by three hundred merchants, complaining of the inadequate protection of British commerce, and Glover afterwards intended to sum up their evidence before the House (*Dict. Nat. Biog.*). Payne is accordingly mistaken in his surmise on this point.

12 5. *Even then.*   He had already published *Leonidas* (1737), and *London, or the Progress of Commerce* (1739).

12 19. *Two accounts.*   Glover had gone into similar statistics (see his speech in *Parl. Hist.*, xviii., 461–478, especially 463–470).

12 20. *State.* Statement.

12 28. *Davenant.*   Charles Davenant (1656–1714), political economist, eldest son of Sir William D'Avenant, the poet. In 1705 he was appointed Inspector-General of Exports and Imports.

12 33. *The African.*   The slave-trade.

13 23. Dodsley sums up incorrectly, as 6,024,171 *l.*

14 6. Most, if not all, of the editions, calmly transcribe this as 6,024,000, though the error in **13** 23 is already corrected in the *Parl. Hist.*

14 23. *Sixteen millions.*   So Glover (*Parl. Hist.*, xviii., 466, 467), who reaches practically identical results concerning the proportion of Colony trade.

14 29. Note the mode of transition to the new paragraph. Burke had a perilous rhetorical flight to attempt, and opinions are even yet divided as to the success of his undertaking. Goodrich, for example, objects : "It may be doubted whether this amplification, and the more graphic one which follows in respect to the fisheries of New England, are not out of place in an argument of this kind before the House of Commons.   They would have been perfectly appropriate in an address like that of Daniel Webster on the landing of the Pilgrims at Plymouth, since the audience had met for the very purpose of being delighted with rich trains of thought, beautifully expressed.   We who read the speech at the present day dwell on such passages with unmingled gratification, because we peruse them much in the same spirit.   But they would certainly be unsafe models for a business speaker."

However, if we grant the propriety of inserting this "purple patch," we may instructively consider the means of introducing it.   Burke first represents the historic, statistical survey just completed as being metaphorically made from an eminence which permitted an extensive view of the past.   This eminence

is gained by the speaker in the most skilful way, through the
agency of a sentence, "It is good for us to be here," which is
perfectly appropriate in its literal sense, but which, through
its connotation (*cf. Matt.* xvii. 4; *Mk.* ix. 5; *Lk.* ix. 33), suggests the *Mount* of Transfiguration. In two sentences, therefore, immense progress has been made away from statistics
and towards poetry, this progress being due not only to the
suggestion of altitude, but to the heightening of sentiment
arising from the use of Scriptural language. With equal skill
the Scriptural tone is maintained in words ("Clouds, indeed,
and darkness ") which suggest another mount—the Mount of
the Giving of the Law (*cf. Deut.* iv. 11), with all its majestic
associations, and the even more sublime conception of the
Almighty's dwelling-place (*Ps.* xcvii. 2). Once arrived at
this point, the poet—for such Burke now is—can do what
he pleases.

What he pleases to do is to depict an imaginary vision
which shall traverse the historic field just covered, and to
make the agent of the revelation a genius, or guardian spirit,
whom, for the sake of preserving the Scriptural tone, he first
calls an angel (*cf. Acts* xii. 15, but especially *Matt.* xviii. 10).
Here Burke may well have been indebted to his favorite Milton (*cf.* Introduction, pp. lv, lvi), who has Michael lead Adam
to the summit of

> a hill
> Of Paradise the highest, from whose top
> The hemisphere of Earth in clearest ken
> Stretched out to the amplest reach of prospect lay,

and from thence reviews the future fortunes of mankind (*P.
L.*, xi., 370-901, xii., 1-606). So in the *Æneid* (vi., 752 ff.),
Anchises and Æneas mount an eminence,

> unde omnis longo ordine posset
> Adversos legere, et venientum discere vultus,

and thence Anchises shows Æneas the long train of Alban
kings, his future descendants, and in fact the whole course of
Roman history.

15 6. *Lord Bathurst.* Allen Bathurst, Earl Bathurst
(1684–1775), died on September 16, 1775, less than six months

after this speech was delivered, in his ninety-first year. A few particulars concerning him may be extracted from the *Annual Register* for 1775, probably from the pen of Burke himself (pp. 22–25) :—

"He added to his public virtues all the good breeding, politeness, and elegance of social intercourse. Dr. Freind, Congreve, Vanbrugh, Swift, Prior, Howe, Addison, Pope, Arbuthnot, Gay, and most men of genius in his own time, cultivated his friendship, and were proud of his correspondence. Pope, in his Epistle to him on the Use of Riches, thus addresses him :

> The sense to value riches, with the art
> To enjoy them, etc. . . .

Sterne, in his Letters to Eliza, thus speaks of him : [Here follows a charming account of Lord Bathurst's introducing himself to Sterne]. 'This nobleman, I say, is a prodigy, for at eighty-five he has all the wit and promptness of a man of thirty ; a disposition to be pleased, and a power to please others, beyond whatever I knew.' . . . His Lordship, in the latter part of his life, preserved his natural cheerfulness and vivacity, always accessible, hospitable, and beneficent. Lately he delighted in rural amusements, and enjoyed with a philosophical satisfaction the shade of the lofty trees he had planted himself. . . . His Lordship having, about two years ago, invited several of his friends to spend a few cheerful days with him at his seat at Cirencester, and being very loth to part with them ; on his son the present Chancellor's objecting to their sitting up any longer, and adding that health and long life were best secured by regularity, he suffered him to retire ; but, as soon as he was gone, the cheerful father said, 'Come, my good friends, since the old gentleman [who was thirty years younger than his father] is gone to bed, I think we may venture to crack another bottle.'"

15 7. *Of an age.* Since he entered Parliament in 1705, this assertion might safely be hazarded. "In thus alluding to Lord Bathurst, Mr. Burke undoubtedly thought of him only as advanced in years, without reflecting on his exact age."—GOODRICH.

15 9. This should read,

> Facta parentum
> Jam legere, et quæ sit poteris cognoscere virtus,

where some editions have *parentis.* Why is *facta* better than Burke's *acta* ? On what word is *legere* here made to depend?

On what does *cognoscere* depend ? In the original both depend upon the same word.

The quotation (Virgil, *Ecl.*, iv., 26–27) is most felicitous, since it may almost be said to continue the Scriptural strain, the theme of the Eclogue from which it is taken being "the birth of a wondrous child, who is to be king of the world in this age of peace. . . . The Eclogue is best known on account of the resemblance of its language in some passages to descriptions in the Hebrew prophets, especially Isaiah. . . . But the vague looking forward to a golden age in the future has been hardly less universal than the dream of it in the past; and though the language used in describing the birth and career of the child who is to be the universal king is certainly sometimes striking, yet there seems no sufficient reason to connect the legends employed by Virgil with the prophecies of the Old Testament " (Lonsdale and Lee, *The Works of Virgil,* pp. 9, 10). The same writers have (p. 4): "Some of the Fathers regarded the fourth Eclogue as a prophecy of the Messiah taken from the ancient writings of the Cumean Sibyl; and it was said that St. Paul, coming to Naples, wept over the ashes of the heathen poet, grieving that he came too late to convert him to the faith of Christ." As a commentary on the foregoing, read Pope's *Messiah.*

15 11. *Auspicious.* Fortunate. What is the derivation of its Latin etymon? *Cf.* with

15 15. *In the fourth generation, the third Prince.* "The third Prince" is of course George III.; "the fourth generation," because the son of George II., and father of George III., died before he succeeded to the throne.

15 16. *Twelve years.* George III. came to the throne in 1760.

15 18. *Moderate and healing counsels.* Observe how, even here, Burke impresses his main theme, conciliation.

Was to be made. Because the vision is assigned to 1704, whereas Scotland and England were not finally united to form Great Britain until 1707.

15 19. *Lord Chancellor.* So created on January 23, 1771, with the title of Baron Apsley.

15 20. *Turn back the current.* Explain the figure.

15 21. *A higher rank.* Within less than a year after the son, Henry, had been made Lord Chancellor, the father, who had been hitherto only Baron Bathurst, was made an Earl (August 12, 1772).

15 26. *Then.* Adverb as adjective, like τότε, νῦν, in Greek. This usage goes back to Old English times.

15 27. Observe that the "angel" of l. 11 has now become a "Genius," and that, conformably to the material character of the "glories" displayed, the Biblical strain more and more gives place to a heathen one, worthy of Cicero and the Roman Republic.

15 32. *Stories of savage men.* "See Part II. of Burke's *Account of America.*"—PAYNE.

15 34. *Taste of death.* A New Testament Hebraism. See *Matt.* xvi. 28: "Verily I say unto you, There be some standing here, which shall not *taste of death*, till they see the Son of man coming in his kingdom."

16 9. *Require.* Should not this be *have required ?*

16 10. *Enthusiasm.* Enthusiasm was generally regarded with disfavor in Burke's century; see the history of the word in the *New Eng. Dict.* What was there in the character of the age unfavorable to enthusiasm? Did Burke conform or not to this spirit of the age? Did he manifest the spirit of any earlier or any later period, rather than that of his own time?

16 11. *Fortunate man.* Virgil and Cicero break out into similar exclamations. Thus Virgil, in an often-quoted passage (*Ecl.*, i., 47): "*Fortunate senex ;*" Cicero (*Pro Quinctio*, xxv., 80), "*O hominem fortunatum, qui ejus modi nuntios seu potius Pegasos habeat ;*" and especially his much ridiculed verse, "*O fortunatam natam me consule Romam.*"

16 12. A warning of the danger of following the policy then pursued by the Government. See if you can find a similar figure in Campbell's *Lochiel's Warning.*

16 13. *Setting.* Quintilian says (xii., 10, 16, 17): "The distinction between Attic and Asiatic orators is of great antiq-

uity, the Attics being regarded as compressed and energetic
in their style, the Asiatics as inflated and deficient in force;
in the Attics it was thought that nothing was redundant, in
the Asiatics that judgment and restraint were in a great
measure wanting. . . . The people of Attica, being pol-
ished and of refined taste, could endure nothing useless or redundant, while the Asiatics, a people in other respects vain
and ostentatious, were puffed up with fondness for a showy
kind of eloquence.'' Already he had said of Cicero (xii., 10.
12): ''The men of his own time presumed to censuré him as
timid, Asiatic, redundant, too fond of repetition, indulging
in tasteless jests,'' etc.

In what parts of this oration does Burke approach the Attic style most nearly? in what the Asiatic?

16 14. Was it better that Burke should now resume statistics, or that he should have finished with them before making
his rhetorical excursus?

16 27. *Are apt to heighten.* Prove and illustrate.

16 29. *Fiction lags after truth.* Of what proverb does this
remind you?

16 34. *Deceive.* A Latinism. *Cf.* Horace, *Sat.*, ii., 2, 11–
13 :—

> Seu pila velox,
> Molliter austerum studio *fallente* laborem,
> Seu te discus agit. . . .

(And if the swift-flying ball or the quoit is your pleasure,
your interest in which gently *beguiles* the severity of the
toil.) *Cheat* is sometimes thus used; so Scott, *Rokeby*, i., 4 :—

> The tuneless rime
> With which the warder *cheats* the time.

16 35. *Burthen.* O. E. byrthen. Burke prefers this ety-
mologically correct form; prove this statement.

17 1. *Springs.* Define.

17 17. *Roman charity.* Readers of poetry will be at once
reminded of *Childe Harold*, IV., cxlviii.–cli. The story, as
related by Festus (*De Verb. Signif.*, xx.) and others, tells of a
father who, having been condemned to death by starva-

tion, is visited in his cell by his daughter, who nour-
ishes him with milk from her own breast. According to
other authors, it was a mother, instead of a father (*cf.* Pliny,
Nat. Hist., vii., 36 ; Valerius Maximus, v., 47). Under the
name of the "Caritas Romana," this incident has furnished
the subject of several pictures. Byron says : —

> And sacred Nature triumphs more in this
> Reverse of her decree than in the abyss
> Where sparkle distant worlds.

Was there not an illustration of this when America sent
shiploads of provisions to starving Ireland ?

17 18. *Exuberance.* Propriety of this word ? Does it
illustrate **16** 26, 27 ?

17 21. *At your bar.* By various persons, as detailed in
Parl. Hist., xviii., 423–430. Seth Jenkins, a Quaker, testified "that he was a mariner, and is well acquainted with the
island of Nantucket ; that the number of inhabitants upon
the said island is between 5 and 6,000, who are almost all employed in the fisheries ; that the number of vessels belonging
to the said island is 140 sail, eight of which are employed in
the coasting trade, and the rest in the fisheries ; .   .   .
that the limits of the whale fishery extend to *Falkland's Isl-
and and the coast of Africa ;* that their fishing vessels are
generally 12 months on their voyage, sometimes 14 months ;
. . . that the vessels from England have little or no success in it, owing to their not understanding it ; . . . that
the money arising from this [the New England] fishery
amounts to about 330,000*l.*" Another witness testified that
the net produce of the *British* fishery on the Newfoundland
coast amounted to about 500,000*l.* According to Payne, "At
this time Massachusetts alone employed 183 vessels, carrying
13,820 tons, in the North, and 120 vessels, carrying 14,026
tons, in the South Atlantic fishery. . . . See an interesting article in the *Quarterly Review,* vol. lxiii., p. 318."

17 30. *Mountains of ice.* What is the meaning of *iceberg ?*
Why, for rhetorical reasons, is *mountains of ice* to be preferred ? Do icebergs *tumble ?*

18 2. *Serpent.* "The Hydrus, or Water Serpent, is a

small constellation lying very far to the South, within the Antarctic Circle.''—GOODRICH.

18 3. *Falkland Island.* How far to the south? Locate it (or rather them) on the map. What does the Encyclopædia tell you about them? The Falkland Islands had for a dozen years been the object of peculiar interest to Englishmen, and indeed to the whole civilized world (see Lecky, iii., 167). Trace their history from 1763 on. Note whence Burke derived his information ; *cf.* under **17** 21.

Too remote. In 1771 Dr. Johnson was engaged by the Ministry to answer Junius's forty-second letter, in which he taunts the Government for its pusillanimity in dealing with Spain about the Falkland Islands. Dr. Johnson deprecates war for any such object, and says :—

''What have we acquired ? What but a bleak and gloomy solitude, an island thrown aside from human use, stormy in winter and barren in summer, an island which not the Southern savages have dignified with habitation ?'' Then, in one of the noblest passages ever penned against the iniquity and horror of war, a passage that England and America might well have pondered then, and more than once subsequently, he continues : ''As war is the last of remedies, *cuncta prius tentanda,* all lawful expedients must be used to avoid it. As war is the extremity of evil, it is surely the duty of those whose station entrusts them with the care of nations, to avert it from their charge. There are diseases of animal nature which nothing but amputation can remove ; so there may, by the depravation of human passions, be sometimes a gangrene in collective life for which fire and the sword are the necessary remedies ; but in what can skill or caution be better shown than [in] preventing such dreadful operations, while there is yet room for gentler methods?

''It is wonderful with what coolness and indifference the greater part of mankind see war commenced. Those that hear of it at a distance, or read of it in books, but have never presented its evils to their minds, consider it as little more than a splendid game, a proclamation, an army, a battle, and a triumph. Some indeed must perish in the most successful field, but they die upon the bed of honour, *resign their lives amidst the joys of conquest, and, filled with England's glory, smile in death.*

''The life of a modern soldier is ill represented by heroic fiction. War has means of destruction more formidable than the cannon and the sword. Of the thousands and ten thousands that perished in our late contests with France and Spain, a very small part ever felt the stroke of an enemy ; the rest languished in tents and ships, amidst damps and putrefaction ; pale, torpid, spiritless, and helpless ; gasping and groaning, unpitied among men made obdurate by long continuance of hopeless misery ; and were at last whelmed in pits, or heaved into the ocean, without notice and without remembrance. By incommodious encampments and unwholesome stations, where courage is useless and enterprise impracticable, fleets are silently dispeopled, and armies sluggishly melted away.

"Thus is a people gradually exhausted, for the most part with little effect.   The wars of civilized nations make very slow changes in the system of empire.   The public perceives scarcely any alteration but an increase of debt ; and the few individuals who are benefited are not supposed to have the clearest right to their advantages.   If he that shared the danger enjoyed the profit, and, after bleeding in the battle, grew rich by the victory, he might show his gains without envy.   But, at the conclusion of a ten years' war, how are we recompensed for the death of multitudes and the expense of millions but by contemplating the sudden glories of paymasters and agents, contractors and commissioners, whose equipages shine like meteors, and whose palaces rise like exhalations?   These are the men who, without virtue, labour, or hazard, are growing rich as their country is impoverished ; they rejoice when obstinacy or ambition adds another year to slaughter and devastation, and laugh from their desks at bravery and science, while they are adding figure to figure, and cipher to cipher, hoping for a new contract from a new armament, and computing the profits of a siege or tempest.   .   .   .

"Of victory indeed every nation is confident before the sword is drawn ; and this mutual confidence produces that wantonness of bloodshed that has so often desolated the world.   But it is evident that, of contradictory opinions, one must be wrong, and the history of mankind does not want examples that may teach caution to the daring and moderation to the proud."

18 9. *Coast of Africa.*   See Burke's probable source in note on **17** 21.

18 10. *Run the longitude.*   Properly, run east or west, but, more generally, any direction inclining east or west.

18 11. *No sea*, etc.   Suggested by *Æn.*, i., 459–460 : —

Quæ regio in terris nostris non plena laboris ?

18 12. *Vexed.*   A Latinism ; so Ovid speaks of winds that *vex* (*i.e.*, agitate) the clouds (*Met.*, 11, 435). Here perhaps in the metaphorical sense, "disturbed." *Cf. King Lear*, IV., iv., 2 : "As mad as the *vexed* sea."

18 16. *Hardy.* Daring, venturesome.

18 20. Paragraph 31 is continuous with the preceding in Dodsley and all subsequent editions. It is evident, though, that "these things" refer to more than the contents of paragraph 30.

18 25. *Generous.* Not munificent, but high-spirited. What is the meaning of Lat. *generosus ?*

18 27. *To us.* In what way ?

18 31. Quintilian thinks (iv., 2, 116) that "the Statement of Facts requires, as much as any part of a speech, to be adorned with all the attractions and grace of which it is susceptible. . . . There should be no figures borrowed from poetry, . . . but such only as lessen tedium by variety, and relieve attention by change." Has Burke's Statement of Facts thus far exemplified these principles ?

19 1. Quintilian allows of a brief digression from the Statement of Facts (Bk. iv., chap. 3), "provided that the dissertation aptly follows and adheres to what precedes, and is not forced in like a wedge, separating what was naturally united ; for no part of a speech ought to be more closely attached to any other part than the Proof is to the Statement, unless, indeed, the digression be intended either as the end of the Statement *or as the beginning of the Proof.*" In this case, it is of course a part of the proof, and in that sense a beginning of it.

19 8. *Complexions.* Temperaments ; now a rare use.

19 11. *Wield the thunder.* Cf. **26** 20.

19 21. *Cf.* Milton, *Par. Lost*, i., 648.

19 25. *Armament.* What became, for instance, of the Spanish Armada ?

19 27. *Conciliation.* Again Burke strikes his keynote.

19 30. *Can never be begged.* See Burke's *First Letter on a Regicide Peace:* "Power, and eminence, and consideration, are things not to be begged. They must be commanded ; and they who supplicate for mercy from others can never hope for justice through themselves."

19 31. *Violence.* Note this use of an abstract term. Is it justifiable ? What is gained by it ? Find other instances.

20 3. *To consume its strength.* On March 6, in one of the debates on the "penal bill," Burke had said (*Parl. Hist.*, xviii., 389, 390) " that the scheme of Parliament was new, and unheard-of in any civilized nation, 'to preserve your authority by destroying your dominions.' It was rather the idea of hostility between independent states, where one not being able to conquer another, thinks to reduce its strength gradually by destroying its trade and cutting off its resources. That this mode was never used by princes towards their subjects in rebellion ; the maxim in such cases always was to cut off the rebels, but to spare the country, because its strength is the strength of the sovereign himself. Here the principle was reversed : the force used against the rebels was trifling (though very expensive), but the trade, which was the wealth of the country, was to be destroyed."

20 5. *Foreign enemy.* What nation was Burke thinking of ?

20 11. *Experience.* Burke is always appealing to this.

20 16. *Our fault* . . . *our penitence.* Effective antithesis. Give other examples from the speech.

"These four arguments show how admirably Mr. Burke could *condense* when he saw fit."—GOODRICH.

20 32. *Restive.* Refractory, unruly.

20 34. *Chicane.* Define.

21 4. *Powerful causes.* "We here see the causes of Mr. Burke's richness of thought. It consisted, to a great extent, in his habit of viewing things in their *causes*, or tracing them out to their *results.* Let the reader study these pages with reference to this fact. Let him observe how Mr. Burke brings out the leading characteristics of the colonists, not as isolated facts, but as dependent upon certain *forming influences* in the mind of the English people ; their early contests, civil and religious ; the necessary results of certain relations of society and forms of mental development. Such habits of thought, if well directed, furnish an endless variety of valuable remarks in filling out a subject. If not abstract in their statement, but rendered intelligible and striking by a proper reference to individual cases, they always interest at the same time that they instruct."—GOODRICH.

21 10. *Respects.* Sarcasm.

21 11. *Emigrated from you when,* etc. Illustrate this statement from American and English history.

21 16. *Abstract liberty.* *Cf.* Burke, *Letter to the Sheriffs of Bristol :* —

"There are people who have split and anatomized the doctrine of free government, as if it were an abstract question concerning metaphysical liberty and necessity, and not a matter of moral prudence and natural feeling. They have disputed whether liberty be a positive or a negative idea; whether it does not consist in being governed by laws, without considering what are the laws, or who are the makers; whether man has any rights by nature; and whether all the property he enjoys be not the alms of his government, and his life itself their favour and indulgence. . . . Civil freedom, gentlemen, is not, as many have endeavoured to persuade you, a thing that lies hid in the depth of abstruse science. It is a blessing and a benefit, not an abstract speculation; and all the just reasoning that can be upon it is of so coarse a texture as perfectly to suit the ordinary capacities of those who are to enjoy, and of those who are to defend it. Far from any resemblance to those propositions in geometry and metaphysics which admit no medium, but must be true or false in all their latitude, social and civil freedom, like all other things in common life, are variously mixed and modified, enjoyed in very different degrees, and shaped into an infinite diversity of forms, according to the temper and circumstances of every community. The *extreme* of liberty—which is its abstract perfection, but its real fault—obtains nowhere, nor ought to obtain anywhere. Because extremes, as we all know, in every point which relates either to our duties or satisfactions in life, are destructive both to virtue and enjoyment.''

21 18. *Every nation,* etc. *Cf.* Goldsmith's *Traveller* (1764), 98–96 : —

> Hence every state, to one loved blessing prone,
> Conforms and models life to that alone;
> Each to the favourite happiness attends,
> And spurns the plan that aims at other ends.

21 22. *From the earliest times.* What is an early example?

21 25. *Balance.* Swift has much to say on this topic in his *Discourse on the Contests and Dissensions between the Nobles and the Commons in Athens and Rome* (1701).

21 28. *Ablest pens*, etc. "Pym, Hampden, Selden, St. John, etc. See Raleigh's *Prerogative of Parliaments in England.*"—PAYNE.

22 1. *Blind.* Define.

22 3. *Further.* Does Burke make any distinction between *further* and *farther*? Should any distinction be drawn?

22 14. *Fixed.* Used intransitively.

22 19. *Sick.* Observe that Burke does not think it necessary to use "ill."

22 21. *It is not easy*, etc. Explain.

22 29. *Provincial legislative Assemblies. Cf.* Burke, *Letter to the Sheriffs of Bristol :—*

"On the other hand, the Colonies, advancing by equal steps, and governed by the same necessity, had formed within themselves, either by royal instruction or royal charter, Assemblies so exceedingly resembling a Parliament in all their forms, functions, and powers, that it was impossible they should not imbibe some opinion of a similar authority. At the first designation of these Assemblies, they were probably not intended for anything more (nor perhaps did they think themselves much higher) than the municipal corporations within this island, to which some at present love to compare them. But nothing in progression can rest on its original plan. We may as well think of rocking a grown man in the cradle of an infant. Therefore as the Colonies prospered and increased to a numerous and mighty people, spreading over a very great tract of the globe, it was natural that they should attribute to Assemblies, so respectable in their formal constitution, some part of the dignity of the great nations which they represented. No longer tied to by-laws, these Assemblies made acts of all sorts and in all cases whatsoever. They levied money, not for parochial purposes, but upon regular grants to the Crown, following all the rules and principles of a Parliament to which they approached every day more and more nearly."

So in the *Speech on American Taxation :—*

"She had, except the commercial restraint, every characteristic mark of a free people in all her internal concerns. She had the image of the British Constitution. She had the substance. She was taxed by her own representatives. She chose most of her own magistrates. She paid them all. She had in effect the sole disposal of her own internal government. This whole state of commercial servitude and civil liberty, taken together, is certainly not perfect freedom ; but comparing it with the ordinary circumstances of human nature, it was a happy and a liberal condition.''

And see Johnson's *Taxation no Tyranny :—*

"As men are placed at a greater distance from the Supreme Council of the kingdom, they must be entrusted with ampler liberty of regulating their conduct by their own wisdom. As they are more secluded from easy recourse to national judicature, they must be more extensively commissioned to pass judgment on each other. For this reason our more important and opulent Colonies see the appearance and feel the effect of a regular Legislature, which in some places has acted so long with unquestioned authority that it has forgotten whence that authority was originally derived.''

22 31. *Merely popular.* Wholly democratic.

22 34. *Aversion from.* Like Lat. *aversus ab.* In the Bible we have *averse from* (*Mic.* ii. 8). *Averse, aversion to* is now more common. See the *New Eng. Dict., s. v.* Averse, and *cf. Averseness* . . . *from,* **23** 10, 11.

23 11. *Dissenting churches.* Meaning?

23 14. *At least coeval.* When was the Roman Catholic religion introduced into England, for example?

23 28. *Dissidence of dissent,* etc. *Cf.* Matthew Arnold, *Culture and Anarchy,* chap. 1:—

" Nowhere has Puritanism found so adequate an expression as in the religious organization of the Independents. The modern Independents have a newspaper, *The Nonconformist,* written with great sincerity and ability. The motto, the standard, the profession of faith, which this organ of theirs carries aloft is : 'The Dissidence of Dissent and the Protestantism of the Protestant religion.' There is sweetness and light, and an ideal of complete harmonious human perfection ! One need not go to culture and poetry to find language to judge it. Religion, with its instinct for perfection, supplies language to judge it, language, too, which is in our mouths every day. 'Finally, be of one mind, united in feeling,' says St. Peter. There is an ideal which judges the Puritan ideal : 'The Dissidence of Dissent and the Protestantism of the Protestant religion ! '"

23 30. *Communion.* Participation.

24 1. *This spirit was high.*   *Cf.* John Morley, *Edmund Burke*, pp. 127–130 : —

"Independence was the grand root from which the old Colonies had sprung. It was their most ancient tradition. The Puritans, out of whose loins the chiefs of the rebellious Colonists had come, began by throwing off the yoke of authority, whether it was embodied in the traditions of an invisible and eternal Church, or in the less mystic form of a dignified hierarchy. It is true that they soon forgot their own principle, imposed illogical restrictions on their own doctrines, and applied themselves to the organization of an authority not less arbitrary and oppressive than that of Bonner or of Laud. Some episodes in the history of Puritanism in America are at least as revolting as any of the crimes which interested polemists are accustomed to lay at the door of Catholicism or Anglicanism in England. But the principle of a system continues to work apart from temporary distortions and perversions. The Puritans might forget for a time that they owed their very existence to the vindication of the right of free judgment. Still, the old tradition of throwing off the episcopal yoke survived through all this to colour their lives and opinions. Their disrespect for human authority in theology led by a natural association of ideas to a no less warm disapproval of arbitrary authority in the political sphere. This connexion was inevitable. . . .

"In England in the seventeenth century the social conditions were not ripe for the general movement to which the Puritan sentiment, thus expanded and transformed, seemed clearly to point. The preparation of public opinion was incomplete. . . . In the Colonies the case was widely different. The Puritan idea, alike in its own theological order and in the political order where it had struck a firm root, was checked by no encounter with an old social state too deeply laid to be speedily modified. The Colonies offered an open field for its free spread and unrestrained development. Feudalism had never been transplanted, for hereditary privilege and the multiform ideas which spring from the legal recognition of primogeniture were too exclusively the product of European development to bear removal into a strange and keener air. There was no Church in alliance with a territorial aristocracy, ready to purchase the patronage of the State by the degrading advocacy of absolutist principles, eager by the dissemination of despotic doctrine to earn deaneries and bishoprics. Thus the lapse of a century and a half gave time for the spirit of independence to grow ineradicably into the national character. The American Rebellion was the third and last illustration of the regenerative forces of Protestantism. The

Dutch Revolt and the English Civil War has been more religious than political. The third was political in form and in
instances, but its impulses and momentum came from the
distinct struggle of old days and the right of private judgment. For the third and last time the wave of Protestantism
swept forward and submerged a political system."

24 11. *Establishment.* What is an " Established
Church?"

24 23. *Broad and general as the air.* Adapted from
Macbeth, III., iv., 23.

24 33. *Gothic.* Germanic ; an incorrect use, common in
the eighteenth century.

24 34. *Were the Poles.* The first of the three parti-
tions of Poland took place in 1772, and thus Polish independence came to an end.

25 8. *The law.* No doubt Burke is right in his views on
this subject, but he passes over without a word the education
of the Colonists in other branches, and in general. See Lecky,
iii., 315, 316 : —

" Owing to the admirable parish libraries, there were New
England parishes 'where almost every householder has read
the works of Addison, Sherlock, Atterbury, Watts, Young,
and other similar writings, and will converse handsomely on
the subjects of which they treat ;' and Boston, New York,
Philadelphia, and Charleston, would in almost all the elements of civilization have ranked high among the provincial
towns of Europe. . . . By the close of 1765 at least forty-
three newspapers are said to have been established in America.
There were seven important colleges, and there were at least
four literary magazines. . . . In the Northern Colonies
. . . education was both very widely diffused and very
equal. The average was exceedingly high, but there were no
eminences."

As to the study of the law, *cf.* Noah Webster's *Essays*
(quoted in Lecky, iii., 302), under the year 1787: "Never was
such a rage for the study of law. From one end of the
continent to the other the students of this science are mul-
tiplying without number, an infallible proof that the business is lucrative." And Lecky, p. 305: "They [the lawyers

of New York, in 1765–1767] had formed an association for the purpose of directing political affairs. In an Assembly where the majority of the members were ignorant and simple-minded farmers, they had acquired a controlling power; they knew the secrets of every family. They were the chief writers in a singularly violent press. They organized and directed every opposition to the Governor, and they had attained an influence not less than that of the priesthood in a bigoted Catholic country."

25 16. *Plantations.* Define.

25 18. *Blackstone's Commentaries.* First edition, 1765–1769.

25 23. *By successful chicane.* See the account in Bancroft's *Hist. United States*, iv., 49: "Boston held a town-meeting. Gage reminded the selectmen of the Act of Parliament restricting town-meetings without the Governor's leave. 'It is only an adjourned one,' said the selectmen. 'By such means,' said Gage, 'you may keep your meeting alive these ten years.' He brought the subject before the new council. 'It is a point of law,' said they, 'and should be referred to the Crown lawyers.'"

Again (*Annual Register* for 1775, p. 11): "This proclamation [Gage's of June 29, 1774] had no other effect than to exercise the pens and the judgment of those who were versed in legal knowledge, by endeavouring to show that the association did not come within any of the treason laws, and that the charges made by the Governor were consequently erroneous, unjust, and highly injurious."

25 24. *Constitutions.* Laws, ordinances.

25 25. *Smartness of debate.* What would be a concrete expression for this abstract one?

25 29. *Honourable and Learned Friend.* The Attorney-General, Thurlow. At the conclusion of his speech, "Mr. Burke was answered by the Attorney-General, who displayed great dexterity and address in his observations on the plan" (*Parl. Hist.*, xviii., 538).

25 30. *Animadversion.* Define.

25 32. *Win over.* *Cf.* the attempts to bribe Samuel Adams, as related in Wells' *Samuel Adams*, ii., 192–196.

26 1. *Litigious.* As were the Normans who conquered England. See Michelet, *Histoire de France*, ii., 160 : —

" The warlike and litigious spirit, foreign to the Anglo-Saxons, which made of England, after the Conquest, a nation of soldiers and of scribes, is the very spirit of Normandy. . . . The father, on his return from the fields [in Normandy], takes delight in explaining to his children, who listen intently, a few articles of the Civil Code. . . . Lorraine and Dauphiné cannot rival Normandy in respect to litigiousness. The Breton spirit, harder and more negative, is less greedy and absorptive. . . . ' The Normans are so addicted to the study of eloquence,' says an author of the eleventh century, ' that the very babies talk like orators.' "

26 6. *Abeunt studia in mores.* Ovid, *Her.,* xv., 83 : "One's habitual pursuits pass over into character."

This study renders men, etc. Cf. Burke's remarks on Grenville (*American Taxation*) : " He was bred to the law, which is, in my opinion, one of the first and noblest of human sciences, a science which does more to quicken and invigorate the understanding than all the other kinds of learning put together ; but it is not apt, except in persons very happily born, to open and to liberalize the mind exactly in the same proportion." On another occasion and for another purpose (*Reflections on the Revolution in France*) Burke is less complimentary to lawyers, at least of the inferior sort : "The general composition [of the States-General] was of obscure provincial advocates, of stewards of petty local jurisdictions, country attorneys, notaries, and the whole train of the ministers of municipal litigation, the fomenters and conductors of the petty war of village vexation. . . . Who could conceive that men who are habitually meddling, daring, subtle, active, of litigious dispositions and unquiet minds, would easily fall back into their old condition of obscure contention, and laborious, low, and unprofitable chicane ? "

26 9. *Snuff the approach.* Payne notes that this is suggested by lines in Addison's *Campaign.*

26 16. *Seas roll, and months pass.* This has been called a fine illustration of zeugma. Explain.

26 20. *Winged ministers of vengeance.* Ultimately de

rived from Horace, *Odes*, IV., iv., 1, "winged minister of
the thunderbolt," because Jove's messenger.   But a study of
the period shows that Burke was frequently indebted to
speeches made by himself and others in Parliament, and did
not always go directly to ultimate sources ; and so it is here.
In a speech delivered on January 22, 1770, Lord Chatham had
said (Goodrich, p. 116) : "They have disarmed the imperial
bird, the *ministrum fulminis alitem*.   The army is the thunder of the Crown.   The ministry have tied up the hand which
should direct the bolt."   Burke, it will have been seen,
transfers the figure to the navy.

It is instructive to see how a further step is taken by Can-
ning, in his speech at Plymouth, in 1823 (Goodrich, p. 874).
He is, of course, applying the image to a man-of-war :—

"You well know, gentlemen, how soon one of those stu-
pendous masses, now reposing on their shadows in perfect
stillness—how soon, upon any call of patriotism or of necessity, it would assume the likeness of an animated thing, instinct with life and motion ; how soon it would ruffle, as it
were, its swelling plumage ; how quickly it would put forth
all its beauty and its bravery, collect its scattered elements of
strength, and awaken its dormant thunder.   Such as is one
of these magnificent machines when springing from inaction
into a display of its might, such is England herself while,
apparently passive and motionless, she silently concentrates
the power to be put forth on an adequate occasion."

26 21. *Pounces.*   Why better than "claws," or "talons?"

26 23. *So far*, etc.   *Job* xxxviii. 11 : "Hitherto shalt thou
come, and no further ; and here shall thy proud waves be
stayed."

26 28. *In large bodies.*   Is such an analogy demonstrative?

26 30. *The Turk*, etc.   See Payne's remarks (*Burke's Select Works*, I., xxxix.-xl.) :—

"It is a well-known canon of rhetoric that, in the selection
of words with a view to energy, we must always prefer those
terms which are the least abstract and general.   Campbell
and Whately have pointed out as a remarkable instance of
this rule, the well-known passage, 'Consider the lilies, how
they grow,' etc.   To illustrate the effect produced by its sys-

tematic employment, we will take a passage from the present volume, and compare it with a passage to the same purpose, in the ordinary style, from an early work of Lord Brougham :

" 'In large bodies, the circulation of power must be less vigorous at the extremities. Nature has said it. The Turk cannot govern Egypt, and Arabia, and Curdistan, as he governs Thrace ; nor has he the same dominion in Crimea and Algiers which he has at Brusa and Smyrna. Despotism itself is obliged to truck and huckster. The Sultan gets such obedience as he can. He governs with a loose rein, that he may govern at all ; and the whole of the force and vigour of his authority in his centre is derived from a prudent relaxation in all his borders. '

" 'In all the despotisms of the East, it has been observed that, the further any part of the empire is removed from the capital, the more do its inhabitants enjoy some sort of rights and privileges ; the more inefficacious is the power of the monarch ; and the more feeble an·l easily decayed is the organization of the government,' etc. (Brougham's *Inquiry into the Colonial Policy of the European Powers*).

"This particularising style is of the essence of poetry ; and in prose it is impossible not to be struck with the energy which it produces. Brougham's passage is excellent in its way ; but it pales before the flashing lights of Burke's sentences."

26 31. *Kurdistan.* Dodsley, *Curdistan.*

26 33. *Brusa.* In Northwestern Asia Minor. *Despotism itself*, etc. Notice the contrast between the beginning and the close of this sentence. Does this make it more impressive ?

26 35. *As he can.* In Armenia, for instance ?

27 3. *Spain, in her provinces.* In Cuba ?

27 11. *First mover.* From the Latin *primum mobile.* In the Ptolemaic astronomy the heavenly bodies were conceived of as "set in a series of spheres, having the earth as their common centre. The outermost of these spheres was called the 'primum mobile' or 'first moved.' It completed its revolution in twenty-four hours, and communicated its movement to the inner spheres." *Cf. Par. Lost*, iii., 483, and Longfellow's notes on the *Divine Comedy, Paradiso*, i., 1.

27 13. *Grown with the growth.* From Pope's *Essay on Man*, ii., 136.

27 20. See Quintilian, Bk. v., chap. 10 ff., for a detailed consideration of this division of a speech.

27 20, 21. A transitional sentence, as this and the following paragraph are transitional paragraphs. Observe that from this point to **28** 3 everything is retrospective and resumptive, with the exception of the question in **27** 31.

27 29 ff. This sentence is usually misprinted, *but* being prefixed to *what*.

28 1. *With all its imperfections on its head.* Adapted from *Hamlet*, I., v., 79.

28 3. Here Burke becomes distinctly anticipative of **30** 23 ff., but in the meantime he devotes nearly two paragraphs to showing that America seems capable of self-government, probably as a means of illustrating and emphasizing what has preceded, and of so arousing the apprehensions of his hearers as to make them attentive to his solution of the problem.

28 9. *Untractable.* Now generally "intractable."

28 11. *Monsters.* Metaphor. Explain the meaning.

28 18. *Popular part.* What is meant?

28 23. *Operose.* Difficult; an archaic word, from Lat. *operosus*, employed by Cicero.

28 35. *Lord Dunmore.* John Murray, fourth Earl of Dunmore (1732–1809). Made Governor of New York in 1770, and subsequently of Virginia. Dissolved the Virginia Assembly in March, 1773, and again in May, 1774, because of its measures of sympathy with the other Colonies. In June, 1775, he took refuge on board a man-of-war. As a result the Burgesses resolved that he had abdicated, constituted themselves a convention, and vested the executive in a Committee of Safety. He afterwards carried on hostilities against the colony, reducing Norfolk to ashes on January 1, 1776.

29 20. *Wholly abrogated*, etc. The act was finally passed on May 11, 1774, and constitutes chap. 45 of 14 George III.

(see note on **62** 25). It is entitled, "An Act for the better regulating the Government of the Province of the Massachu-setts Bay, in New England." It is thus characterized by Lecky, iii., 431–432 :—

"By another Act, Parliament exercised the power which, as the supreme legislative body of the Empire, Mansfield and other lawyers ascribed to it, of remodelling by its own authority the Charter of Massachusetts. The General Assem-bly, which was esteemed the legitimate representative of the democratic element in the Constitution, was left entirely un-touched ; but the Council, or Upper Chamber, which had been hitherto elected by the Assembly, was now to be ap-pointed, as in most of the other Colonies of America, by the Crown, and the whole executive power was to cease to ema-nate from the people. The judges and magistrates of all kinds, including the sheriffs, were to be appointed by the royal governor, and were to be revocable at pleasure. Jury men, instead of being chosen at popular elections, were to be summoned by the sheriffs. The right of public meeting, which had lately been much employed in inciting the popu-lace against the Government, was seriously abridged. No meeting except election meetings might henceforth be held, and no subject discussed, without the permission of the gov-ernor."

Of this measure Bancroft says (iii., 477) : "Lord North placed himself in conflict with institutions sanctioned by royal charters, rooted in custom, confirmed by possession through successive generations, and infolded in the affections and life of the people."

29 25. *Anarchy is found tolerable.* Contrary to the pre-diction of Dr. Johnson (*Taxation no Tyranny*) :—

"The charter . . . by which provincial governments are constituted may be always legally, and, where it is either inconvenient in its nature or misapplied in its use, may be equitably repealed. By such repeal the whole fabric of sub-ordination is immediately destroyed, and the constitution sunk at once into a chaos ; the society is dissolved at once into a tumult of individuals, without authority to command, or obligation to obey; without any punishment of wrongs but by personal resentment, or any protection of right but by the hand of the possessor."

Has now subsisted. On the manner in which it subsisted, *cf.* 'Vells' *Samuel Adams*, ii., 145 : "While this memorable

Parliament were perfecting their measures, the Legislature was prorogued in Massachusetts, and, as usual, the Committee of Correspondence continued to act in open defiance of the King's disapprobation.   The Province, in fact, was virtually under the control of this democratic body of Provincial statesmen.   Hutchinson's authority, as he admits, was little more than nominal.   'All legislative as well as executive authority,' he says, 'was gone.'"

30 10 ff. *Endeavouring to subvert.   Cf.* the following passage from Burke's *Address to the King:*—

"It is not, Sire, from a want of the most inviolable duty to your Majesty, not from a want of a partial and a passionate regard to that part of your Empire in which we reside, and which we wish to be supreme, that we have hitherto withstood all attempts to render the supremacy of one part of your dominions inconsistent with the liberty and safety of all the rest.   The motives of our opposition are found in those very sentiments which we are supposed to violate.   For we are convinced beyond a doubt that a system of dependence which leaves no security to the people for any part of their freedom in their own hands cannot be established in any inferior member of the British Empire, without consequentially destroying the freedom of that very body, in favour of whose boundless pretensions such a scheme is adopted.   .   .   .

"To leave any real freedom to Parliament, freedom must be left to the Colonies.   A military government is the only substitute for civil liberty.   That the establishment of such a power in America will utterly ruin our finances (though its certain effect) is the smallest part of our concern.   It will become an apt, powerful, and certain engine for the destruction of our freedom here.   Great bodies of armed men, trained to a contempt of popular assemblies representative of an English people; kept up for the purpose of exacting impositions without their consent, and maintained by that exaction; instruments in subverting, without any process of law, great ancient establishments and respected forms of governments; set free from, and therefore above, the ordinary English tribunals of the country where they serve;—these men cannot so transform themselves, merely by crossing the sea, as to behold with love and reverence, and submit with profound obedience to the very same things in Great Britain which in America they had been taught to despise, and had been accustomed to awe and humble.   All your Majesty's troops, in the rotation of service, will pass through this discipline, and contract these habits.   If we could flatter ourselves that this would not happen, we must be the weakest of men ; we must be the worst, if we were indifferent whether it happened or not. What, gracious sovereign, is the empire of America to us, or the empire of the world, if we lose our own liberties? We deprecate this last of evils—we deprecate the effect of the doctrines which must support and countenance the government over conquered Englishmen.''

30 25. *There are but three ways.* Genung (*Practical Elements of Rhetoric*, p. 432) calls the mode of proof here adopted the Method of Residues. ''This name,'' he says, ''is given to that form of argument which, first enumerating all the possible aspects of the question, then proceeds to eliminate, one by one, until only the true aspect is left. . . . For the successful employment of this method the alternatives should be thoroughly classified and limited in number ; to clear away too many false positions complicates the argument, and gives rise to a feeling of insecurity lest the true state of the case should, after all, have been overlooked.''

30 32. *That of giving up the Colonies.* This course, which we now see to have been inevitable, was strongly urged by Joseph Tucker (1711–1799), who must therefore be considered, in the light of history, the wisest Englishman then living, so far as the whole matter of the Colonies was concerned. A most interesting tract is his *The True Interest of Britain,* of which the Yale University copy bears the date of Philadelphia, 1776. However, he advocated his views for a series of years, and in several pamphlets ; Lecky thus sums up his arguments (iii., 421–423) :—

''Tucker, the Dean of Gloucester, a bitter Tory, but one of the best living writers on all questions of trade, maintained a theory which was then esteemed visionary and almost childish, but which will now be very differently regarded. He had no respect for the Americans ; he dissected with unsparing severity the many weaknesses in their arguments, and the declamatory and rhetorical character of much of their patriotism ; but he contended that matters had now come to such a point that the only real remedy was separation. Colonies which would do nothing for their own defence, which were in a condition of smothered rebellion, and which were continually waiting for the difficulties of the mother-country in order to assert their power, were a source of political weakness and

not of political strength, and the trade advantages which were
supposed to spring from the connection were of the most delusive kind. Trade, as he showed, will always ultimately flow
in the most lucrative channels. The most stringent laws had
been unable to prevent the Americans from trading with foreign countries if they could do so with advantage, and in case
of separation the Americans would still resort to England for
most of their goods, for the simple reason that England could
supply them more cheaply than any other nation. The supremacy of English industry did not rest upon political
causes. The trade of the world is carried on in a great measure by British capital. British capital is greater than that of
any other in the world, and as long as this superiority lasts it
is morally impossible that the trade of the British nation can
suffer any very great or alarming diminution. No single fact
is more clearly established by history than that the bitterest
political animosity is insufficient to prevent nations from ultimately resorting to the markets that are most advantageous
to them, and as long as England maintained the conditions
of her industrial supremacy unimpaired she was in this respect perfectly secure. But nothing impairs these conditions
so much as war, which wastes capital unproductively and
burdens industry with a great additional weight of debt, military establishments, and taxation. The war which began
about the Spanish right of search had cost sixty millions, and
had scarcely produced any benefit to England. The last war
cost ninety millions, and its most important result had been,
by securing the Americans from French aggression, to render
possible their present rebellion. Let England, then, be wise
in time, and before she draws the sword let her calculate what
possible advantage she could derive commensurate with the
permanent evils which would inevitably follow. The Americans have refused to submit to the authority and legislation
of the Supreme Legislature, or to bear their part in supporting the burden of the Empire. Let them, then, cease to be
fellow-members of that Empire. Let them go their way to
form their own destinies. Let England free herself from the
cost, the responsibility, and the danger of defending them,
retaining, like other nations, the right of connecting herself
with them by treaties of commerce or of alliance.

"The views of Adam Smith, though less strongly expressed,
are not very different from those of Tucker."

In the tract above mentioned, Tucker had declared, "I
make not the least doubt that a separation from the Northern
Colonies . . . will . . . take place within half a
century."

There was still another alternative, of which Burke here makes no mention, though he had discussed it at length in his *Present State of the Nation*, and was to touch upon it in paragraph 89. This was to have the Colonies represented in Parliament. According to Lecky (iii., 349): "A few voices were raised in favour of the admission of American representatives into Parliament; but this plan, which was advocated by Otis and supported by the great names of Franklin and of Adam Smith, would have encountered enormous practical difficulties, and it found few friends in either country. Grenville himself, however, appears to have for a time seriously contemplated it." One of the foremost champions of this measure was Francis Maseres (1731–1824), who had gained American experience as Attorney-General of Quebec from 1766 to 1769, an office he had filled with the highest estimation. In 1770 he published a pamphlet entitled, *Considerations on the Expediency of Admitting Representatives from the American Colonies into the British House of Commons*. His views were combated by Tucker in the above-mentioned tract.

31 5. *Radical.* Payne comments: "It was Burke who brought the term into parliamentary if not into general use—not Pitt, as commonly asserted : *cp.* Fischel, *English Const.*, p. 551."

31 20. *Avarice of desolation.* Explain.

31 30. *Annual tillage.* Look up Hor., *Odes*, iii., 24, 14, and see if you think Burke here owes anything to that passage.

31 35. *Five hundred miles.* To the Great Lakes on the north, and the Mississippi on the west. *Cf.* Bancroft, *Hist. United States*, iii., 467: "An intrepid population, heedless of proclamations, was pouring westward through all the gates of the Alleghanies; seating themselves on the New River and the Greenbrier, on the branches of the Monongahela, or even making their way to the Mississippi; accepting from nature their title-deeds to the unoccupied wilderness. Connecticut kept in mind that its charter bounded its territory by the Pacific, and had already taken courage to claim lands westward to the Mississippi."

32 2. *Change their manners with the habits of their life.*
A Latin construction, *with* signifying *under the influence of.*

This whole passage calls out the following comment from
Goodrich : "It is in descriptions of this kind that Mr. Burke
is more truly admirable than in those of a brilliant and imaginative character which precede."

32 12. *Increase and multiply.* From *Par. Lost*, x., 730 ;
ultimately from *Gen.* ix. 1.

32 14. *Express charter. Ps.* cxv. 16: "The earth hath he
given to the children of men." The Hebraic expression,
children of men, is used in the oldest existing fragment of
English literature, Cædmon's Hymn, in the form "ælda
barnum." See *The Bible and English Prose Style* (Boston,
1892), p. x.

32 20. *Mysterious virtue.* Is the phrase used sarcastically,
or otherwise ?

32 31. *To arrest.* Referring back to the "penal bill," **3** 9.

33 9. *Unserviceable. Cf.* paragraph 35, and note on **20** 3.

33 19. *Spoliatis arma supersunt.* Juv., viii., 124. This
may be rendered in free paraphrase, "Though you rob them of
everything else, they will still find means to procure weapons."
Juvenal has been speaking of the way in which Roman provinces were plundered, and adds, "Beware lest any glaring
wrong be done to men both brave and destitute ; " upon
which follows our sentence.

33 27. *Your speech would betray you.* Adopted from *Matt.*
xxvi. 73, with substitution of *betray* for *bewray*, the latter
word meaning merely "reveal, make known."

This whole paragraph is one of the most powerful in the
speech.

33 35. What do you know of the Inquisition ?

34 3. *Bottom.* Foundation, basis.

34 4. *Books of curious science.* Who were they, in *Acts*
xix. 19, who burnt their books, and why did they do it? In
the Biblical passage, *curious* means nearly the same as "oc-
cult."

34 10. *The army. Cf.* note on **30** 10.

34 18. *Its advocates.* Like Dr. Johnson, who said (*Taxation no Tyranny*): "It has been proposed that the slaves should be set free, an act which surely the lovers of liberty cannot but commend. If they are furnished with fire-arms for defence, and utensils for husbandry, and settled in some simple form of government within the country, they may be more grateful and honest than their masters."

34 21. *Would not always be accepted.* This was shown by the action of Lord Dunmore (see on **28** 35), according to Massey (*History of England*, ii., 199–200): —

"After some hasty measures, followed by a precipitate retreat from his government, this nobleman proclaimed martial law, and offered freedom to all negroes the property of rebels. The most fearful consequences might have been apprehended from a sudden emancipation of the black people; but happily the persons to whom this proclamation was addressed, regarding Lord Dunmore as having no longer the power to perform his promises or to execute his threats, paid but little attention to it. A few hundreds only joined his standard."

34 30. *Have had recourse.* Here Payne has a valuable note:

"See Aristoph., *Ran.*, 27, from which it appears that the slaves who had distinguished themselves at the battle of Arginusae were presented with their freedom. Plutarch says that Cleomenes armed 2,000 Helots to oppose the Macedonian Leucaspedae, in his war with that people and the Achaeans. According to Pausanias, the Helots were present at the battle of Marathon. Among the Romans, as Virgil (*Æn.*, ix., 547) tells us, it was highly criminal for slaves to enter the army of their masters, but in the Hannibalian War, after the battle of Cannae, 8,000 of them were armed, and by their valour in subsequent actions earned their liberty. See Livy, Book xxiv."

35 2. *Their refusal.* Speaking of the Virginia burgesses, under date of May, 1769, Bancroft says (iii., 348): "Such, too, was their zeal against the slave-trade that they made a special covenant with one another not to import any slaves, nor purchase any imported." Among the signers were Washington, Jefferson, and Richard Henry Lee. Before this, the Colonies had made ineffectual attempts to restrict the slave-trade; *cf.* Lecky, iii., 325–326: "In 1761 the Assembly of South Carolina, being sensible of the great social and political danger arising from the enormous multiplication of negroes in the colony, passed a law imposing a heavy duty upon the importation of slaves ; but as the slave-trade was one of the most lucrative branches of English commerce, the law was rescinded by the Crown. In the same year instructions were sent to the Governor of New Hampshire to refuse his assent to any law imposing duties on negroes imported into the colonies.''

35 14. *Ye gods,* etc. Quoted in *Martinus Scriblerus* (1741), which was chiefly the work of Arbuthnot.

35 19. *Alterative.* Define.

35 28. *Should.* Why not *would ?*

36 3. *I do not know,* etc. Frequently quoted with admiration ; *cf.* Introduction, p. xxxix.

36 6. *Insulted.* I give a specimen of the language employed by Coke (1552–1634), who is here designated as *Att.,* *i.e. Attorney.* The extract is from Howell's *State Trials* (ed. 1816), ii., 26 : —

"*Raleigh.* You have not proved any one thing against me by direct proofs, but all by circumstances.

"*Att.* Have you done? The king must have the last.

"*Raleigh.* Nay, Mr. Attorney, he which speaketh for his life must speak last. False repetitions and mistakings must not mar my cause. . . .

"*Att.* The king's safety and your clearing cannot agree. I protest before God, I never knew a clearer treason. . . . Go to, I will lay thee upon thy back, for the confidentest traitor that ever came at a bar. . . .

"*Lord Cecil.* Be not so impatient, good Mr. Attorney, give him leave to speak.

"*Att.* If I may not be patiently heard, you will encourage traitors, and discourage us. . . .

"*At the repeating of some things, Sir Walter Raleigh interrupted him, and said he did him wrong.*

"*Att.* Thou art the most vile and execrable traitor that ever lived.

"*Raleigh.* You speak indiscreetly, barbarously, and uncivilly.

Att. I want words sufficient to express thy viperous treasons.''

36 18. *Under one common head.* See Burke's *Speech on
American Taxation:* —

"I look, I say, on the imperial rights of Great Britain, and
the privileges which the Colonists ought to enjoy under these
rights, to be just the most reconcilable things in the world.
The Parliament of Great Britain sits at the head of her extensive empire in two capacities : one as the local legislature of
this island, providing for all things at home, immediately, and
by no other instrument than the executive power. The other,
and I think her nobler capacity, is what I call her *imperial
character;* in which, as from the throne of heaven, she superin-
tends all the several inferior legislatures, and guides and con-
trols them all, without annihilating any. As all these provincial legislatures are only co-ordinate to each other, they ought
all to be subordinate to her; else they can neither preserve mutual peace, nor hope for mutual justice, nor effectually afford
mutual assistance. It is necessary to coerce the negligent, to
restrain the violent, and to aid the weak and deficient, by the
overruling plenitude of her power. She is never to intrude
into the place of the others, whilst they are equal to the common ends of their institution.''

36 30. *Ex vi termini.* From the force of the term ; from
the very meaning of the word.

37 2. [*That.*] Though found in Dodsley, this word is evidently superfluous, for which reason I have enclosed it in
brackets.

37 10. *It may not always*, etc. Sarcasm. Collect other
instances of sarcasm from the speech.

37 14. *Cf.* note on **67** 11.

37 22. *Against the superior.* *Cf.* Burke's *Present Discontents:*—

"In all disputes between the people and their rulers the
presumption is at least upon a par in favour of the people.
Experience may perhaps justify me in going further. When
popular discontents have been very prevalent, it may well be
affirmed and supported that there has been generally something found amiss in the constitution or in the conduct of
government.''

37 28. *Injustice.* In allusion to the law maxim quoted by Cicero, *De Officiis*, 1., 10, 33, *Summum jus summa injuria*, "The extreme of law is the extreme of injustice."

38 10. *An act of Henry the Eighth.* See on **62** 30, **63** 35.

38 25. *Numerous.* How many can you enumerate?

38 31. *Correctly.* Exactly.

39 3. *No way is open.* Have we seen that there were no alternatives but these three?

39 22. *Nothing at all to do.* Burke has now arrived at one of the most difficult portions of his task. He is to move for the repeal of an act imposing taxes upon the Colonies (see **61** 34 ff.); he is aware that this proposal will meet with strong opposition, and that he will immediately be confronted with the argument, already trite, that, since Parliament has a right to tax English subjects, there is no occasion to repeal an act by which that right is exercised. If he denies the right, his view will be controverted by some of the best lawyers in the kingdom ; the dispute will be endless ; and nothing will be done while the dispute continues. What method does Burke adopt? What were his views, in general, about *rights*?

Payne's note is interesting : —

"It is difficult to select any passage in this oration for special notice in point of style : but no one can fail to be struck with fresh admiration at the method of this paragraph, in which the 'right of taxation' is excluded from the discussion. The delicate irony with which the theorists are passed over gives place, by way of a surprising antithesis ('right to render your people miserable'—'interest to make them happy '), to the earnest remonstrance with which the passage concludes. The continuous irony of the first part of the paragraph seems to contribute to, rather than detract from, the general elevation of treatment."

39 28. *Startle.* *Cf.* Addison, *Cato*, v., 1 : —

> Why shrinks the soul
> Back on herself, and startles at destruction?

40 6. *High and reverend authorities.* For a summary of these discussions, see Burke in *Annual Register* for 1766, or *Parl. Hist.*, vol. xvi.

40 9–11. *Par. Lost*, ii., 592–594.

40 26. *The assertion of my title is the loss of my suit.* Explain.

40 30. *Unity of spirit.* From *Eph.* iv. 3; *cf.* 1 *Cor.* xii. 6 ff. Has not Burke here seized upon an immutable principle, which is that of every artistic creation, as well as that upon which a confederation like the United States reposes? There are those who look for its wider extension in practice. *Cf.* Tennyson, *Locksley Hall:*—

> Till the war-drum throbbed no longer, and the battle-flags were furled,
> In the Parliament of man, the Federation of the world.

Or take this, as perhaps more feasible, from the close of a recent oration delivered at the Harvard Law School by Sir Frederick Pollock, a distinguished legal authority, on *The Vocation of the Common Law* (quoted from *The Dial* of May 1, 1896):—

"Dreams are not versed in issuable matter, and have no dates. Only I feel that this one looks forward, and will be seen as waking light some day. If any one, being of little faith or over-curious, must needs ask in what day, I can answer only in the same fashion. We may know the signs, though we know not when they will come. These things will be when we look back on our dissensions in the past as brethren grown up to man's estate and dwelling in unity look back upon the bickerings of the nursery and the jealousies of the class-room; when there is no use for the word 'foreigner' between Cape Wrath and the Rio Grande, and the federated navies of the English-speaking nations keep the peace of the ocean under the Northern Lights and under the Southern Cross, from Vancouver to Sydney, and from the Channel to the Gulf of Mexico; when an indestructible union of even wider grasp and higher potency than the federal bond of these States has knit our descendants into an invincible and indestructible concord."

41 3. *Million.* Elsewhere millions; *cf.* **10** 25, etc.

41 6. *The general character,* etc. Note the aphorism.

41 12. *Into an interest in the Constitution.* What does this mean, in concrete terms?

41 29. *American financiers.* Explain.

41 31. *Exquisite.* Determine its meaning here from its etymology.

42 3. *Trade Laws.* The various Acts of Navigation, etc.

42 7. *A gentleman of real moderation.* George Rice (1742–1779), M.P. for Newton, in the County of Carmarthen, from 1754 to 1779, and Lord Lieutenant of that county. By his marriage to the Baroness Dinevor, he became the great-grandfather of the present Baron Dinevor (born January 24, 1836). On April 19, 1774, speaking on the Repeal of the Tea Duty Act, Mr. Rice had said, "Whenever we have made the least concession, they have always required more; they will think that we acknowledge that we have no right, if we should repeal this law" (*Parl. Hist.*, xvii., 1211–1212).

42 18. *Shall.* Why used, instead of *will* ?

42 21. *Acts of Navigation.* See Introduction, p. xi.

43 7. *The pamphlet.* By Dean Tucker; see note on **30** 32.

43 9. *Idolizing.* Speaking of Grenville, Burke had said (*American Taxation*): "Among regulations, that which stood first in reputation was his *idol.* I mean the Act of Navigation. He has often professed it to be so."

What do you think of these Navigation Acts?

43 27. *There is not a shadow of evidence for it.* Was there not?

44 9. *Will go further.* Cf. Burke, *American Taxation :—*

"But still it sticks in our throats—'If we go so far, the Americans will go farther.' We do not know that. We ought, from experience, rather to presume the contrary. Do we not know for certain that the Americans are going on as fast as possible, whilst we refuse to gratify them? Can they do more, or can they do worse, if we yield this point? I think this concession will rather fix a turnpike to prevent their further progress. It is impossible to answer for bodies of men. But I am sure the natural effect of fidelity, clemency, kindness in governors, is peace, good-will, order, and esteem on the part of the governed. I would certainly, at least, give these fair principles a fair trial; which, since the making of this act to this hour, they never have had."

Cf. the affirmative statement with the figure of interrogation. Which is the more effective?

44 23. Why all three synonyms?

44 30. *I set out,* etc. *Cf.* paragraph 6. Note the combined (oratorical) modesty and irony of this sentence. Why ought this statement to have disposed his critics to accept his plan?

45 4. Observe the mode of connecting this paragraph with the preceding, and with the following. It is well explained by Payne (*Burke's Select Works*, I., xlii.–xliii.):—

> "The modern or French method is to unite the members of the passage by a connexion of ideas ; as Dr. Whately expresses it, 'to interweave or rather *felt* them together,' by making the thought pass over from one member to the other ; by concealing the sutures, and making the parts fit into and compliment each other. This method leaves better opportunities for marking boldly the transitions in the argument, and, if appropriate, making corresponding changes in the style. In the literary art, as in all others, unprepared transition from one main member of the composition to another is an unfailing mark of barbarism. The Speech on Conciliation, which is the most remarkable of the works in this volume as a specimen of method, is full of illustrations of this canon. Of the boldness with which Burke sometimes broke through his method for the sake of the method we have a striking instance . . . where he inserts in the first part, which consists of a description of the condition of America, and of American character, a series of objections to the employment of force against the Colonists, properly belonging to the second part of the speech."

What *word*, occurring in both paragraphs 78 and 79, serves to unite the two?

45 18. *Ireland.* Consult Green's *Short History of the English People.*

45 29. *Magna Charta.* When adopted ? Quote from Green (chap. iii., sect. iii.) one of its provisions.

45 35. *All Ireland.* "The English settlers in Ireland, after the invasion of Strongbow, kept themselves within certain limits, distinct from the natives, called the 'Pale.' They enjoyed English law, while the natives were denied it ; and this gave rise to incessant contentions. By an act of James I., the privileges of the Pale were extended to all Ireland."—GOODRICH.

46 4. *Davies.* Dodsley, *Davis.* The reference is to his *Discoverie of the true Causes why Ireland was never entirely subdued, nor brought under Obedience of the Crown of*

England, until the beginning of his Majestie's happy Reign,
1612. By the time he was thirty he had published two poems,
Orchestra (1574) and *Nosce Teipsum* (1599). Extracts from these
may be read in Chambers' *Cyclopædia of English Literature*.
From 1606 to 1619 he was Attorney-General for Ireland. His
works have been edited by Grosart in the Fuller Worthies
Library, 1869–1876.

46 23. *Glorious.* Why ?

46 26. *Strength and ornament.* Is Burke guilty of no exaggeration here ? What was and is the real truth ?

46 32. *An exception to prove the rule.* From the Latin
proverb, *Exceptio probat regulam.* Explain.

47 10, 11. *Henry the Third; Edward the First.* Dates?
Cf. Green's *Short History.*

47 16. *Lords Marchers.* *Cf.* Tout, *Edward the First*, pp.
17–18 :—

"The Norman Conquest of England was followed by the
Norman Conquest of Wales. A swarm of Norman adventur-
ers crossed over the border, and drove the Welsh from the fair
plains to the barren uplands. The mutual jealousies of the
petty Welsh kings and princes made national union impossible, and without union effectual resistance to the Normans
was hardly to be thought of. But the Norman conquerors
were as little united as the Welsh that they displaced. As in
Ireland, the ideal of feudal lord and clan chieftain had this in
common, that it involved an infinite division of political
power. The Norman conquerors of Wales fought for their
own hands, and were almost independent of the kings of England. They set up therefore a whole host of petty states, over
which they ruled like little kings. These small Norman prin-
cipalities on Welsh ground were known as the Lordships
Marcher [properly, Marchers], and the whole district as the
Marches of Wales, though the original idea of the March as a
border was largely lost sight of in an age when the Welsh
Marches included the districts so remote from the English border as a great part of the modern Pembrokeshire."

47 23. *Restive.* Have we had this word before?

47 28–29. *Cf.* Payne, *Burke's Select Works*, I., xli. :—

"Burke commonly practises the method of *Interpretatio* by
first expanding the sense, and then contracting it into its most
compendious and striking form. This device is indispensable

when the author is dealing with a subject which is presumed to be unfamiliar to his readers. 'The hearers,' says Dr. Whately, 'will be struck by the forcibleness of the sentence which they will have been prepared to comprehend ; they will *understand* the longer expression, and *remember* the shorter.' Nor does any writer, not even Macaulay, excel him in producing effect by that less methodical interspersion of short, pointed, and forcible sentences throughout the performance, which is so necessary to the energetic and suggestive style.''

47 35. *The sending arms.* Is the syntax good ? Other examples in Burke ?

48 3. *By an instruction.* To General Gage.

48 5. *As you have done.* By what Act ?

48 18. *Rid.* Trace the history of the verb *ride*, and explain how this form arose.

48 25. *Vexation to violence.* For the thought, *cf. Ps.* vii. 16.

48 27. *Husbandry.* Define.

48 30. *Against a whole nation.* *Cf.* **36** 3–5.

48 32. *Twenty-seventh year.* A.D. 1535.

49 13. *Day-star.* From 2 *Pet.* i. 19.

49 16 ff. Hor., *Odes*, i., 12, 27–32. The poet is singing the praises of Castor and Pollux :—

> Soon as whose clear effulgent star
> Upon the shipman gleams, amid the tempest's war,
>
> Down from the rocks subsides the weltering spray,
> The winds in zephyrs creep,
> The clouds disperse that veiled the gladsome day,
> And on the wild and wasteful deep
> The threatening waves—such power is theirs—are lulled to sleep.

49 22. *County Palatine.* ''Counties *Palatine* are so called . . . because the owners thereof . . . had in those Counties *jura regalia* [royal rights], as fully as the king hath in his *palace.*'' BLACKSTONE, *Commentaries*, Introd., § 4.

49 28. *Archers.* Holinshed says, under the year 1397 (ii., 838) : ''The king fearing what might be attempted against him by those that favoured these noblemen that were in durance, sent for a power of Cheshire men, that might day and night keep watch and ward about his person. They were about two thousand archers, paid weekly, as by the annals of Britain it appeareth.''

When was Richard II. deposed, and for what reason?

49 32 ff. The petition has been modernized in spelling from the *Statutes of the Realm*, ed. 1817, iii., 911, forming part of chap. 13 of 34 and 35 Henry VIII. (1542–1543). Dodsley and the other editions are less accurate.

49 33. *Shewen.* The East Midland plural of the present tense in Middle English is in *-en*. See Lounsbury, *Hist. Eng. Lang.*, p. 406.

50 5. *Disherisons.* Disinheritings, deprivations.

50 16. *Ne.* Nor. This is the regular OE. form, *nor* being a comparatively late substitute.

50 22. *Common wealth.* Public welfare. Ruskin illustrates this when he says (*Fors Clavigera*, Letter vii.) : "The question is mainly whether you are striving for a Common-Wealth, and Public Thing, or . . . for a Common-Illth, and Public Nothing." *Cf.* Lat. *res communis, res publica.*

50 23. *Bounden.* Obliged, beholden. Did the original past part. have *-en*, or not?

50 25 ff. How does Burke artistically manage to create at once a climax and a surprise in this paragraph?

50 31. *Temperament.* How is the meaning here to be inferred from that of the Lat. verb *temperare*?

51 6. *Pale.* See note on **45** 35.

51 20. *No way resembling.* "And also by cause that the people of the same Dominion have, and do daily use, a speech nothing like ne consonant to the natural mother tongue used within this realm," etc. (*Statutes of the Realm*, as above, p. 563).

51 23. *Judge Barrington's.* Daines Barrington (1727–1800). Appointed Justice of the counties of Merioneth, Carnarvon, and Anglesey, in 1757. "A mind of restless activity, which turned wide though not accurate learning to most ingenious uses " (*Dict. Nat. Biog.*).

51 32. *Virtually represented.* *Cf.* Johnson, *Taxation no Tyranny:*—

" It is urged that when Wales, Durham, and Chester were divested of their particular privileges or ancient government, and reduced to the state of English counties, they had representatives assigned them.

" To those from whom something had been taken, something in return might properly be given. To the Americans their charters are left as they were, nor have they lost anything except that of which their sedition has deprived them. If they were to be represented in Parliament, something would be granted, though nothing is withdrawn. The inhabitants of Chester, Durham, and Wales, were invited to exchange their peculiar institutions for the power of voting, which they wanted before. The Americans have voluntarily resigned the power of voting, to live in distant and separate governments— and what they have voluntarily quitted they have no right to claim. It must always be remembered that they are represented by the same virtual representation as the greater part of Englishmen ; and that if by change of place they have less share in the legislature than is proportionate to their opulence, they by their removal gained that opulence, and had originally, and have now, their choice of a vote at home or riches at a distance."

52 13. *Opposuit natura.* From Juvenal, *Sat.,* x., 152, " Nature barred his path by Alps and snow," referring to Hannibal ; but Juvenal adds, " He rives the rocks and bursts the mountains."

52 15. *I do not know to be possible.* But Franklin thought it was. See his letters to Governor Shirley of December 22, 1754, and to Lord Kames, April 11, 1767, and his *Observations on Passages in 'An Inquiry,'* etc., London, 1769. However, in the second of these he remarks : " Ireland once wished it, but now rejects it. The time has been when the Colonies might have been pleased with it ; they are now *indifferent* about it ; and, if it is much longer delayed, they too will refuse it."

52 20. *Is not shortened. Isa.* lix. 1.

52 31. *Republic.* This was the original of all Utopias from Plato's day to the present, including Bellamy's *Looking Backward.*

52 32. *Utopia.* Repeat some excellent suggestion, as yet unrealized, from the *Utopia.*

52 34–35. Inaccurately quoted from *Comus*, 634 – 635. Meaning of *clouted shoon* ? Collect evidences of Burke's fondness for Milton. How early did it begin ?

53 9. *By grant. Cf.* paragraph 106.

53 10. *Legal competency. Cf.* paragraph 98.

53 13. *Dutiful and beneficial exercise. Cf.* paragraph 100.

53 15. *Benefit of their grants. Cf.* paragraphs 101–103. *Futility of parliamentary taxation. Cf.* paragraphs 105, 106.

53 18. *Three more resolutions. Cf.* paragraphs 109–116.

53 22. *Six massive pillars.* Propriety of the figure ?

53 23. *Temple of British concord.* Alluding to the Temple of Concordia at Rome, famous in connection with the Catilinarian conspiracy ; *cf.* Sallust, *Cat.*, 46, 4 ; Cic., *Cat.*, iii., 9, 21. Did Burke mean to intimate that, if his propositions were accepted, he, like Cicero, ought to be regarded as the saviour of his country ?

53 29 ff. This is the triumph of oratorical ability, to eliminate the personal element, and cause the views promulgated to appear a mere statement of the very nature of things.

54 6–9. *Cf.* **50** 1–3.

54 15 ff. *Cf.* **50** 9–24.

54 21–26. *By lack . . . the same.* Omitted by amendment ; see note 1 on p. 81.

54 27 ff. "A paragraph in Burke's best style. The copiousness of thought and the economy of words are equally remarkable, and both contribute to the general effect of weight and perspicuity."—PAYNE.

54 33–34. Hor., *Sat.*, ii., 2, 2–3 : "Nor is this my own doctrine, but these are the precepts of Ofellus, a rustic sage, wise without rules, a man of homespun wit."

55 3. *Rust that rather adorns.* Probably Burke was thinking of Juv., *Sat.*, xiii., 148, *pocula adorandæ robiginis.* The passage runs : "Compare, too, those who carry off some ancient temple's massive chalices *with their venerable rust.* a nation's gift, or crowns that a monarch of old days dedicated." The rust would thus be regarded as the sign of a genuine and

valuable antique ; so in Plin., *Ep.*, iii., 6, 3 : "The brass itself, to judge from its colour, which is of the right sort, must
be antique."

55 5. *Exod.* xx. 25 : " And if thou wilt make me an altar
of stone, thou shalt not build it of hewn stone, for if thou lift
up thy tool upon it, thou hast polluted it."

Observe how the idea of the temple, **53** 23, is maintained ;
even the suggestion from Juvenal contributes.

55 7. *Ingenuous and noble roughness.* No doubt suggested
by Juv., iii., 18–20 : " How much better would the spirit of the
stream make his presence felt, if turf but fringed the waters
with a marge of green, and if no marble profaned the native
(*ingenuum*) tufa."

55 13. *Not to be wise beyond what was written.* "τὸ μὴ ὑπὲρ
ὃ γέγραπται φρονεῖν. St. Paul, 1 *Ep. to Cor.* iv. 6. Whether
Burke is the author of this elegant mistranslation, which has
now become a classical phrase, or whether he adopted it from
some English divine, I cannot say. The authorized transla-
tion seems to be correct, though Professor Scholefield supports
that given by Burke."—PAYNE. The Revised Version ap-
proximates more nearly than the Authorized to Burke's ren-
dering.

55 14. *The form of sound words.* 2 *Tim.* i. 13.

55 26. *Touched and grieved.* See **54** 22.

56 7. *Sixth of George the Second.* See Introduction, p. ʔii.

56 13. *Lord Hillsborough.* Wills Hill (1718–1793), first
Marquis of Downshire, Secretary of State for the Colonies
from 1768 to 1772. After the latter date, "though out of office, he continued to act with the Court party in giving the
most determined opposition to any concessions to America "
(*Dict. Nat. Biog.*).

56 31. *Is impossible.* See note on **52** 15.

57 13. *Those who have been pleased.* Meaning Grenville.
Cf. Present Discontents: " He was of opinion, which he has
declared in this house a hundred times, that the Colonies
could not legally grant any revenue to the Crown, and that
infinite mischiefs would be the consequence of such a power."

57 16. *Wished.*   Advised.

58 16 ff. *Journals of the House*, vol. **xxii.**

58 28 ff. *Journals*, vol. xxvii.

59 32. *The misguided people.*   Of England.

60 6. *Mr. Grenville.*   George Grenville (1712–1770), Prime Minister from 1763 to 1765.   It was he who originated the Stamp Act.

"Grenville was an able but narrow-minded man, of considerable financial ability, unflagging industry, and inflexible integrity, both in private and public life. . . .   Stern, formal, and exact, with a temper which could not brook opposition, and an ambition which knew no bounds, Grenville neither courted nor obtained popularity.   Utterly destitute of tact, obstinate to a degree, and without any generous sympathies, he possessed few of the qualities of a successful statesman. . . .   His ill-considered attempts to enforce the Trade Laws, to establish a permanent force of some ten thousand English soldiers in America, and to raise money by parliamentary taxation of the Colonies, in order to defray the expense of protecting them, produced the American Revolution " *(Dict. Nat. Biog.).*

Cf. the quotation from *American Taxation* in note on **26** 6.

60 11. *State.*   Statement ; as in **12** 22.

61 35. *Intituled.*   Entitled ; an archaic form, such as legal documents frequently employ.

62 1. *An act for granting certain duties.*   This is chap. 46 of 7 George III. (1766), and thus begins (*Statutes at Large*, ed. 1767, 8vo, xxvii., 505) :—

"Whereas it is expedient that a revenue should be raised, in your Majesty's dominions in America, for making a more certain and adequate provision for defraying the charge of the administration of justice, and the support of civil government, in such Provinces where it shall be found necessary, and towards further defraying the expenses of defending, protecting, and securing, the said dominions ; we, your Majesty's most dutiful and loyal subjects, the Commons of Great Britain, in Parliament assembled, have therefore resolved to give and grant unto your Majesty the several rates and duties hereinafter mentioned ; and do most humbly beseech your Majesty that it may be enacted, and be it enacted by the King's most excellent Majesty, by and with the advice and consent of the

Lords Spiritual and Temporal, and Commons, in this present Parliament assembled, and by the authority of the same, That from and after the twentieth day of November, one thousand seven hundred and sixty-seven, there shall be raised, levied, collected, and paid, unto his Majesty, his heirs, and successors, for and upon the respective goods hereinafter mentioned, which shall be imported from Great Britain into any Colony or Plantation in America which now is, or hereafter may be, under the dominion of his Majesty, his heirs, or successors, the several rates and duties following ; that is to say,

"For every hundred weight avoirdupois of crown, plate, flint, and white glass, four shillings and eight pence." Etc.. etc., etc.

62 11. *An act to discontinue*, etc. Chap. 19 of 14 George III. (March, 1774), beginning (*Statutes at Large*, xxx., 336–337) :—

"Whereas dangerous commotions and insurrections have been fomented and raised in the town of Boston, in the province of Massachusetts Bay, in New England, by divers ill-affected persons, to the subversion of his Majesty's government, and to the utter destruction of the public peace, and good order of the said town ; in which commotions and insurrections certain valuable cargoes of teas, being the property of the East India Company, and on board certain vessels lying within the bay or harbour of Boston, were seized and destroyed : And whereas, in the present condition of the said town and harbour, the commerce of his Majesty's subjects cannot be safely carried on there, nor the customs payable to his Majesty duly collected ; and it is therefore expedient that the officers of his Majesty's customs should be forthwith removed from the said town : May it please your Majesty that it may be enacted, and be it enacted by the King's most excellent Majesty, by and with the advice and consent of the Lords Spiritual and Temporal, and Commons, in the present Parliament assembled, and by the authority of the same, That from and after the first day of June, one thousand seven hundred and seventy-four, it shall not be lawful for any person or persons whatsoever to lade [,] put, or cause or procure to be laden or put, off or from any quay, wharf, or other place, within the said town of Boston, or in or upon any part of the shore of the bay, commonly called The Harbour of Boston, between a certain headland or point called Nahant Point, on the eastern side of the entrance into the said bay, and a certain other headland or point called Alderton Point, on the western side of the entrance into the said bay, or in or upon any island, creek, landing place, bank, or other place, within the said bay or headlands, into any ship, vessel, lighter, boat, or bottom,

any goods, wares, or merchandise whatsoever, to be trans-
ported or carried into any other country, province, or place
whatsoever, or into any other part of the said Province of
the Massachusetts Bay, in New England ; or to take up, discharge, or lay on land, or cause or procure to be taken up,
discharged, or laid on land, within the said town, or in or
upon any of the places aforesaid, out of any boat, lighter,
ship, vessel, or bottom, any goods, wares, or merchandise
whatsoever, to be brought from any other country, province,
or place, or any other part of the said Province of the Massachusetts Bay in New England, upon pain of the forfeiture of
the said goods, wares, and merchandise, and of the said boat,
lighter, ship, vessel, or other bottom into which the same
shall be put, or out of which the same shall be taken, and of
the guns, ammunition, tackle, furniture, and stores, in or belonging to the same : And if any such goods, wares, or merchandise, shall, within the said town, or in any the places
aforesaid, be laden or taken in from the shore into any barge,
hoy, lighter, wherry, or boat, to be carried on board any ship
or vessel outward-bound to any other country or province, or
other part of the said Province of the Massachusetts Bay in
New England, or be laden or taken into such barge, hoy,
lighter, wherry, or boat, from or out of any ship or vessel
coming in or arriving from any other country or province, or
other part of the said Province of the Massachusetts Bay in
New England, such barge, hoy, lighter, wherry, or boat, shall
be forfeited and lost.'' Etc., etc., etc.

62 19. *An act for the impartial administration of justice.*
Chap. 39 of 14 George III. (May 18, 1774) ; *Statutes at Large,*
xxx., 367–373. Of this Lecky says (iii., 432) :—

"It was more than probable that such grave changes would
be resisted by force, that blood would be shed, and that English soldiers would again be tried for their lives before a civil
tribunal. The conduct of the Boston judges and of the Boston
jury at the trial of Captain Preston and his soldiers had re-
dounded to their immortal honour ; but Government was resolved that no such risk should be again incurred, and that
soldiers who were brought to trial for enforcing the law against
the inhabitants of Boston should never again be tried by a
Boston jury. To remove the trial of prisoners from a district
where popular feeling was so violent that a fair trial was not
likely to be obtained, was a practice not wholly unknown to
English law. Scotch juries were not suffered to try rebels,
nor Sussex juries smugglers ; and an act was now passed 'for
the impartial administration of justice,' which provided that
if any person in the Province of Massachusetts were indicted

for murder or any other capital offence, and if it should appear to the Governor that the incriminated act was committed in aiding the magistrates to suppress tumult and riot, and also that a fair trial cannot be had in the Provinces, the prisoner should be sent for trial to any other Colony, or to Great Britain.''

62 25. *An act for the better regulating,* etc.   Chap. 45 of 14 George III. (May 11, 1774) ; *Statutes at Large,* xxx., 381–390. See an analysis of it in the note on **29** 20.

62 30. *An act for the trial of treasons.*   Chap. 2 of 35 Henry VIII. (1543–1544). Modernized in spelling and punctuation, it is here given from *Statutes of the Realm,* iii., 958 :—

" An Act concerning the Trial of Treasons committed out of the King's Majesty's Dominions.
" Forasmuch as some doubts and questions have been moved, that certain kinds of treasons, misprisions, and concealments of treasons, done, perpetrated, or committed out of the King's Majesty's Realm of England and other his Grace's dominions, cannot ne may by the common laws of this Realm be inquired of, heard, and determined within this his said Realm of England :   For a plain remedy, order, and declaration therein to be had and made, Be it enacted by authority of this present Parliament that all manner of offenses, being already made or declared, or hereafter to be made or declared by any the laws and statutes of this Realm to be treasons, misprisions of treasons, or concealments of treasons, and done, perpetrated, or committed, or hereafter to be done, perpetrate, or committed by any person or persons out of this Realm of England, shall be from henceforth inquired of, heard, and determined before the King's Justices of his Bench for pleas to be holden before himself, by good and lawful men of the same Shire where the said Bench shall sit and be kept, or else before such Commissioners, and in such Shire of the Realm, as shall be assigned by the King's Majesty's Commission, and by good and lawful men of the same Shire, in like manner and form to all intents and purposes as if such treasons or concealments of treasons had been done, perpetrated, and committed within the same Shire where they shall be so inquired of, heard, and determined as is aforesaid.   Provided always that if any the Peers of this Realm shall happen to be indicted of any such treasons, or other offenses aforesaid, by authority of this Act, that then, after such indictment, they shall have their trial by their Peers in such like manner and forme as hath been heretofore accustomed.''

62 33. *The Boston Port Bill.* See note on **62** 11.

63 1. *The Restraining Bill.* See note on **3** 9.

63 17. *The act which changes the charter of Massachusetts.*
The same referred to in **62** 25 ; *cf.* note on **29** 20.

63 30. *Probable duration.* By the last section of the Act it
was provided that it should take effect on June 1, 1774, "and
be and continue in force for and during the term of *three
years.*"

63 35. *The act of Henry the Eighth.* Two years later, in 1777,
in his *Letter to the Sheriffs of Bristol*, Burke commented on this
Act, in enclosing one which had in that year been passed by
Parliament. Here, therefore, is his mature thought on this
subject :—

> "The second professed purpose of the act is, to detain in
> England for trial those who shall commit high treason in
> America.
> "That you may be enabled to enter into the true spirit of
> the present law, it is necessary, gentlemen, to apprise you,
> that there is an act, made so long ago as in the reign of Henry
> the Eighth, before the existence or thought of any English
> Colonies in America, for the trial in this kingdom of treasons
> committed out of the realm. In the year 1769, Parliament
> thought proper to acquaint the Crown with their construction
> of that act in a formal address, wherein they entreated his
> Majesty to cause persons, charged with high treason in Amer-
> ica, to be brought into this kingdom for trial. By this act
> of Henry the Eighth, *so construed and so applied*, almost all
> that is substantial and beneficial in a trial by jury is taken
> away from the subject in the Colonies. This is however say-
> ing too little ; for to try a man under that act is, in effect, to
> condemn him unheard. A person is brought hither in the
> dungeon of a ship's hold ; thence he is vomited into a dun-
> geon on land ; loaded with irons, unfurnished with money,
> unsupported by friends, three thousand miles from all means
> of calling upon or confronting evidence, where no one local
> circumstance that tends to detect perjury can possibly be
> judged of ;—such a person may be executed according to form,
> but he can never be tried according to justice."

Johnson's remark is (*Taxation no Tyranny*) : "When they
apply to our compassion by telling us that they are to be carried from their own country to be tried for certain offenses,

we are not so ready to pity them as to advise them not to
offend. While they are innocent they are safe."

64 13. *Settled salary.* As to the position of the Colonial
judges, see Lecky, iii., 330–331:—

"The Government would gladly have secured for the judges
in Massachusetts a permanent provision, which would place
them in some degree beyond the control of the Assembly, but
it found it impossible to carry it. The Assemblies of North
Carolina and New York would gladly have secured for their
judges a tenure of office during good behaviour, as in England, instead of at the King's pleasure, but the Home Government, fearing that this would still further weaken the Executive, gave orders that no such measure should receive the
assent of the governors, and in New York the Assembly having
refused on any other condition to vote the salaries of the
judges, they were paid out of the royal quit-rents."

With this compare Bancroft, ii., 551–552 :—

"New York was aroused to opposition, because within six
weeks of the resignation of Pitt the independency of the ju-
diciary was struck at throughout all America. On the death
of the Chief Justice of New York, his successor, one Pratt, a
Boston lawyer, was appointed at the king's pleasure, and not
during good behaviour, as had been done 'before the late
king's death' [in 1760]. The Assembly held the new tenure
of judicial power to be inconsistent with American liberty.
. . . Pratt himself, after his selection for the vacant place
on the bench, wrote that, 'as the Parliament at the Revolution thought it the necessary right of Englishmen to have the
judges safe from being turned out by the Crown, the people
of New York claim the right of Englishmen in this respect.'
But, in November, the Board of Trade reported to the king
against the tenure of good behaviour, as 'a pernicious proposition,' 'subversive of all true policy,' 'and tending to lessen
the just dependence of the Colonies upon the government of
the mother country.' The representation found favour with
the king ; and, as the first fruits of the new system, on the
ninth of December 1761, the instruction went forth, through
Egremont, to all Colonial governors, to grant no judicial commissions but during pleasure. To make the tenure of the
judicial office the king's will was to turn the bench of judges
into instruments of the prerogative, and to subject the administration of justice throughout all America to an arbitrary and
irresponsible power. The Assembly of New York rose up
against the encroachment, deeming it a deliberate step tow-

ard despotic authority ; the standing instruction they resolved should be changed, or they would grant no salary
whatever to the judges.''

And add Bancroft, ii., 557 :—

'' When New York refused to vote salaries to Pratt, its Chief
Justice, unless he should receive an independent commission,
the Board of Trade, in June 1762, recommended that he should
have his salary from the royal quit-rents. 'Such a salary,' it
was pleaded to the Board by the Chief Justice himself, 'could
not fail to render the office of great service to his Majesty, in
securing the dependence of the Colony on the Crown, and its
commerce to Great Britain.' It was further hinted that it
would insure judgments in favor of the Crown against all in-
trusions upon the royal domain by the great landed proprie-
tors of New York, and balance their power and influence in
the Assembly. The measure was adopted. In New York, the
king instituted courts, named the judges, removed them at
pleasure, fixed the amount of their salaries, and paid them independently of legislative grants. The system, established as
yet in one only of the older Provinces, was intended for all.
'The people,' said the Chief Justice, who was transplanted
from Boston to New York, 'ought to be ignorant. Our free
schools are the very bane of society ; they make the lowest of
the people infinitely conceited.'''

It will be remembered that Burke was Agent for New York,
and therefore must have been well acquainted with the state
of affairs in that Colony.

64 28. *Courts of Admiralty.* See Bancroft, ii., 553 :—

'' The great subject of discontent [in 1762] was the enforce-
ment of the Acts of Trade by the Court of Admiralty, where a
royalist judge determined questions of property without a
jury, on information furnished by Crown officers, and derived
his own emoluments exclusively from his portion of the forfeit-
ures which he himself had full power to declare. The governor, too, was sure to lean to the side of large seizures ; for
he by law enjoyed a third of all the fines imposed on goods
that were condemned.''

To explain why these Courts of Admiralty should exist, we
must remember (Bancroft, iii., 397): ''The extent of the
American illicit trade was very great ; in particular, it was
thought that, of a million and a half pounds of tea consumed

annually in the Colonies, not more than one-tenth part was sent from England.''

64 33. *For the more decent maintenance.* Dodsley has this note : '' The Solicitor-General informed Mr. B., when the resolutions were separately moved, that the grievance of the judges' partaking of the profits of the seizure had been redressed by office ; accordingly the resolution was amended.'' *Cf.* note 1 on p. 81.

65 10. *Consequential.* Define.

65 17. *Building.* Continuing **53** 23.

65 19. On Refutation in general, see Quintilian, Bk. **v.**, chap. 13.

65 22. *Preamble.* See **49** 32 ff.

66 4. *Advocate for the sovereignty of Parliament.* *Cf.* Bancroft, iii., 165 : '' Grenville declared the paramount authority of Parliament throughout the British dominions to be the essence of the Revolution of 1688.''

66 6. *Lord Chatham.* William Pitt, first Earl of Chatham (1708–1778). See Macaulay's *Essays.*

66 15. *Durham Act.* *Cf.* **51** 4.

66 19. *De jure.* Legally. *De facto.* Actually.

66 25 ff. To be interpreted in the light of **65** 25 ff.

66 34. *Illation.* Define.

67 3. *Tired.* *Cf.* **73** 26.

67 11. *Must give away*, etc. *Cf.* Burke's *Reflections on the Revolution in France :* —

'' One of the first motives to civil society, and which becomes one of its fundamental rules, is that no man should be judge in his own cause. By this each person has at once divested himself of the first fundamental right of uncovenanted man, that is, to judge for himself, and to assert his own cause. He abdicates all right to be his own governor. He inclusively, in a great measure, abandons the right of self-defense, the first law of nature. Men cannot enjoy the rights of an uncivil and of a civil state together. That he may obtain justice he gives up his right of determining what it is in points the most essential to him. That he may secure some liberty, he makes a surrender in trust of the whole of it.'' *Cf.* **21** 16 ff.

67 16. *The immediate jewel of his soul.* Adapted from *Othello,* III., iii., 156 ff. What is the meaning here (*cf.* l. 20)? There is a parallel in the *Fourth Letter on a Regicide Peace:* "Our ruin will be disguised in profit, and the sale of a few wretched baubles will bribe a degenerate people to barter away the most precious jewel of their souls."

67 17. *A great house,* etc. From Juvenal, v., 66: "Every great house is full of haughty slaves." How often, in this speech, has Burke alluded to Juvenal? What is there in Juvenal which appeals to Burke, and is so serviceable for quotation?

67 32. *The cords of man. Hos.* xi. 4: "I drew them with *cords of a man,* with bands of love."

67 34. *Aristotle. Nicomachean Ethics,* Bk. i., chap. 3 :—

"Our statements will be adequate if made with as much clearness as the matter allows. Abstract accuracy is no more to be expected in all philosophical treatises than in all products of art. . . . We must consequently rest well satisfied if, in treating of such matter, and with premises thus uncertain, we can exhibit a rough outline of the truth, and if, since our premises are mere generalities, and our matter akin to them, we can derive from them conclusions of a like generality. And it is in the same spirit that all our statements ought to be received. A man who has been well trained will not in any case look for more accuracy than the nature of the matter allows; for to expect exact demonstration from a rhetorician is as absurd as to accept from a mathematician a statement only probable."

68 8. *That power.* See note on **36** 18.

68 11. *I feel not the least alarm. Cf.* paragraph 76.

69 6. *These methods.* Note the clever transition.

I recollect. How many distinct objections has Burke refuted in this part of the speech (since **65** 19)?

69 7. *I promised. Cf.* **9** 16.

69 8. *The proposition. Cf.* note on **8** 13.

69 16. *Already.* On February 20 (*Parl. Hist.,* xviii., 335-337).

69 23. *Experimentum in corpore vili.* Usually, *Fiat experimentum,* etc. Let the experiment be made upon a worthless object.

69 33. *State auctioneer. Cf. auction of finance,* 8 20.

70 13. *Quarrelling. Cf.* 8 17 ff.

70 32. *Quantum.* Define.

71 3. *Proportions of payments.* Burke had thus expressed himself on the subject (*Parl. Hist.*, xviii., 336; *cf.* note on **69** 16):—

"The Colonies are to be held in durance by troops, fleets, and armies, until, singly and separately, they shall do—what? —Until they shall offer to contribute to a service which they cannot know, *in a proportion which they cannot guess*, on a standard which they are so far from being able to ascertain, that Parliament, which is to hold it, has not ventured to hint what it is they expect."

71 16. *Composition.* Define.

71 28. *The tobacco of Virginia.* Bancroft, ii., 19 : "Taxes were paid in tobacco ; remittances to Europe were made in tobacco ; the revenue of the clergy, the magistrates, and the Colony was collected in the same currency."

72 23. *Extent.* A writ issued against the body, lands, and goods of a Crown debtor.

72 25. *Restraining laws.* Alluding to what Act?

72 29. *Intestine fire.* An image drawn from what natural phenomenon ?

72 31. *Empire of Germany.* Comprised what States at that time ?

72 33 ff. Why not read, "Her revenue and her army are the worst in the world ? "

73 5. *Designed for breaking the Union. Cf.* note on 8 18.

73 21. *Certain Colonies only. Cf.* **71** 18 ff.

73 26. *Tired you by a long discourse.* Of three hours. *Cf.* **67** 3.

73 35. *In every stage.* What were some of his earlier deliverances on the subject ?

74 17. *Posita luditur arca.* From Juvenal, i., 90 : "When did avarice open her purse wider ? When had gambling such spirit ? Why, now men don't go to the hazard of the table with their cash-box by their side, but *they stake the whole chest and play !* ''

74 18. *Time of day.* Meaning?

75 2 ff. *Voluntary flow of heaped-up plenty.*

'' ' He that will milk his cattle, must feed them well ; and it encourages men to gather and lay up when they have law to hold by what they have.' N. Bacon (*Henry VIII.*). So Lord Brooke, *Treatise of Monarchie*, sect. x. : —

> Rich both in people's treasures and their loves ;
> What Midas wish, what dreams of Alchimy
> Can with these true crown-mines compared be ?

Burke's metaphor is borrowed from the wine-press. The 'mustum sponte defluens antequam calcentur uvae' was highly valued by the ancients, and is still prized in some varieties of modern wine. 'Among the many excellent parts of his speech, I find you have got many proselytes by so cleverly showing that the way to get most revenue, is to let it come freely from them.' Duke of Richmond to Burke, June 16, 1775. ''—PAYNE.

75 18. *Gamesters. Cf.* note on **74** 17.

75 21. *Ease would retract*, etc. '' It should be ' recant.' *Par. Lost*, iv., 96. Quoted by Mr. Gladstone from Burke, April 12, 1866. ''—PAYNE.

75 25. *The immense, ever-growing, eternal debt.* '' ' The debt immense of endless gratitude.' *Par. Lost*, iv., 53. ''— GOODRICH.

76 18. *The enemies.* What countries?

76 22. In the Peroration an appeal to the feelings is admissible. On the whole subject of the Peroration, see Quintilian, Bk. vi., chap. 1.

76 23 ff. *For that service, for all service*, etc.

'' No passage affords a more curious illustration of the manner in which Burke, in his more impassioned appeals, refunds 'rich thievery' of the Bible and the English poets. The remarkable independence of Burke's usual style makes the contrast striking. The concluding sentence is a reminiscence of Virg., *Æn.*, vi., 726, etc. :—

> The active mind, *infus'd* thro' all the space,
> *Unites* and mingles with the *mighty mass.*
> Dryden's Transl., ll. 984, 985.

Burke evidently borrowed this use of it from Bacon, *Adv. of Learning*, xxiii., 47, where it is applied to government in general : ' We see, all governments are obscure and invisible ;

Totamque infusa per artus
Mens agitat molem, et magno se corpore miscet.

Such is the description of governments.' South uses it in the same way : ' The spirit which animates and acts the universe is the spirit of government' (*Sermon on the Episcopal Function*). Shakespeare and the Bible supply most of the other phrases in the passage. ' My trust is in her,' etc., Psalms. ' Light as air, strong,' etc., *Othello*. ' Grapple to you,' *Hamlet*, etc. ' No force under heaven will be of power to tear you,' etc., St. Paul. ' Chosen race,' Tate and Brady. ' Turn their faces toward you,' 1 *Kings* viii. 44–45 ; *Dan*. vi. 10. ' Perfect obedience ; ' ' mysterious whole,' Pope."—PAYNE.

76 27. *Light as air. Othello*, III., iii., 322.

76 28. *Links of iron. Jul. Cæs*., I., iii., 94.

76 30. *Grapple. Hamlet*, I., iii., 62.

77 7. *Sacred temple.* Has this image occurred before ?

77 9. *Turn their faces towards you.*

"This is one of those beautiful allusions to the Scriptures with which Mr. Burke so often adorns his pages. The practice among the Jews of worshipping toward the Temple in all their Dispersions was founded on the prayer of Solomon at its dedication : If thy people go out to battle, or whithersoever thou shalt send them, and *shall pray unto the Lord toward the city which thou hast chosen, and toward the House that I have built for thy name*, then hear thou in heaven their prayer and their supplication, and maintain their cause.—1 *Kings* viii. 44–45. . . ."—GOODRICH.

77 17. *Of price. Cf. Matt*. xiii. 46.

77 21. Genung, *Practical Elements of Rhetoric*, p. 466, uses the passage from here through paragraph 139 in illustration of the following principle : " The appeal to worthy motive is not always explicit. It is often made even more effective by being pervasive, permeating structure and style, phrase and word, so that the hearer is at every step inspired by lofty standards and aims. It is this that makes a true oration preeminently ethical ; it is an embodied appeal to what is righteous in man."

77 25. *Sufferances.* A sufferance is a permit for the ship-
ment of certain kinds of goods.

77 26. *Cockets.* A cocket is a document sealed by the officers of the custom-house, and delivered to merchants as a cer-
tificate that their merchandise has been duly entered and has
paid duty. In the Boston Port Bill, certain vessels are exempted from the provisions of the Act, "provided the vessels
wherein the same are to be carried shall be duly furnished
with a *cocket and let-pass.*"

77 30. *The mysterious whole.* *Cf.* note on **76** 23 ff.

77 34. *It is the spirit,* etc.

"The reader of Virgil will trace the origin of this beautiful
sentence to the poet's description of the Animus Mundi, or soul
of the universe, in the sixth book of the *Æneid,* lines 726–727:—

> Spiritus intus alit ; totamque infusa per artus
> Mens agitat molem, et magno se corpore miscet.

Mr. Burke's application of this image to the Spirit of Freedom in the English Constitution is one of the finest con-
ceptions of his genius. The thought rises into new dignity
and strength when we view it—as it lay in the mind of Burke
—in connection with the sublime passage by which it was
suggested."—GOODRICH.

78 5. *Land Tax Act.* The Acts here mentioned were all
passed annually, and will be found among the first for each
year in the printed statutes.

78 7. *Mutiny Bill.*

"'The people of England, jealous on all subjects which
relate to liberty, have exceeded, on the subject of the army,
their usual caution. They have, in the preamble of their
annual Mutiny Bill, claimed their birthright ; they recite
part of the Declaration of Right, "that standing armies
and martial law in peace, without the consent of Parliament, are illegal ; " and having stated the simplicity and
purity of their ancient Constitution, and having set forth a
great principle of Magna Charta, they admit a partial and
temporary repeal of it ; they admit an army, and a law for its
regulation, but they limit the number of the former, and the
duration of both ; confining all the troops themselves, the
law that regulates, and the power that commands them, to *one
year.* Thus is the army of England rendered a Parliamentary
army ; the constitutional ascendancy of the subject over the

soldier preserved; the military rendered effectually subordinate to the civil magistrate; the government of the sword
controlled in its exercise, because limited in its duration;
and the King entrusted with the command of the army during
good behaviour only.' Grattan, *Observations on the [Irish]
Mutiny Bill*, 1781."—PAYNE.

The Mutiny Bill was superseded in 1879 by the Army Discipline and Regulation Act; this is brought into force annually by a short act called the Army Annual Act.

78 16. *Profane herd.* Adapted from the *profanum vulgus*
of Horace, *Odes*, III., i., 1.

78 22. *These ruling and master principles. Cf. Present
Discontents:* —

"Nations are not primarily ruled by laws ; less by violence.
Whatever original energy may be supposed either in force or
regulation, the operation of both is, in truth, merely instrumental. Nations are governed by the same methods and on
the same principles by which an individual without authority
is often able to govern those who are his equals or superiors,—
by a knowledge of their temper and a judicious management
of it."

78 30. *Auspicate.* Initiate with a ceremony calculated to
insure prosperity or good luck. What is the Latin? Is it in
the best taste to use a word of heathen associations when
about to refer to the most solemn portion of Christian worship? Have we noted such a blending of paganism and
Christianity in any earlier pages?

78 31. *Sursum corda.* Lift up your hearts. In the Mass,
or the English Communion Service, this phrase, or its English
equivalent, is used when the preliminary portion has been
concluded, and the priest or clergyman is proceeding toward
the preparation of the sacred elements. It is immediately followed by the Sanctus, unless a Proper Preface should be interposed.

78 34. *High calling. Phil.* iii. 14.

79 9. *Quod felix faustumque sit. May it be happy and
prosperous.* An invocation in use by the Romans at the beginning of an important undertaking.

79 10. *Temple of Peace. Cf.* **53** 23.

79 11 ff. *Cf.* **54** 3 ff., pp. 80–82.

An instructive commentary upon the question of the taxation of America by England is furnished by the following editorial paragraphs from the *Saturday Review* of July 25, 1896 (p. 77): —

"The Royal Commission appointed to inquire into the financial relations of Great Britain and Ireland published its Report weeks ago. Ten out of the thirteen Commissioners agree that we have taken £2.750,000 a year more from Ireland than Ireland ought to have paid. And this fleecing of England's weaker sister has been going on at this rate for something like half a century. According to the finding of a Commission mainly composed of Englishmen, we owe Ireland considerably over £100,000,000 sterling, a sum that, wisely expended on light railways, harbour extensions, and drainage schemes, would go far even now towards making Ireland prosperous. Had this sum been left in Ireland to fructify, it is more than likely that Ireland would never have suffered as she suffered in the early eighties, and then we should have had Home Rule in a much milder form.

"But what is to be done now? The politicians have paid no attention to this Report; it is, in fact, being met with silence—the 'Todesschweigen' that allows no whisper to disturb the grave wherein unpleasant things are buried. For our part, as we have already said, we rejoice in this Report; it shows that the cry for Home Rule has not its root in sentiment, but in material grievances, and a rich country like England can easily turn these grievances into gratitude. But will England even now act generously in this matter? That's the rub. We hope so, and shall press the point in and out of season. This Report has yet another bearing : it explains the existence of the physical-force party in Irish politics, just as the illegal levy of ship-money explained Hampden's revolt."

INDEX

ADDINGTON, xxxiii.
Addison, xlix, 108, 121, 123, 136.
Address to the Throne, 102–103.
Admiralty, Courts of, 152–153.
Alliteration, 95- 96.
Annual Register, 82–84, 97, 98, 103, 108, 122, 136.
Arbuthnot, 108, 134.
Aristophanes, 133.
Aristotle, 85, 154.
Arnold, Matthew, 119.
Asiatic and Attic oratory, 110–111.

BACON, FRANCIS, xxxvi, lv, 92, 157.
Bacon, N., 156.
Bancroft, 103, 104, 122, 127, 131, 133, 151, 152-153, 155.
Barré, xxii, 97.
Barrington, Daines, 142.
Bathurst, Lord, 107–108, 109, 110.
Beattie, xxxiii.
Bellamy, *Looking Backward*, 143.
Bible, liv, lviii, 91, 95, 96, 107, 110, 119, 124, 132, 137, 141, 143, 145, 154, 157, 159.
Blackstone, 122, 141.
Bolingbroke, xlvii.
Boston Port Bill, xxxiii, 147–148, 158.
Brooke, *Treatise of Monarchie*, 156.
Brougham, Lord, 125.
Buckle, xxiii–xxvi, xxviii–xxxiii.
Burke, xiii–xiv, xv, xvii, xviii, xxi, xxii, xxvii, 116, 136, 152, 155.
    Address to the King, 128–129.
    American Taxation, xxxvi, xxxviii, 86, 92. 118–119, 123, 135, 138, 146.

Burke, anecdote respecting, lix–lx.
    a philosopher in action, xliii.
    aphorisms, xliii, liv, 137.
    Appeal from New to Old Whigs, xxxviii.
    argument on the " penal bill," 116.
    charm, deficient in, liii.
    Conciliation with America, xv, xxxvi, xxxvii, xxxviii–xxxix, l, li, 86–87, 90, 139; Fox's opinion of, 87; reception of, by the House, 82–84.
    conversational powers, lix–lx.
    diligence in study, lvii.
    early education, lviii.
    flexibility, lacking in, liii.
    imagery, xlv.
    imagination, lviii.
    intellectual independence, xl–xli.
    language, xlvi.
    Letter on Regicide Peace, First, 115.
    Letter on Regicide Peace, Fourth, 154.
    Letter to a Noble Lord, 101.
    Letter to Sheriffs of Bristol, xxxvi, 91, 95, 117, 118, 150.
    memory, lviii.
    method, xliv.
    Nabob of Arcot's Debts, li, 87.
    oratory, didactic, xliv.
    perception of cause and effect, xlii, lvi.
    perception of resemblance, xlii.
    power of generalization, xxix, xlii–xliii.
    Present Discontents, xv, xxxvii, 93, 135, 145, 159.

11